JUDAS

By

Gary Browne

An *Apostles Series* Book

Copyright © Gary Browne 2011.

The right of Gary Browne to be identified as the author of this work has been asserted in accordance with the Copyright, Designs and Patents Act of 1988. All rights reserved. No part of this publication in any form may be reproduced, stored in a retrieval system, or transmitted, in any form or by any means, electronic, mechanical, photocopying, recording or otherwise, without the prior permission of the publisher.

This book is a work of fiction and, outside of historical facts, any resemblance to actual persons, living or dead, is purely coincidental.

ISBN-13: 978-0-957058224 (BCB Media)

The Apostle Series of books are published by the BCB Media Group, 32 Homewood House, Milford Road, Pennington, Lymington, Hampshire SO41 8EZ. United Kingdom. Please email **bcbmedia@live.co.uk** for submission enquiries.

Table of Contents

PART ONE: Resurrections   page 4

PART TWO: Revelations   page 127

PART THREE: Fruits   page 203

PART FOUR: Fulfillments   page 397

PART ONE

RESURRECTIONS

1

My life was never the same after that kiss late Thursday night, April 3, 30 A. D.

*

'Malchus!' I whispered, motioning with my right hand. 'Keep those men back!'

'Stay closer!' he said to the others and repeated my motion. 'And be quiet!'

'You're sure he'll be up here?'

'I'm sure.'

'God, this brush is thick! You could get lost in here!'

'Why do you think he chose it?' I replied, looking at him. The stupidity of men never ceased to amaze me.

'But you know this area, don't you? That's why they paid you?'

'Can you keep these men quieter? Don't you know sounds carry further at night?'

'Shhh! Malchus! Tell the men to be quieter!' I whispered again.

'Its getting thicker up here.' One of them tried to whisper.

'It's all right. He knows the way,' another whispered.

'That's why they hired him,' a third grinned.

Further away, a man wearing all white was kneeling in a tiny clearing when he heard them coming. I told Judas where I'd be, he thought as he looked up. Please continue giving me your strength, father.

'Tell that man with the rope to stay closer!' I whispered again. God! City people! Living indoors too long! But we're getting closer now.

'Malchus, keep the men closer together.'

Malchus called to some by name; others by what they carried. 'Tighten up!' he said. 'Tighten up!'

The man in white heard the sounds more loudly now. Coming closer. He stood up, his sweaty clothes sticking to him, and walked over to the sleepers under a tree. And was disgusted. I bring you to help me and you can't even stay awake! He said to himself and looked up at the starry sky: hopeful, expectant, fearful. The night was cool but he felt his sweat. Beads of it cling to his beard and coat. I could never have done this on my own. I'm glad I asked him to help me. Suddenly he heard a twig snap to his left. 'Wake up! Wake
up!' he yelled.

The approaching men stopped suddenly. As if paralyzed.

'Did you hear that?'

'I heard someone yell over there!' One whispered loudly and pointing ahead.

'Yes. This way!' Another whispered loudly, and point right to where he was facing, nose in the air. 'It won't be far. Spread out a little.'

The scruffy bearded man woke first and saw the man in white drenched in sweat. 'I'm sorry. Must've been the big meal.' Then he heard them. He shook the one next to him. 'Wake up! Wake up! They're here!' he
said getting to his feet. He turned to the man in white, saw his clothes were wet and smelled his fear. And then saw lights through the brush. They brought lanterns!

'I see swords and clubs!' whispered another former sleeper behind him.

'And ropes,' said another, rubbing his eyes.

Suddenly, they saw men with lanterns, torches, swords and ropes enter the clearing.

'Remember to identify him.' Malchus whispered to their leader with red steaks in his hair.

'Hello, Jesus,' red streaks called out.

'Judas!' Scruffybeard recognized him. And Malchus, the High Priest's servant!

Judas walked slowly and smiling to the man in white as his followers fanned out to surround him and big beard.

'May I give you the kiss of peace?' It seemed so unnecessary to big beard and in slow motion.

'Friend, do what you came for,' said the man in white. They embraced and Malchus stepped forward sword in hand.

'No!' Shouted big beard drawing his sword and sliced downward as he moved forward.

'Put up your sword!' said the man identified as Jesus, turning to him. 'It must happen in this way.' Then, turning back to the armed men surrounding him, he said, 'what do you think? I'm leading a rebellion? Don't you know me? Haven't you seen me teaching in Temple every day? You could have arrested me then!'

But the circle of armed men closed in around him. And that's when the man in white's so-called friends ran away. One was even naked.

'Remember, I'm going with you,' said red streaks.

2

Resurrections are difficult even in the best of times, but mine took two years and, if I'm honest, even longer; but I'll never forget that night until I die. The horror, deceit and murder reverberated through my mind for the rest of my life.

Why? Not because of guilt but because it wasn't supposed to happen that way. After identifying Jesus the plan was to accompany the Sanhedrin's men to the High Priest's house to negotiate. That's all. Just talk. But no: High Priest Joseph Caiaphas and Annas, his father-in-law, were waiting for us with Annas' other sons and sons-in-law, Ezra other chief priests, and my own brother! They all betrayed us! And then to the Romans!

None of it was supposed to happen that way, but we didn't know it until we got to the High Priest's house and I was told to leave! Me!

'Yes, Leave!' Annas said, 'or get what he's going to!'

That's when I knew it was a set-up; so I did; and warned Peter, who was warming his hands by the fire in the courtyard to get out while he could. They betrayed us! I whispered to him and wasted no more time; I almost ran toward the Damascus gate and the Jericho road! Desperate to reach the King's Highway and didn't know where the others ran off to. Or want to.

Instinct and familiarity drove me. I headed for the big caravansary on the south side of Damascus, one of my old haunts about a week's walk away. I needed to make sense of all the images and fragments of conversations that were racing through my mind. I kept smoothing my hair back but that didn't help: they wouldn't go away. I was so intent that it was only when I noticed the few people on the road looking at me that I realized I was muttering. And I was disgusted with all the time we wasted. We thought we knew what we were doing. We knew we were flying in the face of the Sanhedrin's entrenched power: it's authority and hierarchy of spies, informers and secret information. We knew the rulers, elders, scribes and even Pharisees in the towns write to each other and send monthly reports to Jerusalem's supreme council. We knew they corresponded with the local Councils and they with them; and we knew the backbone of our society was its genealogy, its four generation rule: no one could hold any sort of responsible public office unless one first documented four generations of male descent. From true Hebrews. Records were kept: and none of us qualified. Me, especially, being from Idumea, a second class citizen of Israel, one notch above a Samarian.

But why? Why did the High Priest and his friends double-cross us after offering such a magnificent bribe? That question plagued me all that night and the entire next day after I joined other travelers for safety and camaraderie. Only after bedding down that second night did it strike me: it was over the Disapora! I woke to the stars; drenched in sweat. Caiaphas and the others were afraid of the thousands of pilgrims! They prevented Judea's rulers from seizing Jesus in the Temple! The Jerusalemites didn't!

He threatened the Sanhedrin's power over the Diaspora! Where would Jerusalem be without the hundreds of thousands coming every year to worship at Judaism's center of power? Why didn't I think of that before? The city made nothing and wasn't even on the caravan routes! Without the pilgrims Jerusalem would be bankrupt: financially, religiously and politically! That's why they double-crossed us! To preserve their power! And that's really why they involved the Romans! Not because Rome alone could decide death in capital crime cases! But because Annas and Caiaphas wanted to tell the pilgrims they weren't responsible for his death!

Judas rubbed his eyes and looked around at his fellow sleepers and nodded: raw, naked power, that's what matters in this world! Even to priests. He remembered the serpent pool outside the Essene gate and thought that was the real Jerusalem! I'll never go back! He decided. I hate them all!

But now I have to find a job.

*

DAMASCUS; FOUR YEARS LATER

I returned to caravanning because that's what I did before I joined Jesus. Doing something and concentrating on it has always kept me sane. And whole. So I returned to my former way of earning a living because it gave me the security of the familiar while I tried to forget Jerusalem.

But I couldn't; and even though I tried that for the next four years my past caught up with me.

'A good trip?' 'Good' in caravan lingo means profits after incidents and my employer, Amos, was most interested in profits.

'Yes. We should do well. I bought extra pepper and coffee this time figuring prices usually rise at this time of the year.'

Middle-aged Amos smiled. A traditional Jew, he had been kindly to me and didn't care about my connection with Jesus. Or even about Jesus, himself. Or so I thought.

'They have,' he replied and hesitated. 'We have another van leaving next week. I know it's sooner than usual but do you want to take it or wait for the next one?' He knew Judas might need to rest; but he also knew that something beyond money drove him.

'Yes, if you can find me fresh mounts.' I wanted – no, I *needed* - to be busy, active, engaged.

'I'll have them ready for you.' Then Amos looked up from what he wrote. 'By the way, there's a surprise waiting for you at home.'

I stared at him, instinct told me this wasn't about business.

'He's been there since yesterday. Ahib's been taking care of him. He's blind.'

I felt my brow furrow.

'His name is Saul. From Jerusalem. They him brought him to your house because he knew exactly where you live. They said he told them how to get there. You must know him.' They're all wearing some sort of military uniform and he was struck blind on the road coming here.'

'No, I don't,' I replied and didn't like the sound of it. 'Since yesterday, you say?'

Amos raised his eyebrows. This was the first time he knew Judas to have a visitor whom Ahib made a point of saying was *not* a vanner; and hospitality dictated he couldn't be refused; especially given his condition.

'I've never heard of him and you know as well as I do that many people suffer from the sun.' Judas got up to go but then turned. 'What day do I leave next week?'

'The third. I'll have fifty droms (dromendary camels; more vanner lingo) packed with glassware and textiles and a list of commodities to get. Take your usual guards and helpers. When you return cinnamon, cloves, and frankincense prices should be at their peak.'

'Sounds good. You'll arrange the packing for the return leg as well?'

'Yes.'

'See you the day before, then.'

*

I was right; I didn't know him. He was a young man dressed in strange military garb that wasn't the Temple Guards. 'Don't be afraid,' I said when I entered my house. My name is Judas and I've never seen you before in my life.'

'I know. The Lord sent me here. He told to ask you to contact a man named Ananias, a follower of Jesus' way, and ask him to come here to me.'

I was taken aback and confused, to put it mildly. 'The Lord? Who do you mean? King Aretas?' Ananias had told me the rumors about Jesus' resurrection, but most people called their local king, Lord. 'Did he tell you about me?'

'No. Jesus did.'

Luckily, there was a stool handy so I sat down and asked him to tell me all about it. I was bewildered because I figured Jesus has been dead for nearly five years. But his friends came in just then, wearing the same strange uniforms; and we nodded to each other. Then I stood up and said, 'now, don't be afraid. I'm going to reach over with my two hands and feel your face. When I do, I want you to reach up and feel mine. All right?'

They did and as Saul stood up, his hands remained on my face. But as we stood feeling each other's faces someone knocked very loudly on the front door.

'Do you hear that?' I asked, hoping it wasn't anyone I knew who would see us like this.

'I'm blind, not deaf,' Saul replied.

'I'm going to answer it,' I said and asked two of his friends to help him sit back down. I went over and opened the door.

'Hello, Judas,' said Ananias. 'Is Saul all right?' Ahib left a message for me.

'Yes.' I replied, even more bewildered by how these people knew things I didn't, and introduced Saul to him. I told Saul that Ananias was one of Jesus' followers here and that we've been friends for three years. Then I turned to Ananias and said, 'you will probably want to talk with him and I have some work to do. So why don't I show you Saul's room so you can come and go as you please.'

Two mornings later, I was going over my accounts in my back room office off the atrium when Saul walked in, looked at me and shouted, 'I can see!' I dropped my pen and stood up. 'I can see you! Thank the Lord and you!'

I didn't know what to say, so I asked him to sit down. 'Now, how did you know to come here? I mean to my house specifically.'

'The Lord told me. Judas' house on Strait street.'

So this was meant to be! I thought; and then asked him, 'why do you call him Lord?'

'Because he commands me. I think he has things for us to do.'

I thought 'us?' and looked into Saul's eyes which now looked back at me like two lights centered in piercing blackness.

'Who do you mean by us?"

'Ananias and I. He's coming to take me to synagogue this morning.'

'Oh.' I looked down. 'I'm afraid I have to leave tomorrow. You know I work in the caravan trade, don't you?'

'Yes.'

'I won't be back for a few months but I want you and Ananias to feel free to come and go while I'm gone.'

*

This was Judas' eleventh return trip and he was making good money because Amos allowed him – and a few others – to act as a supercargo: shipping a few goods of their choice, paying all their own expenses, and sharing their profits – but not their loses - with Amos and his partner, Esau. Judas realized quickly that greater profits lay with higher priced luxury goods and that the two-hump dromedaries were cheaper means of transporting them than the single-humped bactrians. So, his profits from his first six trips, together with Amos' backing, bought more camels and gear as well as that small house on Strait street; those from the seventh and eighth bought more camels and gear and paid Amos' loan off that had financed him. And now, after a third trip at full profits, he would be able to finance and direct his own complete caravan venture as a junior partner of Amos and Esau.

They had been good to him, taking him on because of his brother's recommendation but more because of his own experience and abilities with languages. But they themselves were nephews and junior partners of Simon and Jacob in Antioch, which was the headquarters of the firm because of its more direct connections with Rome, their most important selling market, and because of it direct connection with the eastern trade. Damascus was their subsidiary station aimed at their southern trade to Egypt and Arabia, and for the repacking and re-distribution of goods to different markets.

Gradually, Judas learned that the bigger picture was directed from Antioch where uncles Simon and Jacob had been born, bred and inherited their caravan trade that stretched south to Egypt and Arabia and further east through the great Roman encampment of Zeugma on the Eurphrates river to Dura Europas. Rome was their principal overseas market. Concentration on the supply side of luxury goods made their business prosperous; but their connections with the east – chiefly for silks but other exotic goods as well – was tenuous at best because Roman military controls stopped at Dura.

Judas understood why. The eastern trade was completely different from the Arabian and Egyptian that he was familiar with for two reasons: banditry and the Parthians. He understood the greater the danger the greater the risk; and particularly of lucrative, luxury goods like silks.

*

His round trip from Damascus to Petra and back took four months; and they had just settled into Damasus' southside caravansary to spend their last night on the trail around the campfire when his chief guard and old friend, Sa'ad, settled next to him.

'Are you serious about taking an eastern trip?' he asked. Slightly older than Judas and having spent his working life in the caravan trade, Sa'ad helped re-acclimate him into the work but didn't understand the business end of it. His highest ambition was to manage a van trip and liked to ask Judas to explain what he did. 'Eastern goods don't come to Damascus as much as Antioch because Simon and Jacob send them mainly to Rome and the other seaports of the empire.'

But Judas noticed that Sa'ad didn't mention fear of the Parthians as a factor or the fact that the Roman's maintained a greater military presence in Antioch than Damascus. 'I understand it's more dangerous . I was just curious about it,' he replied. 'Who's involved in it in Damascus?'

'The only one I know is Titianus.'

'Never heard of him,' Judas replied.

'That's his Roman name. His real name is Maes.'

'That's not an Arab name!'

'No. And he's neither Jewish nor Roman either. He's a Parthian or a sere or something. You have to see him. He moved here to concentrate on the marketing end of it. But his eastern connections have dwindled because he's too old to make those trips very often.'

'So, it's a young man's game. Is that why he took the Roman name?'

'I'd say so. If you want to market anything in the empire Roman citizenship is the best and safest thing to have.'

Just then, one of the caravansary manager rode up to them, slowed his camel down and shouted 'take them into pen number sixteen,' and then moved on down the line of other campfires shouting the same thing.

'Are you going to oversee the transfer again?' Judas asked. (More vanner info: after the camels were penned, the goods were transferred onto donkey-driven carts and wagons for shipment to their company's warehouses which gave caravan workers extra work if they wanted it.)

Sa'ad smiled. 'With four kids and a wife, what do you think? Not everyone's as free as you.'

'If you help me unload mine first I'll pay you double what they do,' and smiled when he saw Sa'ad nod. It's the way of the world, Judas thought. Too bad Jesus never saw it that way.

3

CARVED into a mountain pass about thirty five miles south of the *Mortuum Mare*, Petra had been the crossroads of a north-south caravan trade along the King's Highway for centuries as far as I knew. Just north of Petra, an eastern route branched off past Elousa - south of Beershevba where I was born in the Negeb - to Gaza and on into Egypt. City goods - manufactured glass, iron and textiles came east and south to be exchanged for commodities - especially spices – going west and north. Literally carved into the mountains, Petra was a traders' mart as well as a stop-over and it was at the animal pens where we were packing our goods for the return trip to Damascus that I first saw the younger version of myself. I was thirty five; he looked eighteen.

His name was Malia. His mother was Arab, his father Jewish and he was hungry for life. But I didn't understand his sensitivity nor his sadness because I didn't share it. He had two spare camels, wanted to join a caravan going to Damascus and had the desperate look of the loner.

'I have no brothers and only one sister,' he explained. 'My father died three years ago and I just learned that my mother's been murdered there and my sister's disappeared,' he said. 'I need to find her.'

'You can come with us,' I replied. But I want your two camels to carry my goods and we'll split the profits from them in Damascus. You'll work for found.'

'Fifty-fifty?' He asked, eyes wide and hopeful.

I tried to gauge him. He looked in his early twenties but was probably five years younger. What struck me most about him was his lack of fear. Not fearlessness; just a lack of fear. 'Agreed,' I replied. And smiled.

*

I didn't know it at the time, but meeting him changed my life. It turned out that he was twenty three (so much for my powers of observation) and had been caravanning for seven years. He had even been east as far as Ctesiphon, Parthia's capital. Sa'ad took to him immediately.

'Don't use droms if you're going there,' he told me. 'Bacs (bactrian camels) are better.'

That surprised me. 'Will their spindly legs hold up all that way?'

'Not at all and their smaller hooves track better because the ground's harder out there. Rockier. They'll carry four hundred pounds the same distance that droms do their three hundred. Besides, the bacs thicker coats are also an advantage.' I looked at Sa'ad who nodded.

'Why is that an advantage?' I asked.

'It's far more mountainous there and colder. Bacs can go without food and water for a week.'

What he said made a lot of sense; so I shot an arrow in the dark: 'do you know Titianus then?'

'Of course. That's who I went with though it was years ago.' We walked on in silence a bit before he asked, as I expected him to, 'are you planning on going east soon?'

'I wouldn't say soon. There's too much I have to learn first.'

'Well, I'll be glad to help you and I'd like to return there.' He looked at the horizon. 'But I must find my sister first.'

*

I've liked the rhythm of caravan work since I started working at as a boy. You're intensely busy when buying, selling and packing and unpacking, but then you have these long stretches of walking and sometimes riding which allowed you to think. I don't know why, but they reminded me of my northern tour with Jesus. But that was with donkeys, not camels.

The stabs at conversation that I had with Mal - as I started calling him - reminded me of Jesus and how we disagreed over some topics but saw eye to eye on others. It was painful, but recalling those disagreements made me realize what a good man he was - and how I contribute nothing to the larger life I was now part of. He gave literally everything to it; yet here I was, still taking and receiving - and doing quite well by my accounts - but without being accountable. To anyone beyond Amos and myself that is, and certainly not to God. What bothered me was not that Jesus had shown me how to be accountable to ourselves and one another, but that I hadn't taken it to heart in nearly five years.

Saul's visit and then the little that I heard about his evangelism in Damascus before I left made me realize how far I had strayed from Jesus' way - not into evil ways but into do-nothing ones. And no matter how much I protested to myself that I did no harm, the more I realized how much good I did not do. That's when I began to form an idea of how I could be good by being myself.

But it was complicated and required a lot of thought. While walking; and sometimes riding. But mainly walking.

Yes, vanners have to be practical. And my chief concern now was our return trip. How one moves in arid lands is from water to water and that's why all caravan routes are planned according to where water is. Crossroads are usually found there and travelers like us meet various people – I'm tempted to say from all walks of life - in these spots. Oases are only that: points for rest, water and socializing; and that's why our routes follow them and are anywhere from a three to five day walk apart.

*

When we entered the last oasis south of Damascus' caravansary I heard a familiar voice.

'Tent and leather repairs! Jesus will save you! Tent and leather repairs! Jesus will save you!'

'Saul! Remember me? Judas, from Damascus! You stayed at my house!'

'Of course. Of course. Jesus protect and guide you. I wondered where you went!'

'I've been to Petra to visit the Arabs. But why are you here? I left you in Damascus with Ananias!'

His look told me something was wrong. 'I began preaching the word of the Lord and it was all right for a few weeks. But then the ruler and elders of the synagogue turned against me. They were going to kill me. Imagine! A fellow Jew!'

'Obviously they didn't, so what happened?'

'They had men watch me. Even put them at the city gates. So Ananias took me to a friend who lives in one of those houses on the city walls - you know which ones I mean?'

'Yes, yes.'

'They lowered me from one of the windows in a basket over the wall in the middle of one night. I didn't know where to go but figured they wouldn't think to look for me here. So here I am, living by what my father taught me.'

'And Ananias? Is he all right? Have they harmed him?'

'No. They weren't after him, just me. He didn't preach to the public as much as I did.' He looked down and put a finger in the sand and made swirls. 'I was the turncoat, you know.'

'Yes, I understand what people think of them. But you don't intend to stay here, do you?'

'No. But I'm not sure what to do next. I can't go back to Damascus and I can't return to Jerusalem. I don't want to return to Tarsus.' He stopped and looked down. 'I don't know what to do. But I do know that I want to preach how Jesus has come into my life.'

Then, you need to be around his disciples. They call themselves apostles now. But they can tell you about him. Aren't they're all still in Jerusalem?'

'As far as I know.'

'Eat with us tonight, Saul. We'll be under the trees over there,' I pointed, 'but we have to secure our animals first.'

When he arrived I introduced him to Sa'ad, Mal and the other vanners, and then sat down to our meal around our campfire. I had already thought about his situation and the more I did the more it made most sense that he join Peter and the others in Jerusalem. But then after Saul told me about what he did before and during Stephen's stoning I thought that wouldn't work: if Annas or Ezra found out they might kill him. But then I had another idea.

'You should definitely talk to Peter or John or Philip or Thomas. Or who's ever left there. And in secret. I've heard about James but don't know him well.' I didn't want to tell him about his opposing Jesus and heard about his changing sides – like Saul - afterward.

But he got in the first question: 'Did you really betray him? That's what I heard before I left.'

'Who said that?'

'Jesus people generally, but John in particular.'

Judas had heard that from others. 'Were you in the city when he was crucified?'

'I was a student.' He hesitated. 'Of Gamaliel's.'

Judas didn't say anything. Gamaliel and his friends were part of his brother's world.

'I'm going to have a difficult time proving to them that I want to serve Jesus, won't I?' Saul asked, more to himself than me.

'I would say so. And I would expect them to test you in various ways.'

Saul was quiet for a minute. 'It's frightening.' He stopped and looked up at the night sky. 'And it isn't.'

I looked directly at him and decided to be more positive. 'What can happen? I shouldn't think it would be any more frightening than what you said about your experiences in Damascus!'

'That's true. Thank you for that.' After a silence he asked, 'what was he like in person? I mean did you know him as a person, a real person?'

'He was as real to me as you are. I talked with him many times just like this.'

'But how do you account for--'

'I can't and gave up trying.' Judas paused. 'But I can tell you this. The longer I was with him the more I realized what incredible strength he had! And yet he was a man as we are.' I didn't want to tell him I had trouble believing all that Peter and especially John said about him after his death.

They were both quiet for a moment. Then Judas continued, 'those stories that you've heard about his healing people, even raising them from the dead - I saw him do them, Saul. There wasn't any hand that came down out of the sky that did it. I never heard any voice other than his. I was there when they cut that hole in his roof and lowered that man on his cot into his front room. Jesus healed him; and if it was God who really did it then he did it through Jesus.' He stopped talking and was aware that Saul was staring at him. 'I want to tell you that heaven may have come to earth then, but if it did, it came through Jesus.' He tossed a small twig on the glowing fire. 'Do you think you have that strength? I know I don't.'

'I don't know either. I only know I feel this tremendous urge to tell people about him and what he can do for us.'

They were both quiet for awhile and then Judas asked, 'do you think you'll go to Jerusalem to meet with the others?'

'Yes.'

'I would offer to write a letter of recommendation for you but I think it would hurt rather than help you.'

Saul nodded. 'I understand.'

'But will you take a letter for me?

He nodded.

'Give it to Matthew only and don't tell the others about it. But tell him I think it's important.'

'I will.'

*

Matthew [also known as Levi]
Lower City
Jerusalem
Dear Matt,

As you may know I've been involved in the caravan trade between Damascus and Arabia and Egypt for several years now and have been relatively successful. I think it's time that I try to give back some of the largess that has flowed my way. I don't have anything in detail but am writing to you to ask what you and your <u>particular</u> friends think about my proposition below.

I've encountered a few of our brothers in the different places that I've been. Frankly, they seem confused if not lost in the ways Jesus taught us to live. I can understand, of course, why so many of us seem to have abandoned them. Do you think the others would oppose my encouraging Jesus' teachings?

I do not mean through the single itinerant preachers that Jesus preferred to use. I have in mind settling families to create a truer, more life-like community; to appeal to the total person, not merely to one's intellect which tends to divorce belief from life.

As I say, I haven't worked out the details of my idea but am simply writing to gauge your collective sentiments about such an undertaking.

Please reply to me in care of either Amos or Esau in Damascus as I am away from home much of the time.

Your ever grateful brother in living Jesus' Way,

Judas

4

WHEN we returned to Strait Street I introduced Mal to Ahib and told him that Mal would stay with us for awhile, that he was looking for his sister and would bring her to live here as well when he finds her. Then I went to talk with my employers, Amos and Esau.

I told them that I was ready to make my maiden trip east and that I had a young man - meaning Mal - to assist me. But their absolute refusal to be involved shocked me.

'It isn't our line and we have no connections in the east,' Jacob lied. 'That was what Simon and Jacob did out of Antioch. We don't deal with eastern goods.' So, they refused to provide gear, manpower, supplies or money for such a trip.

When I said, 'suppose I went with one of Maes' vans, what kind of split would you give me on the silks that I returned?' Jacob said forty percent to me. It was clearly meant to insult me and I sensed they were secretly chuffed with me and felt I was ungrateful for all they did for me.

But not as much as I was with them.

So, I followed Mal's advice and went to see Maes. He wasn't what I - or you - expected. To begin with, I never saw a sere before. Here, I am, a healthy Jewish male in my early thirties, slightly above average height and with reddish streaks in my hair; Maes is old — probably twice my age - tiny, thin and virtually hairless, and who barely comes up to my shoulder. And he's not brown like me from the sun; he has a yellowish pallor and parchment skin, a sing-song voice and the strangest eyes I ever saw. A lidded look. Like two black olives lying on their sides. And his ancient body is covered with brown spots. I had the sinking feeling that his trips to the east were over. But we did have one thing in common; we were both unmarried.

Yes, he remembered Mal from a trip three years ago, he said. A smart young lad.

I told him I thought so too and about what happened to his mother and how he was looking for his sister, thinking he might know of something. But he didn't and then said he had been thinking about making one more trip east - his last before dying. That made sense to me. I explained my working for Amos and Esau in the spice trade the past few years and how they let me act as a supercargo, running as many as six camel-loads on my own account. I also told him what financial arrangements I had with A & E, and asked if Mal and I could accompany him on his trip. I agreed to pay for Mal and my expenses. Then he said that my offer to pay him fifty percent of the profits on my goods sounded fair; but I said I would give him sixty if he would teach me what he knew along the way. He liked that; so we parted friends and future partners.

Maes thought about his visitor after he left. Mid-thirties and didn't call me Titianus! Young and respectful. Not like the others. I'm sixty seven, probably not as old as he thinks I am, but I'd like to make one more trip even if it is only half-way home. I'll have two younger and experienced men with me. I don't need the money but I do miss the adventure! He smiled in his memory of long pigtails, polite people and the sounds of sing-song voices when white stockings in black soft slippers, appeared in front of him.

'Oh, there you are, Lu Che,' he said looking up and smiling. I've decided to make one more trip.'

*

The next day, I received a note from Maes saying he looked forward to the trip east with me and wanted to talk about it in greater detail. Just when I finished writing my reply, Mal arrived with terrible news: his sister, Malecha, had been abducted by a local gang of men who kept houses of prostitution. She was forced to live in one of them and beaten if she refused any of the men. Mal said he watched the house all yesterday and heard her occasionally scream. He estimated four to six – and maybe more - men were involved.

Too many for the two of us to handle, I decided after watching the house myself; besides, we'll need hard men to confront hard men. Then I remembered Simon and his friends. Gishchala isn't far from Damascus, a day or two by camel. I knew the route: take the coast road south of our city and branch over to the west side of Lake Guleh. Gischala's just a short distance north from where the road forks south toward Egypt. It's honeycombed with underground caves and tunnels where the Zealots live.

I explained the situation to Simon. 'I know there aren't many Zealots in Damascus. But I don't want your recruiters as much as I need seven or eight hard men who will rescue my friend's sister and kill the men who took her. Beyond that, I don't care who they are or what they've done. I'm willing to pay a good price, of course.'

Simon gave me his enigmatic smile, shook his head and said, 'just like the old days when we were disciples, isn't it?' He paused. 'I always thought you overpaid us for our supplies because you sympathized with our cause,' he said, but I knew he was fishing. So we chit-chatted for awhile until he said, 'I guess you've done all right since you're offering to pay this price. And now you want to go east for more?' He shook his head and smiled again. 'Is it just money you care for? Are you sure you don't want to join us?'

'I'm sure,' I replied. 'But I'd like us to remain friends. I've always thought we have certain things in common.' And when he smiled I thought I saw movement in the shadows. So, I leaned forward and almost whispered, 'you've certainly risen in the ranks. Do you ever see Barabbas?'

'Once in a while. He's was given charge of the city--'

'As a reward, I'm sure. It took great courage to do what he did.'

'Yes.' he replied. We both knew what the reference was to and didn't want to talk about it; it was too painful. 'Do you intend running silks from Damascus to Egypt?' he persisted.

I leaned back and laughed. Our arrangement had been for me to pay an agreed upon percentage of the value of our cargoes for not attacking my van. 'Well, that's being optimistic, thank you. But if I do, I know to come here and clear it first.'

'Yes. You know the good uses we put our funds to.'

I nodded.

'All I can tell you is that we're developing a sideline in the larger cities. Go see Elias and Moab at the Black Bird. Tell them I sent you. They'll get you what you need and do whatever you pay them for. Tell me if they don't.' He paused. 'I probably don't have to tell you this, but once you've made your arrangements with them, do like Jesus told us: stay out of their way. It'll be like our last journey to Jerusalem.'

I nodded again, remembering their involvement.

That's exactly what I did. And they looked bigger and meaner than Barabbas among the others in the tavern near the docks. They were certainly uglier. I told them about Mal, exactly what we wanted, paid them their price in full without haggling, and didn't see them for a week. That's when they showed up at my home with Malecha, a strikingly beautiful girl. No, they said, we won't ever be bothered by the men who took her and left.

It had been a long time since I felt that good about doing the right thing.

Two weeks later, after Mal and I had make our final plans to go east with Maes, I sent word to Elias and Moab that they and their friends could use my home while we were away. Years ago, I had learned Zealots were loyal to their cause, people who helped them and money in that order and figured two out of three wasn't bad. Mal and I felt they now had a protective interest in Malecha.

*

We left with Maes and an eighty-camel van three weeks later. It seemed such a long way to go; but only because I had never been there.

We went north from Damascus but turned east while still south from Antioch and we went through Palmyra, Aracha, Orisa to Soura on the Euphrates river. Maes explained it was shorter but it took us a month and after that we just followed the river through Zenobia to Dura Europas which took one and half weeks. In Dura we rested, however, because the next leg - from Dura to Ctesiphon – followed the river as it broadened but could take as long as three weeks because of all the turns it made. We also knew that we would be passing through the most dangerous part of the journey during the first two weeks out of Dura.

That was because Dura was more than a resting place: it was where west meets east, where Romans met Parthians and a host of many other peoples lived there, including a sizeable community of my people. East of Dura were frontier conditions where banditry was a way of life, especially among a people known as the Scienitae. Northern Galilee was tame in comparison. Also, Parthians, not Romans tried to maintain order because it was their connection with the west; and they had the reputation of not being half as civilized as the Romans. Which I considered a Dura joke after I came to know them and because after that – and the closer you came to Ctesiphon – the more Parthian and safer it became. Almost like taking a van through northern Galilee from Damascus to Egypt, I told myself; but--.

It was as I feared. On the first day of our second week out of Dura we met bandits attacking a group of travelers on the road ahead of us when we rounded the great bend at Haradu. We stopped; I left half of our guards with our van; divided the others into two groups, one led by Maes who had Mal with him, the other by myself, and both of us attacked the bandits from the rear.

That caused them to ride off; but not before an arrow from one of them hit Maes, wounding but not killing him. He took it in the right side of his chest and had to be littered along which slowed us down considerably. But some of the travelers we helped now helped him and through his pigeon-Parthian we learned they were Parthians returning to Ctesiphon, and joined with them.

But that lasted only three miles because a detachment of Parthian cavalry showed up; and I saw why the Romans hadn't pushed further east.

I've seen Roman cavalry; but until you see fully mailed cavalry armed with lances, bows and arrows riding in a broiling desert sun you haven't seen anything; and you don't want to be in their way because they're also mounted on the biggest, mailed war-horses I've ever seen. Later, I learned they were Parthia's shock troops called cataphracts who gave the name 'the Parthian shot' (shooting arrows directly behind them at full gallop which they could do because they had stirrups; the Romans didn't) to their cavalry. But. luckily, they seemed to know our pigeon-Parthian helpers. Curiously, the cavalry officers - a few of whom seemed to know of Maes - thanked us profusely and were most solicitous of our welfare, especially his. They insisted that all of us travel together for the rest of the way which would take approximately two weeks, they said. Their military physician – the equivalent of a Roman medicus - seemed to know all about Maes' wound: he pulled the arrowhead out, cauterized its entry and jabbered about something that sounded serious but didn't understand. Maes didn't either. But he felt better.

We supped with them on three occasions and I never saw such fastidiousness about camping. On two of those occasions, veiled women were present – one of whom kept looking at me - and after the first time, Maes explained to me it was a Parthian hareem. I knew enough not to speak to the women but I tried to learn some Parthian words from the officers who laughed a lot.

That's how the rest of our trip went. We were safe because no one was going to attack us - I mean them.

*

Except for three of the officers, the cavalry left us when we were within sight of the city; then, once inside its walls, the travelers and three officers went their own way and we ours. Mal and I simply followed Maes around and were amazed at how easy and quickly we completed our business. People actually came to us, asked us what we wanted and then provided it: everything from lodging to food, to the trade-goods we wanted. They even gave me more camels and goods than I asked for and called it 'on consignment' - whatever that meant. Maes said it meant we could pay for it later so Mal and I took all we thought we could safely carry and couldn't understand why anyone would not be the eastern trade. It was so easy to be greedy and get rich!

I also saw a few people who looked like Maes. Even younger versions, females and children. And, of course, he spoke with them in a musical language I never heard before. The men wore long pigtails and all of them wore silk everything. What fascinated me was that indoors, they always wore little soft - and invariably black - slippers instead of sandals. Maes stayed with some of them almost every night while Mal and I camped out with the camels because we were used to it.

A month and a half later, we were ready to return to Damascus.

I told Maes, he converted me into an eastern trader but he smiled and replied, 'just wait,' which only mystified me.

*

It wasn't until several days later, on our return trip, did he explain how we received special treatment. Trade wasn't normally this quick or efficient he remarked to us after we were bedding down for the night.

'Why?' I asked him.

'I don't know exactly but I'll tell you what I've observed. Servants wearing royal outfits running around carrying messages.' He raised his eyebrows when he said this. 'And the merchants we dealt with monopolize the royal trade.' He paused. 'Frankly, I'm not sure whether the travelers we helped were members of the royal family or some of the cataphract officers were --.' He stopped and looked into the fire. 'I've been trading here for forty some years but I've never been treated this well. It must be you.' He rubbed his wound which surprised everyone by not healing as quickly as we thought it would. Then he said, 'but tell me your impressions of Parthian society. All markets are pretty much the same.'

'I can only give you my sense of it,' I replied. 'It's much more rough and ready, and far more military. More of a horseback and fighting society that values physical strength and brawn. Not as commercial as ours is, nor as private family organized. And I can't get over their strange bazaar that the royal family seems to dominate. Not even our King Herod has such power in Jerusalem. The Romans only interfere to collect their taxes and Antipas couldn't possibly get away with dominating the markets there are as they are here.' I stopped for a moment. 'I think you were smart to go west. I would rather be a merchant in the west than here.'

Maes didn't comment. Just said he was tired, closed his eyes and turned his head away from the fire.

5

MAES died in Dura Europas after surviving the longest and most dangerous leg of our return to Damascus. The infection, closed in by the cauterization of the wound from the outside, had slowly - and unknowingly to us - become gangrenous. Maes announced that he wanted to rest in Dura and we did for a month; but he grew worse and worse.

What struck me was that he knew he was dying all alone but wasn't afraid to: he would be the last sere in Damascus who couldn't reach either of his homes. So it didn't surprise me that he decided to leave the last of his worldly goods to the two men who made his last adventure possible: the bulk of the estate to me and the remainder to Mal. But sere law did not exist in Dura and the easiest way was to leave it to us in his capacity as a Roman citizen. Eventually, it was agreed that Maes as Titianus would adopt Judas as his son and leave all his estate to him with the contractual stipulation the I – as the new Titianus – would now owe Mal the goods formerly owned by Judas to him. Little did I know that such adoptions and inheritances were standard procedures in Roman law and we had no problems finding Roman notaries filled in the Roman forms.

So, I returned to Damascus as both Judas and Titianus, Jew as well as technically a Roman citizen, a very rich man and still on the sunny side of forty! A month later, I told Mal that I was going to move to Antioch immediately - the center of Rome's legal system in the east - to prove my forms in the Roman courts there and to compare silk prices there to what they fetched in Damascus. But Mal was crucial to my plans; so I proposed a partnership between us and that he and his sister accompany me. I would buy a house large enough for the three of us but I intended to be on the road most of the time. I also proposed Mal become my partner in the eastern trade: he to handle the Antioch end of things while I concentrated on marketing opportunities. When I saw him raise his eyebrows, I said, 'that's right, to hades with Simon and Jacob. We're going to have our own firm.'

*

But Judas, the Idumean Jew, was only vaguely aware of the new Antiochean world he was entering. The city dwarfed Damascus and was the third largest in Rome's empire; it was also the administrative center for the empire's eastern provinces. All governors of Judea were under the jurisdiction of the Governor of Syria. If Judas was to understand things, he would have to as Titianus the Roman: Judas the Jew couldn't.

But little did Judas know that he couldn't have chosen a better time or place to prove his new legal status because the new emperor, Claudius, was appointing new men to imperial offices as fast as he could to get rid of Caligula's old ones. The new Legate (Governor) to Syria had been the leading lawyer in Rome - Cassius Longinus - who deliberately chose to prove the legality of Judas' adoption and inheritance because he wanted to enforce Roman law everywhere within his jurisdiction and especially where he, like most Romans of his class, believed conflict with Parthia was inevitable. Thus, Judas' encounter with Longinus did two things: it demonstrated him how Roman law could be personally beneficial and educated him to the art of gratuities in the Roman system. He came away from it a giant step closer to Titianus.

*

Judas liked Rome's directness and accessibility through money without the need for Jewish Law, so it didn't bother him that Simon and Jacob refused to have anything to do with him after he told them he was establishing his own firm - with an abundance of fresh, original and quality goods to sell into the chain of trade with the prospect of more.

Except for his vanner's eye view of Alexandria during his spice trade days, his experience also told him Antioch was not Jerusalem. He vaguely, but not fully, understood how complex and different pagan marketing was. But he had the correct instinct: business was commercial but more social in Antioch and money defined status and opportunity unlike Jerusalem where religious behavior plus money plus Hebrew blood defined such things. So, he bought the largest villa he could find in Daphne, the southern suburb where the wealthiest elite lived (its residents had their own Daphne Gate directly opening into Antioch's main street - where the Phyrminus river flowed west into the Orontes – and then forked into the Herod and Tiberias streams as Jerusalem's spiritual elite, the Essenes, had their own gate). Although Daphne was distant from the Nymphaeum, the theatre of Caesar, his own warehouse, the Palace, and the Circus on the north side of town, he didn't intend spending much time in them. Nor in the Jewish neighborhood of Keirtron just inside the city wall and southeast of the Daphne Gate. Business was social, he told himself, not convivial nor religious.

Still, the neighbors wondered: he's supposed to be a Roman citizen but calls himself Judas and looks so Jewish.

*

Leaving Mal and his sister in his new house in Antioch, Judas returned to Damascus to end his junior partnership with his business relationship with Amos and Esau, and to hire Sa'ad to manage his vans. But he received a surprise: Esau was ill and not expected to live; so he met with Amos.

'Esau and I have talked this over, Judas,' Amos said, 'and we're sorry to lose you. But you're young and we don't know those eastern goods as well as we do the spice trade. That's the fact of the matter. We've also talked about this because Esau is fifteen years older than I am and has retired. Would you consider taking me on as a partner to handle the spice trade here in Damascus while you and Mal handle the eastern trade? Or, I can move to Antioch if you think that would be better.'

I hadn't thought about that. Amos was in his late forties, his youngest child was just fourteen, and of course he was looking for new challenges; but safe ones that he knew and was quite willing to change geography but not the lucrative trade he was good at.

'What about Simon and Jacob?' I asked.

'What about them?'

'They think I've betrayed them; that I'm a traitor. Can you imagine what they'll think of you?'

'I'm the one proposing this Judas, Esau isn't part of it.'

Actually, Judas had been thinking he wanted to combine both markets but would have to find someone in Antioch; this took care of that and linked him with someone he trusted. So, he smiled, nodded, extended his hand and said, 'done.'

*

Amos moved to Antioch; and Judas began a new life in the spring of 43, but without thinking about urban, middle-class Jewish life and the fact that Amos and Ruth had a fourteen year old daughter, Miriam.

In traditional Jewish families, the father usually chooses a wife for his son and if the son is not able to afford his own abode, the new couple commonly live with husband's parents. Sometimes the girl's brothers might have a say in the proceedings; but the couple's wishes in the matter were usually ignored. Completely.

Miriam had no brothers and my parents were dead. I was thirty five, rich, had seen something of the world, had never been married, and lived in a large house with Mal and Malecha, several servants and extra, unused rooms.

Then whisperings began among the orthodox wives: it isn't right! and after all that Amos has done for him! In their minds, it was a foregone conclusion that he should pay his future father- in-law the mohar, give the gifts to his new wife's family, and live with her in my house after constructing an adjacent one for Mal and Malecha. What amazed me about my own life at the time was how expectations become realities so quickly!

So, ours was a traditional wedding in the autumn (the favorite time for Jewish weddings) of 43. Mal acted as 'the friend' of the groom - a sort of master of ceremonies - and provided the diadem because my mother couldn't.

Guests from Antioch and Damascus attended and heard Amos and Ruth pronounce the marriage blessing in their new home and then accompanied the new, heavily veiled bride and me to our home. The singing, dancing and feasting went on for several days; and though solid walls surrounded our compound (it was a Roman domus style house), some neighbors said it was scandalous what those verses from the Song of Songs said.

But that's how I married Miriam, the only child of Amos and Ruth, who would turn fifteen in the following month. It was one of my declining attempts to hold onto Jewish traditions in spite of Titianus. But I didn't fully understand that much of my confusion was owing to the dead hand of the past still gripping me.

*

You've probably guessed it. Marital happiness didn't last a year. She wasn't to blame; I was. I realized I did both of us wrong by marrying her. We had little in common which made me understand that I married her because I loved the idea but not the fact of her. We had little to talk about. Was I blinded by love? Hardly. More by my eastern trade success. I was drunk with it; and, like most imbibers, I couldn't seem to stop. I wanted everything the world offered. Talk about the foolish man who builds his house on sand.

She was every young Jewish male's dream: young, innocent, devoted to her parents, God and me. She was also the daughter of a successful merchant so at least understood what I talked about; but I was more than twice her age and intent on achieving more out of life. She was perfect according to traditional ideals; but I didn't appreciate them.. And that's why she was a better child of God than I was. I know this sounds like a confession and it is because I should have known better than to have married an image – a dream – instead of a woman.

She announced her pregnancy to her mother two months after we married and then to me. That's when I began thinking of her as a child having a child and saw my failure. I did what I could and whatever I was asked to do. But the midwives told us there was going to be trouble. Then the physicians did. Then she was dead. It was miraculous the child lived. A son. And a Jew eight days after his birth.

'Shall we call him Judas?' Amos asked me one day.

'Let's wait,' I replied (naming children usually waits till it's weaned). 'He's so small and puny. Let's wait to see if he lives.' And he did; and I thanked Jesus.

Later, on his weaning day celebration, Amos asked me again: 'do you want to call him Judas?'

'No,' I replied. 'I think Hero is a more appropriate name.'

None of the orthos liked that Greek name, but I already knew what they thought of me especially for throwing myself into a frenzy of business opportunities.

6

HEROD Agrippa – later called Agrippa I because he, too, had a son survive but was given the same name – provided those opportunities. He had discovered that being a friend of emperor Caligula was more lucrative than being a friend to his uncle Herod Antipas; especially after the emperor revived the old title of King and gave it him.

But Caligula's mysterious illness in October 37 completely changed him; and no one has ever known what did it. He became an unpredictable monster; and Agrippa decided it was time to visit his new acquisition before he lost it. It was a difficult choice because he had been born and raised in Rome and loved Roman ways. So he applauded the new emperor Claudius' attempts to streamline the empire. That's what kept him alive, in Claudius' favor and in touch with Rome's ways.

Judas knew nothing about any of this; nor of the fact that Agrippa arrived in Caesarea just before Judas' marriage with plans remarkably similar to the first King, Herod the Great, the bête noire of Jerusalem's priesthood, to modernize Judea. His new public construction - of roads, amphitheatres, baths, circuses, gymnasiums - stimulate employment and prosperity, increased trade and population and proved politically popular. But that was with Claudius' administration and the poor of the province; not with the Sanhedrin rulers of Jerusalem who were orthodox defenders of the Temple and the sacrificial system of traditional Judaism; and of the definition of God's chosen people as the pure blood line of Hebrews.

Agrippa destroyed the entente between his uncle and the Sanhedrin after Jesus' death and couldn't understand it. He had imbibed Roman ways and didn't understand that economics and politics couldn't function divorced from religion in Judea. That's why it took so long for him to understand that what he meant by 'modernization' was interpreted as 'Hellenization' by the Jewish traditionalist elite. And they would have none of it just as their father's and wanted none of Agrippa's grandfather's – Herod the Great's – program that chipped away at the Hebrew culture of the chosen people.

So, in addition to his building and transportation program, Agrippa took the next step: he encouraged trade through a series of tax moratorium schemes.

All this looked fine in Antioch. Amos told Judas and Judas was one of many merchants who flocked to Agrippa's court in Tiberias to hear the details from Blastus, the minister put in charge of the program to raise taxes by encouraging trade. He liked what Blastus said and signed a three year contract to ship from the north (Damascus or Antioch) through Israel to the south (Alexandria or Petra) and return with the promise of a tax moratorium for those years. And as a sweetner, Blastus added, the normal tax is ten percent ad valorum but we'll accept your valuation with the proviso of our right of inspection. Judas discussed it with the more experienced Amos when he returned to Antioch.

'I suspect that even if you worked something out with the Zealots we won't make that much on the spices,' Amos said. We'll do better running the eastern goods down the coastal road to Egypt.'

'Then why don't we divert all our eastern goods here and ship them down the King's Road along the east side of Israel.'

Amos thought for a moment. 'No. That's worse.' He hesitated. 'Actually, it would be cheapest and less dangerous to ship by water. I mean from Antioch directly to Alexandria and bypass Judea altogether.'

'But that will make Antioch our chief terminus for our eastern goods.'

'Yes. But it gives us access to everywhere else on the Great Sea.' Amos paused. 'You always said you'd like to market the eastern goods in Rome and maybe we should try the shorter route to see how it works. We've never done overseas but it can't be that complicated and ships are easy to hire.'

'What about the spices from the southern trade?'

'I'll investigate that as well.' he replied, scribbling a couple of lines on the note-scroll he always kept in front of him. 'We'll see what it would cost to ship from Petra to Alexandria and then by water here.' It could be cheaper than caravanning overland through the whole of Israel.' Just as Judas opened his mouth to speak, Amos continued. 'I know the set up costs are high and neither of has done water business. So, suppose Mal takes on the spices for a season and I get into the water transport. I think we'll see what will work fairly quickly.'

Judas thought for a moment. He liked the idea of us sharing knowledge about the different businesses. And he said, 'in the meantime, it seems to me we should take advantage of the tax moratorium, especially if I can get Simon to take a fixed amount as a bribe for letting us through the coastal road with the eastern goods.'

'Yes. The tax moratorium on the spice run from Petra to Alexandria will be helpful.'

As matters turned out, the tax moratorium was good for business. And when Simon agreed to a fixed fee for not robbing the vans it was even better.

*

But they were thinking like businessmen instead of politicians, and especially as politicians in a religious culture. Agrippa's modernization offended many: the Sanhedrin and priesthood complained it furthered the Romanization and Hellenization of Jewish culture. It brought more Greeks and Hellenized peoples – as craftsmen and laborers - into Judea who wanted to live non-Jewish ways and urbanized the Holy Land with more circuses, amphitheatres and public baths; and on and on.

But most importantly – and the most curious thing about it – was Agrippa's failure to see that political opposition could only be expressed religiously. So the Sanhedrin's culturally conservative reaction to Agrippa's program coincided with the reaction to the spread of Jesus Judaism. Traditionalists on King Agrippa's Council warned him: orthodox leaders will rail at what they call this secularization of the nation! His defense was predictable (some said he had lived in Rome too long): he jibed. He now encouraged religious divisions by attacking the Sanhedrin's enemies, the Jesus Jews, to win the support of the Sanhedrin.

When Simon wrote him Agrippa's change of policy, Judas admitted to Amos that he had never thought about it like this, and that maybe Simon had been right when he used to argue with Jesus. Maybe Jesus was wrong about divorcing religion from politics. Or was it merely the Zealot's point of view?

*

'The implications of all this are far wider and deeper than merely changing his religious policy,' Simon told Judas when they met. 'Once he starts here, Agrippas's going backwards will have to renege on his entire economic policy which will have long range effects.. I'll continue taking your money if you stay in trade,, of course, but bad times are in both our futures.'

Simon had decided long ago never to reveal anything about the Zealots to any outsiders like Judas. But he figured he would have a long-term relationship with Judas as long as he was careful about advancing his religious politics in tandem with Judas' business interests.

'So, he really had James and Peter arrested?'

Simon nodded. 'Yes, and they're now looking for John and the others. He wants to eliminate the leaders of the Jesus' Jews.' He hesitated. 'He's serious, Jud, because he needs revenues to pay his Roman creditors.'

'Can we get James and Peter out of prison? I'll fund the operation.'

'Thank you for that. The best man for the job is you know who.' Simon saw Judas raise his eyebrows and nod.

'Barabbas! Yes, thank God for Barabbas.' Then Judas had a sudden thought. 'But will he act during Passover?'

Simon smiled and said, 'actually, this is a good time. It'll be a complete surprise to Agrippa's men because they won't expect such an unorthodox move from us.'

'Shouldn't you keep this just between ourselves and Barabbas and his men?'

Simon sat back. 'I told you once before not to question us about our business. It's our business because it's our lives at stake. I'll contact Barabbas first. To see what he says. If he thinks he can do it alone, he can tell James and Peter to say an angel did it.'

*

But it was already a botched job all around. James had already been murdered in a different prison from the one John the Baptist had been in; but it was the wrong James. He was John's brother, James, not Jesus' brother who sometimes acted as head of the church when Peter wasn't around. Then, on the following day, the eve of Passover, Peter was rescued by an 'angel' from Agrippa's prison in Jerusalem and he and his family then disappeared. And when Simon told him about it, the first thought on Judas' mind was why did he flee to Rome?

*

Then, nearly three months later, in Caesarea's amphitheater watching wild animals tear criminals, gladiators and other animals apart, Agrippa died from a burst appendix before thousands of witnesses. Many said it was more spectacular than the ones in the arena and well worth taking the time to watch.

7

AGRIPPA'S very public and dramatic death in Caesarea – under Rome's nose, so to speak - provided the opportunity for the Romans to govern Judea more directly: they used as their excuse his son's minority and residence in Rome. There was time enough for his further education they rationalized (he was seventeen years old); so, they strengthened the Roman governorship by changing its title from Prefect (which Pontius Pilate had been) to Procurator which brought the office more directly under the authority of the emperor and especially more responsible for imperial taxation.

The result was our trade through Israel worsened dramatically not only because the tax moratorium ended but also because the laws were enforced more rigidly. The new Procurator, Cuspis Fadus, a friend and appointee of Narcissus, emperor Claudius' chief secretary, 'woke me up,' Judas later confessed to Amos, 'because I was still thinking like a Jew.'

'So, change!'

'But why is Fadus doing this?' I asked him. 'Why is he so pushy about it?'

'Because he gets a percentage of all the taxes collected. He was just another man-on-the-make in Rome with friends in high places and I'm sure he gives a percentage of his take to Narcissus.'

'What a name for an ex-slave. So now we pay for his profits?'

'That's the Roman way. Get used to it. "Trade and pay or don't and die." That's a business metaphor.' He smiled.

I thought more about that. I understood how we could avoid Judea by stopping our eastern trade at Antioch and taking the Great Sea routes to our markets; but the old problem remained: how could we avoid Judea with our southern spice trade? 'I feel caught,' I told him. 'Until it's solved let's bring the eastern goods to Antioch and ship them by water to the different seaports. Let's set Mal up in Ctesiphon to expand our supplies and keep them coming steadily from there.' Amos nodded again while I had a further, depressing thought, 'it looks like that'll be our main source of profits for awhile.'

'You better go with him to work that all out.'

'I know, Amos, but don't want to admit it. It's just what I need now, another trip to Parthia.'

*

Four months later, I realized how myopic and strictly business-minded my insight was: everything in Judea seemed to fall apart. Banditry increased; then, as trade declined even further and Agrippa's son remained powerless, the Sanhedrin refused to support further costs of transportation and communications improvements. Except for the on-going repairs and construction to the Temple paid for from the Temple tax, non-Temple construction came to a standstill and Roman taxes fell off. That's when I decided I needed a fresh perspective on what was happening from someone who was more actively engaged in it than I was.

I went to Gishchala to talk with Simon after making a contribution to their cause. 'At least I get something for the money I pay you!' I told him. 'The increased taxes we pay the Romans is the real banditry!'

But I was also concerned about something else. 'Is it just me, Simon, or are the moneyed people getting out of trade and investing in land? If this continues Judea will lapse into its old agrarian society.'

Simon grimaced. 'Even banditry pays less and less these days.' He shook his head. 'And I can't help you with the spice trade. Fadus has put troops in the towns along the major trade routes and I don't have to tell you that they'll move into the Nabatean Kingdom before long.'

'There must be a way to get around this.'

Simon stared at me. 'Don't I remember you dealing with opposition and failure by fleeing from it?'

'That worked on our northern tour but Jesus didn't take my advice about Jerusalem.'

'Well, what do you think you should do now?'

I stared back at him and suddenly realized something new. 'Thank you. You've just made me realize I've been thinking about this all wrong.' When Simon raised his eyebrows, I said, 'I've been looking to the Antioch and the water to solve my eastern trade but never even considered it for the southern trade.'

Simon smiled now. The same old Judas, he thought. Get a mile out of an inch. 'But have you given any thought to what this new set of conditions in Judea will lead to?'

I was confused by the question; so I answered, 'no.'

'Only moneyed men will answer in business terms. True Jews will respond religiously.'

Oh, God! I thought. 'You mean because Israel's the holy land, not a Roman province?'

'Never forget that politics here is religious. The Romans either don't or won't understand it. But by now you should know Rome's way is not Jerusalem's and certainly not Jesus." He paused and then said, 'if the Romans persist in their way my people will come into leadership.' He paused again. 'You know what that will mean.'

'Yes. I'll have to choose between Judas and Titianus.'

'That's right. But I have a sweetner for you.'

I looked at him, suspecting he had a proposal. 'What?'

'As our social economy reverses itself religion will become even more important than it is now. Which means its costs will rise which will make the Sanhedrin look for ways to increase their revenues.' I nodded, so he continued, 'naturally, they'll look to raise revenues from the Diaspora where the Romans don't interfere with the Temple tax. But what about here, in Judea?'

I hadn't thought about it. 'What about it?'

'Increasing the number of pilgrims fulfilling our Law by attending Temple three times a year or more will increase their revenues enormously! Right?' I nodded. 'I want to help them.'

My left elbow slipped from the table and I nearly fell off my stool. 'You!' I looked around. 'Pinch me!' I'm afraid I exclaimed (in spite of what you've read about me, I'm not the dramatic type). 'I can't believe I'm hearing this!'

Simon rarely laughed; but he did now. 'And I want you to help me achieve it! I want Amos to establish a line of ships to bring the hundreds of thousands of pilgrims from the largest seaports to Joppa and --'

'Joppa? You mean Caesarea.'

'No. Joppa. It was our Jewish port until the Romans built Caesarea and it will be our port once again for our faithful to fulfill their obligations.' He stubbed his right index finger on the little table between us. 'I can almost guarantee the priesthood will buy enlarging Temple trade. Joppa's only thirty three miles from Jerusalem - no more than a two or three days walk away - and I'll take care of establishing the overland facilities for the trip and—'

'You want me to set up ships to ferry the pilgrims from the big seaports to Joppa!'

'You got it. But I'd suggest you don't use either name, Judas or Titianus.'

'Let's go through Amos, then. He's beyond the reach of the Sanhedrin and handles our shipping anyway.'

'There's one more thing,' he said. 'Remember how we first met?'

'Yes.'

'This is more than mere business. I'll expect you to charge the cost of passage for the pilgrims. But we want it cheap for them. So, don't profit from it. Keep the transport rock bottom but you can sell them food and drink if you want.'

I knew he was serious because Simon understood and agreed with much of Jesus' religious understanding and I owed that to both of them. 'Of course,' I replied. 'I'll instruct Amos to that effect.'

'Good!' he said. 'I knew I could count on you.' He paused. 'Don't worry about the Sanhedrin opposing this. They won't refuse if it's presented properly.'

I didn't want to ask what he was getting out of it. But I knew it would be something; so I just smiled.

'What?' he asked.

'I was just wondering which of us is the better businessman.'

*

I returned to Antioch asking myself what price is information? Simon had told me – obliquely and veiled, but unmistakably - to get out of Judea if I choose Titianus. He knows things I don't and usually it involves the Romans, I thought; and I believe him. He isn't the young messenger for the Zealots anymore; he commands one of Galilee's districts and knows what his compatriots are doing everywhere else. Yes, I should take his advice and get out. Not next week or next year or perhaps even five years from now; but plan now to get out. But why don't I feel right about it? I suddenly realized that it wasn't a matter that one side was right and the other wrong; it was that I didn't know the Roman way well enough. But I should. Especially if I was really going to be Titianus.

The conversations with Simon also made me realize how limited Amos' view of things were. He was just an older, more experienced version of me. A nice man. A good man. And Ruth, his wife, was the salt of the earth. But I decided I'm not going to learn much more from him. The key to my growth is my mind; not the volume of goods I trade. I knew in my soul that personal prosperity would follow. So, learn from those who know more than I do but keep what they know in perspective. Am I being devious? Selfish? I don't think so. It's just keeping my own counsel and noting what others know. Jesus didn't tell us everything he knew. And he sometimes told us riddles. Parables, I mean.

So, I talked with Amos soon after I returned to Antioch.

'I would like to get out of trading through Judea as soon as possible.'

He looked up from his desk in our office over our warehouse. 'Why? What made you decide that?'

'The moneyed people are abandoning trade and investing in land again. I think Roman policy's behind it: trying to drive them into producing foodstuffs for their imperial markets which are urban. We'll be like Egypt in two generations. Lost.' (See how I still identified with Judea?)

'You mean the Sadducees are giving up?'

'On commercialization. Actually, on that part of commercialization which is modernizing Judea into a Roman province. They intend to dominate through religion and their old social economy as they did before Herod the Great.'

Amos was silent for a moment. 'How do you feel about that? I mean about the Romans monopolizing Jewish commerce.' He finally asked.

'We can't stop it. We need to get out while we can.' I sensed that this retreat bothered Amos even more than it did me. Giving up one's heritage is hard to do.

'Flight, then.' He paused. 'I remember how prosperous Antipas and his grandfather made Judea! So many improvements and new people and money coming in! They were exciting times!'

He surprised me. A traditional Jew rhapsodizing about the commercialization of Judea's agrarian and one-God society So unlike Jesus. 'Yes, but they did so by Hellenizing Judea, remember?' I said. 'Didn't they make it Roman and Greek on top of Israel's static economy? I mean long before the Romans changed things in last year.' I stopped because of a sudden thought.

He noticed. 'What?' he asked.

'Remember how I had the idea of diverting our eastern trade to Antioch to get access to the water for overseas trade? Well, how can we apply that idea to the southern spice trade?'

Amos looked off into the distance through the portico doorway he faced. 'It's no secret the Romans are pushing into southern Arabia and eastward by sea. There's even talk that Alexandrians are trying to connect with India through the Red and across the Southern seas. Of course, that's what the Roman's want. Some firms have already established themselves there to do that. But it's just talk and dreams so far.' He shook his head. 'That Southern Sea is still too hit-and-miss for any regular trade. It's too risky for us.'

So, regularity is what we need, I thought. 'Could I ask you to investigate that further, Amos? Ask around and if you have to go to Alexandria do it and take Ruth. On our firm's expenses, of course.'

Amos studied him. 'You're that determined to by-pass Judea? Is it for business reasons or is it personal?'

I knew he and Ruth probably suspected I wanted to escape bad memories; and I wondered whether they heard the rumors about me and Jesus that John talked about. I thought it best to be personal. 'You're right about the personal part, Amos. I feel I want to escape Israel. I do have bad memories about it.' I looked Amos in the eye. 'And, yes, Miriam is one of them. As she is for you too, I'm sure.'

'They're not as bad a memory for us as they probably are for you.' He paused. 'Besides, we have Hero!'

I liked how he included Hero as his and Ruth's. 'Yes.' I replied. 'It's difficult for me to say this. But I wonder if my constant traveling is partly a reaction to him, to accepting him, as it is to my bad memories of Judea. I don't think I blame him for her death. But I noticed that my first thought when confronted by circumstances larger than I am is to flee.'

'You know we love him and will always care for him.'

'Thank you.' I nodded. 'Thank you for saying that.'

'It's a terrible cross you must bear. I've never had to.'

'I wish I didn't. But it seems to be what Jesus wants.'

'Perhaps it's God,' I replied, knowing he wasn't a messianic.

'Yes. But you know I'm beginning to think he was right even though I think I knew him as a man better than anyone.'

Amos looked at me. 'Maybe he wants you to go to Parthia again.'

I stared at him. And blinked three times. That's twice Parthia's called me.

8

MAYBE God wanted me to go. That thought grew on me as Mal, Sa'ad and I planned our second trip, intending to leave Mal there to serve as our procurement manager since his sister was marrying in two weeks. Personally, I had mixed feelings about it because I discovered long ago that repeating a magical moment usually doesn't invoke the same magic as the first time. I only found echoes of it. Or shadows.

But this wasn't true of my second trip to Ctesiphon. It was even more exciting, mysterious and serendipitous when we got there six months later. Servants met us in the bazaar; two of the cataphract officers whom I dimly remembered as Vologases and Pacorus immediately showed up after they left and invited us to dine with them with a vague promise of meeting Tahirir – whom I couldn't quite remember under all those veils- once more. And their surprised response of 'oh!, I'm so sorry to learn of your wife's death; but isn't it wonderful that the child survived. And a boy!'

Now, what was that about?

By the second week of Judas's visit there, he realized Parthian society was similar to Jewish and Palestinian upper class ones: the male heads of the families determined power strategies, their females their social counterparts. And he was woefully slow more out of unpracticed than ignorance. His first dinner invitation, for example, involved himself and Mal being nearly overwhelmed by Vologases' huge family; but his second was alone with Vologases with his younger sister, Tahirir, unveiled this time. And by then, he should have known; but he didn't.

As the conversation became more personal and as Judas learned more about Tahirir, Vologases saw he was attracted to her. 'Tay,' he suggested, 'why don't you take Titianus across the river to see the new arch we're building.' He turned to Judas who just noticed that none of the other Parthians ever called him by that name, 'we're fashioning it after the ones in Rome which I think you may find interesting.' He didn't say what he hoped Titianus would find even more interesting; but Tahirir understood: she was of the hareem.

*

There was a lot more Judas/Titianus didn't know.

For example, several royal families - but chiefly the Gevs, Karins, and the Surens – usually occupied Parthia's throne at different times. This was the time of the Karins; but Judas didn't know exactly who Tahirir was because families were more important than the individuals who composed them. He just assumed she shared the common experience of all the women of those royal families and wasn't familiar with the product of the hareem which didn't exist in Jewish or Greek or Roman cultures. The closest thing was the Jewish allowance of multiple marriages - Rome's Antioch allowed serial ones only – but very few, and only the very wealthiest Jews had multiple wives. The hareem existed for one purpose: sex and the procreation of children; its members were pampered and protected and their status was an automatic given. Individual members who rejected it's conditions were instantly murdered. But even had Judas known this, he probably would have asked, who, in their right mind, would reject such status?

And then there was the militarism of Parthia's culture: it made the male-dominated cultures he experienced pale in comparison; and one found nothing of the softness of Roman Antioch's commercial one in it. Men made war and dominated women much more completely than in the west. Tahirir grew up not merely knowing but participating in it. She had no conception of such female freedoms as divorce or even just saying 'no.' So, when she was thirteen and told that she would marry Vardanes, Vologases' much younger brother, she simply obeyed.

A year later, when Judas hadn't even met Maes, her son, little Vardanes, was born, a prince destined to become king after his father who in turn would succeed his brothers. Seven years later little Vardanes left the hareem to begin his military training. But then his father was killed in one of the incessant wars on Parthia's northwestern frontier and their status of wife and son was socially frozen. Except for Vologases, who hated his two older brothers even more than he loved his younger ones, their loss may have been deeper.

Vardanes was twelve and Tay twenty-six now when Vologases was plotting their, his and Parthia's future. Even as a boy, his father knew Volo was the brain among his other son's brawn. And now Vologases kept his eye on Rome because he understood - as Rome's ruling classes did - that the clash between them would continue for generations; at least until the Romans could figure out how to overcome the Parthian's cataphracts and solve their problems of logistics. 'We sit in a cat bird's seat,' Volo would tell his father and brothers, 'and should wait for them to come to us.' Then he added, 'but we should know what they think as soon as they do.' So during the past three years, he repeatedly told Pacorus, his brother whom he trusted and next in age to him after the slain Vardanes, 'this is a good time to plant one of us in Rome. But I need you here.'

'So, who then?'

Now, he had an answer. 'Perhaps we should learn more about this Judas pretending to be Titianus.' He replied. 'What he's up to and really like. Perhaps help him become Titianus. It wouldn't cost us much and will give Tahirir purpose in her life. And ours.'

*

Judas' third meeting with Tay included an evening walk in the gardens before dinner with only her personal servants as chaperones.

'So, we're both widows with sons.'

'I am a widower. But your meaning is true.'

'And what about love?'

'What about it?' At first, he was confused. 'It's part of life. Well, I don't mean all of it. I mean I'm alive. She's not. And I can't do anything about that.' He stopped because he realized how silly he was being. 'That was too harsh of me. I married a child who died giving birth to a child because I was too stupid to know better.'

'You were in love with a dream?'

Jesus flashed through his mind. 'Yes. I know now that dreams are as good - and sweet and wonderful – as they are realizable.'

'Realizable?' she looked puzzled. 'Achievable? Practical?'

'Yes. In this world. Not separate from it.' He stopped to examine a small palm leaf; plucked it and held it up to her. 'God determined the length and shape of this. Yes, your servants helped with its care but they can only encourage it to grow into the form that God wants. Not what they want.' He let it fall and they walked on.

'Your God is similar to ours then. They don't live here in the world.'

'No, he doesn't. We just have to make the best of it we can--'

'Alone?'

'No. Never alone. Only with his help.'

'But we can't know if he's helping us, can we?'

'I once had a very wise man teach me many things. He told me that when you stop and examine your life you see whether God favors you because he's within you.'

'How do you know that?'

'Through faith. Believing he is.'

'Did you do that with your first wife before you married her?'

'No, I didn't and that's where I went wrong. For her and me. Her name was Miriam. My wise friend never married and never talked much about husbands and wives beyond general things.'

'But if you wait until you're old to find God's favor, it may be too late.'

He smiled. 'I search every day.' He stopped again and turned toward her. 'But I miss being married.'

'What do you miss about it?' She knew it couldn't be sex because secular and religious prostitutes were too readily available to 'miss' that.

'The companionship. The sense of having a home and family that I shared with her. A place that I could come home to - and feel safe and comfortable.'

'And talk with her?'

'If I wanted to or she did. It's the shared honesty of a deep relationship that I miss. And yes, it's sexual. I couldn't share that with a man.' He stopped; then went on. 'But I discovered we didn't share much because I had experienced so much more of life than she did.' So we didn't share what I really wanted.

She nodded and started to walk on. 'There was a gap between you. But tell me about love? How was that different with your wife than with God?'

'It was the closest to God that I'm ever going to get in this world. God created women as well as men and I believe I should honor her relationship with him as she should mine.' He looked off to his left, away from them. 'You see, it bothered me that that same wise man who I mentioned didn't tell me those things and, since then, I've always thought it strange how I didn't discover it until I was his age when he died.'

'Did he teach you everything before he died?'

'I suspect not but I don't know.'

'But you remember him. Do you think he still teaches you? Perhaps in different ways now?'

Judas looked at her. 'I never thought about that.'

'Perhaps he doesn't seem as wise to you now as he once did?'

Judas stared at her and didn't answer immediately; but then said, 'it didn't happen like that. I had already begun seeing his human imperfections I'll call them, after I got to know him better. But he taught me things I would never have known without him--'

'So it's both instead of either or.' She said this in such a matter of fact way that it caused Judas to stop her by putting a hand on her forearm and say more than ask, 'there's a lot more to you, isn't there?'

'And to you, I suspect.' She walked on and he followed. The chaperones lengthened their distance behind them.

*

Of course, she knew what Vologases was up to and allowed herself to wonder what it would be like to be married to a merchant and live in Antioch. Less noisy certainly because his weapons and armor were his mind. Less dangerous too; for the men she knew lived only to fight. And die. But she knew Vologases was different; he wasn't the biggest or strongest; he won because of his mind. Judas was the same but different. But what he lived for perplexed her. Was it for money? Where's the glory in greed? So far, his life seems so flat; so without. . . honor.

'Don't think about living in Antioch,' Vologases said. 'Think about living in Rome. About living as a rich Roman and raising little Vardanes as a wealthy Roman. But educate him wisely. They've already lost their nobility and aristocracy. Everything there is money now. Why, look at the troops they send against us! Mercenaries and even many different peoples they now call Romans! They'll be a mongrel race in our lifetime!'

So she started wondering would it be like to be married to a merchant and live in Rome where hareems didn't exist. The thought of 'no' never crossed her mind.

*

'And love. What did your wise friend say about that?'

It was the day after their sixth meeting, and they were walking in the royal gardens again, but this time chaperones weren't in sight.

'That it means many things and comes in different forms. People marry to have families and to practice love, loyalty, and friendship. As a common purpose in life, I think. And for privacy as well--'

'What's privacy?' They stopped and she turned to him. 'I don't know that word. You mean secret? Hidden?'

'No. Let me give you an example. I am a Jew by birth but also a Roman citizen by choice. God's and mine. I'm a freedman. That means I can do anything I want provided I have money enough but I can't hold public offices. I can't serve in the Senate or as a magistrate or as a judge. I have what's called a private status. I'm free to come and go; to make contracts, and to bring judicial actions but I'm not a member of the aristocracy. I have no special privileges and I'm not above the law.'

'You mean people can't order you to do things?'

'No. Not as long as I pay my taxes and make my annual oath to the emperor I am free to go anywhere in the empire, do what I--'

'Pursue your business you called it.'

'Yes. I think Roman culture allows for great individual freedoms.'

'But within limits, I should think. Is it true they have no hareems?'

'That's right. No hareems. Only one wife at a time.' He smiled. 'And our children inherit.' They walked on.

'Tell me more about your wise friend.'

'He was a Jew, a few years older than I am and a true prophet in our tradition. He lived by our holy books--'

'<u>Torah</u>?'

'That's right. You know it?'

'I know about it. Jews are everywhere.'

He decided not to get into his friend's knowledge of <u>Torah</u> too deeply. 'Well, he knew <u>Torah</u> better than anyone else I've ever known and he tried to live through its rules without being bounded by them.'

'Why do you say 'tried?''

'Because the world killed him for telling others to live the same way, a better way than was generally lived then.'

She thought about the man who just said that for a few moments. 'I don't think you would ever try to do that.'

'You're right. I accept the world as I find it. But he didn't. He was purer than I am--'

'And how do you find the world?' They sat down on a bench under a gazebo.

'It challenges me because there's something new every day . I think of it like your men do; it's a battle. I want to do what's good but there's something in all of us that fights against it--'

'So you want to find goodness in your private family life?' She looked directly at him. 'You seem such a very private person.'

'Just because I've said these things?'

'No. Because I think you're in-between.' She saw this might confuse him. 'We say at twos and threes here. What I mean is that being a Jew is bad enough because you don't know what kind of a Jew you should be; but you're also a Roman even though you don't dress or behave like one. Why not? Are you afraid to be one or the other?' She hesitated, not wanting to go too far. 'I'm not conflicted like you. I do what I'm told because I know who I am and what I'm expected to do.' She looked off. 'I expect my husband to know that about himself as well. Otherwise, husbands and wives are not equal in life – not what you call partners.'

*

While Judas spent the next two days thinking about what she had said, Vologases and Pacorus met with their sister on several occasions.

'So he wants to move to Rome. That's a good thing. Encourage him! It's the center of their power.'

'But how do I live? And Vardanes? It's so very different there!'

'Yes, but don't worry. You'll live wealthy and we'll help you. There, you hire everything done for you or have slaves do--'

'I don't think he'll keep slaves.'

'Then hire servants. As many as you want.'

Pacorus saw the perplexed look on her face. 'Wait, Volo. She's confused,' he said.

Vologases stopped. Then he said, 'look, he's a merchant who understands the commercial nature of Roman society. Romans will pay anything for the silks and trinkets that pass through here. Well, we'll make sure he has more than he ever dreamed of.' Volo smiled. 'It's nothing to us and we'll never tell Mal about it.' He stood up, walked over to her, put his hands on her shoulders, looked her in the eyes and said, 'you must never - never - tell him about what we think! Do you understand?'

'Yes.'

'Swear it. On Vardanes' life.'

She swore.

*

When it became obvious that Judas and Mal were nearing the end of the three-month deadline they set for themselves to do what they came to do, people began to talk. They went from one merchant to another looking at silks, haggling prices and asking about future arrangements to supply more on a continuous basis. But they weren't aware of the men following them nor of their speaking with the merchants they had just talked with. They even made arrangements to rent a warehouse with rooms over the top where Mal would live. Things just fell into place like on their first trip when one day Mal jerked his head up and virtually shouted, 'you're due to leave at the end of next week!'

Judas had already decided.

'I want you and Vardanes to come with me, Tay. We'll marry here and again in Antioch. I'll adopt Vardanes as my son. I know we're different but I think you'll hold your own in our relationship and I think we can talk out whatever differences that come up between us. There's just one thing you should know. As soon as I've settled this trip's business I intend moving to Rome but keeping the Antioch house. Do you object to that?'

'No. But I want to know more about love. You didn't really answer me.'

Judas was afraid she would ask this before she gave her answer, but he knew it was best to be honest up front. 'My heart is and will always be Jewish, Tay. I'll always love you because our one God wants us to have one wife. My Romanness, if I can call it that, reflects the outer me.' She raised her eyebrows. 'Yes, I'm going to dress as the Romans due and behave like them from now on. But to answer your question. My tradition is filled with terrible stories of what being in love can do to people. It's unbridled passion, like an illness that thinks it's too good for the world. Those people live beyond belief because it's not rooted in the world we really live in. Why, I've know people to commit atrocious crimes in the name of love--'

'Like King David with Bathsheba?'

'So you know that story! Yes. It's true.' He paused. 'What I'm trying to tell you is that God is in my life and always will be. Quite literally within me. Not some made-up figure in heaven divorced from the world I live in and certainly not some graven image here on earth.'

She looked at him and now understood how to deal with him. 'I'll want a Parthian wedding, of course.'

'Of course.'

*

A week after Judas was to leave, the announcement was made and the legalities completed, Ziones - one of the merchants they dealt with agreed to serve as Titianus and Mal's partner which would free Mal to return to Antioch. He assured them and signed contractual agreements to supply all the eastern goods they ordered. At their marriage ceremony, Vologases stood up for Vardanes' long-dead father with - as Judas later remembered it - a beatific smile on his face. They then left in a one hundred and twenty camel caravan for Antioch with a formidable detachment of troops disguised as caravan drivers and guards.

Jesus must still smile on me, Judas thought. But Tay knew Vologases did. And Vardanes thought it was the greatest adventure of his life. He took two things with him: a Latin scroll which he couldn't read and his father's Roman sword that he took from a defeated enemy.

9

'**D**EAR Vologases,

The trip and Antioch were not exactly disappointments but almost. I expected to arrive in Antioch pregnant and thought Antioch would be more Roman than what it is. It's very Greek and filled with people from every nation and Syrians in particular. But make no mistake about it: under the Greek toga is the Roman armor that faces you.

About Judas: I have no idea what drives him. We have more than enough wealth to live comfortably but it doesn't seem to give him the same pleasure that planning to get it does. I had mistaken this for greed; after all, what's money for if you don't know what to do with it? But now I think I don't understand his motivation for it. He's driven by something other than the money. This is going to take more time for me to figure out.

So, I'll concentrate on his wanting to move to Rome. And to live like I think we should will take money. A lot of it if Antioch is any judge. But don't worry: I'll insist on Roman citizenship for Vardanes and myself.

In the meantime, I have some minor contradictions to deal with. Hero's grandparents, Amos and Ruth, far out-Jewish Judas so I'll call him Ti - short for Titianus - from now on. We live in a small, non-palatial house in an area where most of Antioch's wealthy people live. The Romans call it an urb of Antioch; the Greeks call it Daphne. But most people within the city walls live in tiny houses. Even what they call apartments. Some won't talk to us and a few – mainly Jews - think we're something called Gentiles. Worse: they think we're terrible for wanting to move to Rome and make a strange clucking noise with their tongues at us. I can't wait to leave.

Your dutiful sister,
Tahirir
PS: I'm not pregnant yet.'

*

Ummidius Quadratus, Claudius' newly appointed governor of Syria tried not to stare at the younger man across the table from him

'I don't have to tell you that citizenship for your two sons and wife will take a long time and be very expensive because it's more complex than yours was. By the way, I see she's Parthian.' He noticed that Titianus looked every much the Roman patrician and noticed the heavy signet ring he wore. 'I should tell you that citizenship is premised on one's wealth.'

Ti knew what he was asking because he had already taken legal advice about it. 'I have sequestered five million sesterces for our citizenship qualifications and have allocated ten percent on top of that for helpful advice. Apart from this, I'm negotiating to purchase a home – a domus – on Palentine Hill.'

Quadratus was taken aback, not expecting such large sums were involved. 'But how will you continue your eastern trade?'

'Through my partners, Amos and Mal, who will be in charge of my operations here in Antioch. These are not problems, sir. We've just returned from Ctesiphon and lead a very open, visible life here and I expect to do so in Rome where I will be coordinating my business operations. But I am somewhat pressured by time. I must settle on my domus before mid-October. Could you help me with that? I understand this shortens my time somewhat but in return I expect to furnish a suitably larger gratuity.'

A domus on Palatine Hill rang in Quadratus' mind: where many of Rome's rich and political lived. Millions of sesterces. And he calculated a proper gratuity in the back of his mind while he replied, 'may I offer some other advice apart from these legal matters?'

Ti understood the game and smiled. 'Please do. I would be most appreciative.'

'You should have a secretary. You have none, I think.'

'That's right.'

Quadratus thought so. 'You should have someone experienced and knowledgeable. Preferably a freedman who would be allowed to take personal interests in things from time to time (supercargo sprung into Ti's mind). One who doesn't merely carry out his employer's wishes, but who anticipates them. But never on his own, never independently of you. Do you follow?'

Ti nodded. He needed someone for social planning, to help his family become Romanized and know the proper social etiquette for conducting business. 'Yes, I do, thank you. Should I look for someone in Rome rather than here?'

Quadratus understood Titianus' situation perfectly. 'As you probably know, I am newly posted here and expect to be here for several years. Consequently I have hired a new one - Hellas, whom you met in the other room - for my work here but I haven't discharged Quintus yet. He's been with me for the past ten years and is extremely able and knowledgeable. He knows Rome and the people there very well.'

'I should be most grateful for the opportunity to employ him.'

'He isn't Jewish.'

'That's an even better recommendation.'

Quadratus nodded. He could see that Titianus was a quick learner. 'I think the citizenship papers should be ready on the fourth day of next week. But I won't know about the Palantine Hill property for a month, maybe two. I'll send my first inquiry on the next ship. But since they know my name there I wouldn't anticipate any difficulties. Would that be agreeable?'

'More than agreeable, sir. Shall I wait to hear from you about these matters then?' Quadratus replied yes as Ti got up to leave but then turned and asked, 'may I bring my eldest son? It's part of his education.'

Quadratus understood. Encouraging these kinds of men was part of his job. 'That's Vardanes, isn't it?'

'It's Marcus now, sir.'

*

'Dear Vologases,

We are preparing to move to Rome and thank you for your generosity. It's quite a feat; like planning for a battle I imagine. First, we got Roman citizenship for myself, Vardanes and Hero. Now we are learning about Rome and Roman ways from tutors Ti has hired - is it appropriate to call them a squad? – to teach us in the evenings. The same with tutors about speaking. One tutor even teaches Vardanes and Hero what games children play in Rome! Oh! Vardanes is now called Marcus. A good, strong Roman name.

And you wouldn't recognize us! We've changed our entire appearance to look like Romans. I wear my hair in ringlets. It's called the Cleopatra look and Titianus has even hired a secretary. One thing is similar to Ctesiphon: you never go anywhere alone. You employ what they call 'retainers' who are servants, not soldiers. But Ti hires only former soldiers, men who carry weapons hidden under their clothes and know how to use them. We've never had trouble in public. We also have banners – we use our design and colors – which the retainers carry.

Until we moved here I didn't know how minimally Jewish Ti was. Amos is much more Jewish but we don't attend synagogue services very often. Ti says he prefers us to be known as 'God-fearers,' Gentiles who loosely follow Jewish ways. It's less confusing for Marcus.

I must tell you that I never thought Marcus would accept Hero as a little brother but he has and seems delighted to watch and play baby things with him. He doesn't seem to have his father's rougher and harsher qualities. I told you Ti has adopted him as a Roman citizen. When we were discussing Roman names Vardanes said he wanted to be called Marcus, so that's what it is. I've taken the name, Tarpeia because I like the legend about her. It also allows Ti to continue calling me Tay which seems to be fixed in his mind. Which I find strange because everything else in his world seems in constant flux.

It's taken me some time getting used living with a merchant. They seem to think and plan a lot and because he does I've tried to make his home surroundings easy and familiar to him. I don't wish to offend you by saying it seems so much easier and peaceful living with him than how I lived before. I think it's because the routine of our home life isn't intruded upon as much as it used to be. But I'm still not pregnant yet.

I've been surprised at how many Parthians live here. I don't know what to expect in Rome.

Ti is planning our move for late September or October. He says he wants us settled for the social season and well before Saturnalia which he says is the festival end of the year celebration there.

Did I tell you he has gotten to know the Legate – called the Governor - here quite well?

Your dutiful sister,
Tahirir (still not pregnant)

*

Titianus and his retainers stopped and stared at the big, black-bearded man walking toward them. He was the last man in the world Ti expected to see as he was walking to his warehouse office to see Amos.

'Matthew? Matthew from Capernaum?'

Black beard looked at him; then at the retainers and standards. 'I don't know you,' he said.

'You used to know me as Judas. I'm Titianus now.'

'Judas?' He blinked several times. 'Judas. I thought you were dead! I mean, that's what John told us. That you hung yourself.'

'Do I look dead?'

'No. Of course not.' He looked right and left and then smiled at Judas.

'I heard you moved here,' Ti said.

'Yes. I have a synagogue and my son and his family live with me.'

'Your wife's dead?'

'Yes. Many years ago.' His big, wide eyes riveted on Judas' face. 'And you?'

'I'm moving to Rome.'

'From here? Have you been living here all the time?'

'I'm leaving from here but I travel a lot.'

'I feel awkward. Are you busy right now?'

'Yes. Unfortunately. But maybe I can see you before I leave. Where's your synagogue?'

'Near the reservoir. Just through the Cherubim gate.'

Ti nodded. 'I'd like to visit you.'

'I'd like that too.' He hesitated; then turned to walk away, stopped and turned back. 'I always liked you, Jud. I didn't think everything that John said about you was right. He was pretty extreme. But there were reasons why we did what we did. You know that, don't you?'

'Yes. I understand.'

'It was necessary. By the way, Peter's returning for our big Council meeting in Jerusalem but if he is still in Rome, talk to him. He'll tell you all about it.'

I nodded. 'Thank you, Matt. I've got to go now.'

We both turned and went our separate ways.

*

'Dear Vologases,

I write to you from Rome but don't know where to begin! It's like nothing you've ever experienced in your life! Ctesiphon is a small town compared to Antioch and Antioch even smaller compared to here! I've never seen so many people crammed together in one place! Nor so many different kinds of people! I hear languages I've never heard. And I think there are more slaves here than in all of Parthia! Ti says they number more than half the city!

We live in a house that Romans call a domus on a little hill called the Palantine within walking distance from the Forum, the heart of the city, and near the imperial palaces. Ti takes Marcus every day to its southeast corner where a man stands on something called a rostrum and reads the news of the day. Then the tablet is hung up for people to read. Ti and Marc go there with our 'retainers.' No, I'm not pregnant yet.

Soldiers are everywhere but our hired attendants carry our pennant which identifies us just like the purple-striped togas do the Senators. We are safe in spite of the many crazy people who give public speeches in the Forum. Which is the reason for the soldiers, I guess. They call the special peace keepers 'vigiles.'

The vast majority of people live close together in what they call apartments - Ti says they're small cramped rooms - and away from the huge public spaces where the Romans have built amphitheatres, gymnasiums and baths! Everyone bathes in public! Can you believe it!

But they're also gossip centers where you go to find out what's really going on. There's also a hippedrome called the Circus Maximus where horses and chariots race. Admission to all these is free; and markets - bazaars they called them in Antioch - are scattered everywhere. That's where our servants go. The streets are also lined with small shops where you can buy food and drink.

But if I had to mention the one thing about Rome that's different from Ctesiphon it's the reading that people do. Everyone reads scrolls or indexes they call books. There's even a special building not far from us called a 'library' which keeps them on wooden shelves. The public like us - Marcus takes Hero there frequently - can go there and read them for a small fee. Scrolls are also sold in the markets like silks. People who write the books are called 'authors.'

Living with a merchant is very different from how I lived in Ctesiphon. Ti purchased a warehouse in the Porticus Aemilia on the Tiber river which has an office on the first floor and is within walking distance from home. He spends most days there and takes Marcus when he wants to go. I see Marcus wanting to be a man more and more and both he and Ti are becoming Romans together. Marcus loves the merchant's life. You should be quite pleased. No, we never changed Hero's name because it's a proper one for a male and it's Greek. Everyone in Rome seems mad for everything Greek. All the Romans seem to want what they aren't. I guess we fit right in.

Your dutiful sister,
Tahirir'

*

'Dear Brother,

I haven't told you about our home or neighbors. First, you were absolutely right about the Romans and money. There's no temple to it but it's their real god and they're absolutely mad for it. So thank Ahuraz that Ti has a natural instinct for it and is encouraging Marcus to develop his own. Ti says the heart of business here is social, that anyone can know numbers or how to calculate profits. So when he came here he bought the largest house in the most prestigious neighborhood he could find and we live very close to the imperial palace. It's a huge, two story block of connected houses arranged in a rectangular around a central courtyard that has a pool. Three or four families could live here but he says we'll grow into it. No, I'm not pregnant yet.

Unlike our home, it has rooftop gardens and animals are kept in pens away from the house but most food and everything else is brought here. There's no reason to leave the house unless for social reasons and then we go with armed guards disguised as servants who carry pennants with the same symbol as his signet ring. That part is very much like how we live in Ctesiphon and Ecarta.

But I must tell you about our closest neighbor, Senator Marcus Publix Agrippa who's too rich and well connected for me to even understand. And he's very odd. He's crippled and shuffles along using sticks. He also has a small army of servants who help him. He reminds me of Claudius, our emperor, and our father after he became ill. Agrippa was injured in accident a few years ago which killed his wife and left him with a three year old daughter and two older sons. She's five or six now, about the same age as Hero.

One of his oddities is he's crazy for cats and keeps two special ones. He had a cage the size of two rooms built so they can go outside and not be bothered by dogs. He actually talks to them, feeds them by hand, sleeps with them, and has them carried in cages to the Senate meetings with him! He even claims they have supernatural powers! Don't the Egyptians do too? It's all very strange; but you never ridicule a Senator in public. He's invited us for dinner next month so I'll know more about him after that and why he seems to love his cats more than his sons.

Very few other neighbors live in separate domus' as we do. Most live in very cramped quarters. But those who do live in domus' are mainly senators from old landed families. We're told that the social season runs from about late September until early May. Quintus, Ti's secretary, has been enormously helpful in knowing what kinds of wines and food to serve and what the appropriate dinner protocol is. Socializing here is very different from Ctesiphon. The men talk politics, geography and empire, the women about the latest fashions and what their latest purchases are. I have never known women to be so consumed by what is the latest fashion, jewelry, clothing and hairstyles! But this commercial culture means you have to buy things so if you send some things that you think are particularly beautiful and exotic I shall wear them to help Ti sell them. I must also tell you how corrupt this society is. Ti and I are hardly prudes – yes, we work really hard and frequently at trying to make a baby - but even we are shocked at the indecent ways men and women here talk and act toward one another in public. Hero is particularly shocked and ashamed, especially by the public toilets which both sexes use for bodily functions, gossiping, meeting the opposite sex, and inviting people to dinner parties. It's unbelievable!

This reminds me, and I don't mean to get off the subject, but the most difficult thing here for Ti has been dealing with the altar in our home. Every house has one dedicated to the Roman gods. But the Romans are like us – Parthians I mean. We have no problems with images and are indifferent about the gods of other peoples. But this bothers him for some reason and he won't talk about it. And he avoids the room; he won't go in it. And yet when we're in someone else's home he has no problem participating in whatever is said and done about the deities. I find it strange, like Publix' craziness about cats.

This is all by way of saying that public life can be very different from private life; and I now understand Ti better when he say he wants little to do with public life and prefers a private one of pursuing private interests.

He's different from what I expected.

Your dutiful but still not pregnant sister,

Tahirir

10

'I want to go to Alexandria for about a month, maybe a month and a half.'

'Whatever for?' A year ago Tay never knew where Alexandria was; or Egypt for that matter. But once settled in Rome Ti had hired a succession of tutors who came in the evenings with maps, charts, and tables and gave talks to them about the Roman world they lived in. Information, Ti told her and the boys, makes getting silks possible.

'For two reasons. One is to examine the grain trade. Alexandria's the basis for it in the empire and it will just grow. Amos has been gathering information about shipping for our exports from Antioch so we're learning a lot about shipping. But the most important reason is that I met an Indian merchant the other day who said that silks are also made in India and that other Indian products are equally valuable. They call pepper 'black gold' in the spice trade and I'd like to see what else comes from India and especially how. Alexandria seems to be developing the Southern Sea route to the east.'

'I remember seeing silks from India when I was girl.'

'He said his nephew in Alexandria imports them and then sends them on here.'

She looked blank knowing Alexandria wasn't near India. 'You mean it's all by water! The southern sea!' She said thinking about the long overland journey to Parthia.

'That's right,' he said, smiling.

She was suddenly frightened. 'You know I'm not a water person.'

'Don't worry. I want you to stay here and be sociable, charming and exotic.' He smiled. 'Your usual self! I just want to scout this out. India's a long way away even by water. But it might solve some of our problems.' So he explained to her the two routes to the east, the northern one to Parthia and the potential southern one by water to India. When he said both would by-pass Israel, she understood better. It was more personal than business and a long, slow fight for him to leave his old self. And it wasn't over.

But then he was quiet. Which she knew meant he had something more on his mind. 'I want to take Marc with me to Alexandria,' he said. 'Hero's only seven so he's too little.'

'But Ti, Marc's only thirteen!'

'Practically fourteen and time to see more of the real world. I was fourteen when I left home. Don't worry. I'll watch after him.'

She just stared at him, remembering him a baby in her arms.

'Look. You know how I have Quintus write out my itinerary with the names of everyone I'm to meet and brief memos about them and why I'm meeting them. He can just give you a copy of it so you'll know where we are on almost every day. And if you have a problem write to where I'm expected to be about a week and a half from the time you write.'

But she worried. 'It will be his first time to be away from me so long.'

'Yes. But I thought we could call it his second big adventure.'

Sons, she thought. So eager to be in the big wide world and it doesn't get much bigger than this. 'All right.' But why can't God give me a daughter? She thought - wished – and longed for.

*

'You're leaving me with Hero but not pregnant, Ti.'

Ti got up from the little table in their bedroom and went over to sit beside her on the lounge. 'I don't know why not. We both have had children with other people. Would you like to see a doctor while I'm away?'

'No. I don't think there's anything wrong physically. I mean I don't have pains and nothing's unusual or different about. . . about anything.' Ti took her hand in his and didn't know what to say. 'Do you think it's spiritual? Is there some reason that God doesn't want us to have children?' He squeezed her hand and drew a deep breath. He had been dreading facing up to this. 'I admit I've tried to escape my Jewishness even before we met. But I've always wanted a wife and children.' He looked her in her eyes. 'I want us to have a child. You know I haven't been holding that back.'

'I know. But it bothers me that I haven't been able to get pregnant.'

'What else can I do?'

'You never go into the altar room.'

He was surprised. 'The household gods!' He paused and looked away. 'I don't put much stock in them.'

'Then pray to your own! Will you do that for me?'

He put his head down so that his chin was on his chest. 'This may seem strange to you. But I've wondered about why you haven't become pregnant. I've had strange ideas about it. Maybe Jesus and God have punished me for not marrying a Jewess. Maybe Jesus has done this for my . . . sin--'

'What sin?'

'Abandoning him to the Romans and disappearing.'

'Oh, that. You told me about it. I can't believe he would do that.'

'Maybe it's a doubt I've carried for many years.'

'Ti, we're not talking about guilt. We're talking about the result of a physical act. There's no mystery about it. And that's what marriage is, a license to have sex and children as much as you want.'

'Then why did you raise it? The part about the mystery and the suggestion that I pray?' When she didn't answer, he said, 'I agree. I'll pray.' He paused. 'Can we agree not to blame each other? Let's not confuse what is now with the past.'

'All right. But I'm not getting any younger.'

'Maybe we should try once more then?' He smiled his come-on smile.

She smiled. 'Let's pray first.'

*

Looking across the water at Alexandria two miles away, I was reminded that Judas the vanner never came to Alexandria by water. He only saw its land side, the side where the Jews and poor lived and where the city melted into brown veins that stretched into the brown desert. Its land arteries were contracting now; and there was even talk of building a canal to connect the city with the Red Sea. I'm sure that will come to pass in a few years, he thought.

And Alexandria's a trader's city: you can almost smell the intrigues that lay behind the haggling in the off-shore wind. Everything for sale - and nothing. Goods - the lifeblood of the city - are bargained for in all the bazaars where information is only promised in quiet whispers.

But Titianus was looking at the water side of the empire's second largest city. It's beautiful and far more Greek than Roman. The lighthouse, the crescent shaped shore line, the houses and tavernas where those merchants live whose merchandise we vanned. There's not a camel in sight, he thought; nor walls nor soldiers.

And only five districts, not fourteen like Rome. It should be easy to locate who I need to. He remembered them ghettoizing the city twelve years ago, Jews shoved into two of the five; everyone else living wherever they could afford to. Manga and the Buddhists probably live among the Jews. I felt a twinge of guilt: I hadn't told Tay about Thomas and Buddhists. Or about Matthew.

What is going on? Is my past catching up with me? First, Matthew in Antioch and now Thomas in Alexandria? What does this mean? I missed Peter in Rome; he had already left for Jerusalem; but Matthew later told me they decided I wasn't going to say anything. We talked about what they did several times when I went to see Amos there.

'Stay invisible,' Matt had said. 'Stay Titianus and do whatever you're doing. Stay socially invisible. You can best serve us as the devil. We discussed all this twenty years ago when Peter and John called us together in Galilee. None of us wanted to go back to the old life. Or abandon Jesus. By admitting he was wrong and we had failed. And we were afraid the Zealots would attack us in revenge for not allying ourselves with them. So Peter and John said we should return to Jerusalem and to build on what he taught us: the church. That was an easy choice. Who wants to live in Capernaum after living in Jerusalem? So we went back there! We knew you had fled as we did. But no one knew where you had gone so Peter suggested that we dispose of you. Just say you were dead. But then John came up with the idea that we say that you were paid to betray him because it better fit our story. Peter and I knew better but figured you'd understand.'

'But Thomas didn't?'

'You know what a doubter he is. He didn't think the story would make sense but the Sanhedrin didn't deny it.'

'Is that why he left?'

'No. And that's what none of us understood. He left later, after we had been successful. Had established a following and began meetings and established some order and procedures. You know how he was. A stickler for the spirit, for the inner God. He kept railing about how Peter and we were just creating a different synagogue order. 'It was just a new formalism,' he said.'

I remember nodding and thinking: that's Thomas all right. 'But he didn't join the other spiritualists? In Antioch or Cyrene?'

'No. We heard he went to Alexandria. And then he just disappeared. Like you did.'

*

I also have to confess telling Tay about Grupa but not Manga. Grupa imported goods from India to his warehouse up river from mine; and I was fascinated with them; They were unusual, exotic and rare and I instantly knew what attracted me most was their very high profits on very low volume with next to no competition.

'Ahhh, uncle says you want to go to India where Romans are?' said the small brown man that Grupa had called nephew. He had the same sing-song voice and slight, dark stature but blacker hair that Grupa did. He also had the same white teeth and constant nodding of his head.

'Yes. But I want to talk to people first. People who have sailed there and maybe lived there.'

'You want to know what it's like? Yes, very wise, very prudent. And you're taking your son?' He turned to Marcus.

'Yes. And my secretary.'

Manga surveyed us as a group and said, 'then you should go with a group.'

'There are groups who sail there?'

'Oh, yes. Merchants and soldiers.' He looked at me with large eyes. 'You choose.'

I was surprised and not surprised. 'How large a city is Muzirus?'

'Not as large as Alexandria. Maybe one,' he held up one finger then four. 'How long will you stay?'

'At least one full year but probably two,' I said. 'To understand the growing seasons.'

'Very wise,' he replied.

I could see that Manga was a careful man; perhaps because, like me, he was a foreigner making his way in a strange culture . 'How long ago did you come here?' I asked.

'Many, many years ago,' he flashed his toothy white smile. 'Grupa brought me as a boy.'

I calculated twenty years ago. When I was with Jesus. 'Then you lived in Rome!'

'Oh, no. We lived here until I was older. Then he moved to Rome.'

It was difficult to judge his age. I guessed around forty since I thought Grupa about sixty. 'So, you have many business contacts here. Are you the only one who trades India goods?'

'Yes. Here in Alexandria. But my uncle's go through me as well. What I mean is that his come to me and he directs me what to do with them.'

I understood it instantly. It was cheaper for Grupa to set up his distribution point in Alexandria than in Rome. 'So, from Muzirus, I could direct goods to you or to Grupa?'

'Yes. But we trade with all the other seaports around the Great Sea.'

'May we see your warehouse?'

His warehouse was arranged as Grupa's was. Textiles separated from the spices, from the gems, from the metal workings, and from the glassware. I was about to comment on how similar his arrangement was to Grupa's when I realized he had probably organized it using Grupa's as the model.

'It's similar to Grupa's,' Marcus whispered.

'He probably set it up originally,' I whispered back. 'Who should I talk to first about going there?' I asked Manga.

He thought a minute. 'I would talk to the ship captains first. They will know when they are going and it's important to get the winds right. They'll know about such things.'

I certainly knew nothing about sailing. 'Do they frequent any particular tavernas?'

'Start with the Dolphin and ask for Aristides or Timaeus or Crestias. They've all sailed there and Timaeus even sailed with Hippalus.'

He looked at me sideways when he said the last name; even I knew he was revered as the god of the Southern Sea.

*

That's where we learned that the Greeks were the geographers of the sea. No, every captain told us, we don't sail to India during the winter but only during the summer when the prevailing winds come from the southeast. Yes, we only return during the winter, most specifically during December and early January when the winds come from the northwest. But the starting point is not Alexandria: it's Aden just east of the Red Sea. Yes, it's the caravan point for Mecca to Petra and where the Romans have established a garrison. If the winds are right, it's a forty day sail to Muzirus. Yes, it's done all the time and merchants who make the run can usually do a round trip in one year.

Once I understood this, I realized new directions for our southern caravan trade would have to be made and we had maybe four months to get ready.

So, I next inquired of the consul about Roman ships sailing the route. There were, he explained, regular sailers and irregular ones. Those from Alexandria to Aden were regular – monthly - and used by the military. When we decided we wanted to leave we could book passage just as we had from Rome to Alexandria. Irregular sailers were what the name said: haphazard about when they left no matter where they were bound for. It all depended on cargo and - less so - on passengers. Yes, the Red Sea was becoming Roman water as much as the Great Sea was, but the Southern Sea remained a free-for-all and full of pirates. His best advice: choose your captain carefully, the fastest sailer and the most heavily armed one. And since you're booking three passengers write to the Roman aedile in Aden, tell him your reasons for going, give him your requirements and give him two and three month choices for the trip from there to Muzirus; then let him make the choice for you.

I understood they wanted to encourage trade and would be solicitous of our welfare; they wanted a steady stream of taxes. I thanked him for his suggestions, followed his advice and told Marcus 'what a difference from how Israel treats us.'

11

I never told Tay about Thomas. Why not? I always liked him and he was among my last friendly links with Jesus' disciples. But now I realize I was never ready to tell her about my experiences with Jesus. And it wasn't because I was ashamed about them or that the stories they told about me were so untrue; it was simply because they were too painful.

I liked Thomas' down-to-earth, sensibly-oriented mind, so opposite the confused one's of most of the other disciples and John's dreamy one. Where John filtered worldly reality through his mind, Thomas didn't. He went the other way and pursued God within his small, wiry and slender body which made what he did seem so much purer when all it was, was merely simpler. 'There are only three sources: the holy spirit, and the last two are false.'

So, it shocked me when Manga told me that he was a well-known follower of the Buddhists. Why? I saw some in Ctesiphon but couldn't imagine a shaven-headed Thomas in dark brown clothes walking along chanting and fingering beads like a Greek or shaking a tambourine or rattling beads like an Indian.

But he wasn't that way and taught me to distrust my imagination. He looked like he did twenty years ago but older. 'Thomas! It's so good to see you after all these years!'

'And you, Judas!'

'I'm Titianus now.'

'And you look every inch of it!' He stepped back and surveyed me. 'I'll admit, I doubted who you were when I first saw you.'

So, it was I who had drastically changed. 'This is my son, Marcus.'

They exchanged greetings and Thomas invited us into his house.

'How long have you lived here?' I asked.

'Four years in this house and eight in Alexandria. I went to Antioch after Jerusalem, then to Cypress and then to Cyrene. But I found those people were too confused and thought God was what they felt. So, I came here.'

'And you feel at home with the Buddhists?'

'I'd say we share a certain identity. Like I did with everyone when we were Jesus' disciples. I discovered I have a lot in common with the Indians.'

'Such as?'

'Seeking the divine within you. They believe in rebirth. Like Jesus talked about our being reborn. They share--'

'That's what we used to talk about!' I interrupted.

He switched subjects. 'You know about the Grand Council Meeting last year, don't you?' Puzzlement suddenly swept over his face. 'Or was it the year before?'

'I heard something about it,' I replied, wondering why he switched so suddenly. 'They were wrangling about whether to preach to Gentiles, weren't they?'

'Yes. This Paul has them confused because he did that in Arabia and Syria with great success.'

'I heard about that in Antioch. When I was there a couple of years ago they were calling the Jesus Jews Christians.'

'It's all the work of a merchant there. Samuel. He was Stephen's father, you know. Oh! I forgot! You weren't!' He shook his head. Samuel and his friends are financing Paul's work but trying to confine him to the seaports where they trade regularly.' He suddenly stopped and stared at me. 'You do know about what Peter and the others did, don't you?'

'Yes,' I nodded. 'So Paul's the spearhead?' I had heard so many stories about how Peter changed the disciples I knew into apostles but didn't want to discuss it.

'Not in the sense of leading them,' Thomas replied. 'Peter favors the Gentiles just as much as he does but I think it's more Samuel than Paul.'

'Is that why Matthew moved to Antioch? To fight it? Remember Matt telling us on our northern tour that he would never preach to the Gentiles?'

'Yes.' Thomas looked nostalgic. 'Those were good times,' he said. 'But it all changed after Peter escaped to Rome and James became the head of the church. He's more a priest type than Peter is.'

He wasn't making much sense and I didn't want to pursue this, so I changed topics. 'Tell me about the Buddhists. You mentioned you felt you shared the divine with them.'

Thomas looked down and slowly replied: 'I think we share looking for the divine within us but that's all. You know how we retain our individuality without obliterating our separate relationships to God? Well, they try to lose themselves in the divine. It's like they want to dissolve themselves in it. It's a strange, isn't it?' He stopped and I could see wanted to say more. 'But it's given me an idea.'

'What's that?'

'If there are a lot of people like that in India, I want to go there. If I share a road with someone it's easier to take them to the true house instead of a wrong one.' Then he looked up at me. 'From the looks of you, you don't proselytize his Gospel anymore.' He turned to Marcus. 'You've never seen him proselytize, have you?'

'No.'

He turned back to me. 'You know they had to make you into the devil when they created their church, don't you? It was John's idea.'

'Yes,' I replied. 'You sound like you disagree with what they did.'

'To be honest, I simply doubt the wisdom of what they did. It made sense at the time but something about it didn't ring right with me.' He hesitated. 'Some continue to say bad things about you.'

'You mean John?'

'And his followers. He seems bent on keeping heaven separate from earth and denying the divinity of man.' He turned to Marcus again. 'I probably shouldn't speak so technically since you're probably not used to it.'

'I don't mind.' Marcus replied.

I didn't say anything because I wanted Marc to see how different the world was and because I was neither ashamed nor proud of having been different in my past from what I am now. And I was sure I would be something different yet again. That was the way of the world if one paid attention to it. Attention as in noticing, not becoming a slave to it. That's what I wanted Marc to learn.

*

Thomas was right: the Buddhists were very different from us. Not just because they worshipped their god differently and all the time; but because the rhythm of their lives were unified as no other group I ever saw. Even when I had been with the other disciples, we didn't share that similarity to the degree which they did. They were in unison; were one; they looked the same in dress, behavior, what they ate and how they replied to our questions. But I couldn't understand their passivity toward life! I can't stand people like that and even Marc commented 'no wonder the Romans are doing everything they can to get to India!' I thought it quite astute of a sixteen year old.

But a few weeks later, while I was going over a list of what I thought we would need from Manga, he cautioned me about them. 'Don't be fooled by my people here. Oh, I'm peaceful enough and quite harmless because I want to live like a Roman. But don't think all our people are like me or Grupa.' When I raised my eyebrows, he added, 'They are disciples of Buddha and only a tiny minority of the people. They're articulate and friendly here, but most Indians are not like them. Be warned.'

*

Hellas, Marcus and I left Manga's warehouse and were walking through the third district's main bazaar when Marcus suddenly yelled, 'look ahead!' and pointed: 'The man in white who just turned into that street!' All three of us were dazzled by the incredible whiteness of his robe: it couldn't have been Egyptian because their cottons are browns - beige at best.

So, Marcus ran ahead and stood pointing down the cross street. 'He went down here.'

When Hellas and I reached the corner, the two ran further on down but no one was in sight and only the first two buildings had shops on the ground floor.

Then white robe emerged from one of them and looked at us. 'Why are you following me?'

I told him I was interested in where he got his robe from and whether he had had it dyed. I was particularly intrigued by the small and discrete 'JC' white insignia embossed on the left shoulder and another one centered on his back.

No, no, he said. He bought it this way off the shelf and told us where.

The mystery deepened a half hour later when the 'where' turned out to be a warehouse at the docks near Manga's and not a shop. No wonder we've only seen this one, I thought, which was confirmed by the man in his office looking older than I am.

'I'm called Joseph,' he introduced himself, 'and no, I don't have coats in any colors other than white.'

'And the J in the JC embossed on your clothes,' I asked, 'does that stand for Joseph?'

He laughed. 'No. For Jesus,' he said. 'As in Jesus Christ. I'm a weaver and since noticing the number of his followers are increasing I thought I would market a line of clothes that would advertise him and me at the same time.'

'Brilliant!' I said and smiled.

He looked at me. 'You're a Roman aren't you?'

'Yes,' I replied and introduced the others.

'The way I figure it, they're now called Christians and spreading throughout the seaports which makes it easy to market to them from here.'

'You need a distribution network,' I replied and saw Marc roll his eyes. 'Do you have someone for Rome?'

'No.' He looked at me in the appraising way that I've long been used to.

'Hellas, please note what Joseph says in answers to some questions I'm going to ask him.' I turned to Joseph and explained, 'he's my secretary. Now, how do you sell the goods. In bolts, leaving it up the merchants to tailor it to their individual customers?'

'Yes. That's what I've been doing.'

'How many wraps are you getting per bolt?'

'Normally, twenty. Thirty makes each one too heavy for shipment and handling.' He paused. 'Where's this going?'

'I like your product and ideas, but I'm doing this mentally. If I think it's worth my while I'll make you an offer right now for an on-going business relationship. We'll make and sign a contract and I'll pay you through a local merchant. I'm returning to Rome in two weeks.'

Joseph stared at him. He never met such a determined man in his life; one who actually *did* what most people only think about it. 'You remind me of someone I once knew. He was no nonsense about life too.'

'It's too short.'

'That's not what he said.'

*

'This will be our longest separation, Ti.'

'I know. But many, many good things could come from it and I'll learn a lot more than merely making money. Besides, Marc should come back a man and this experience is far better than wasting his time going to Athens with the other young men to learn about past glories.'

'I know this is going to be a long time but I can see there will be others. Do you mind if I do some remodeling?'

'Some remodeling?' I'm sure how I felt appeared on my face: puzzled. 'Of our house?'

'Yes, but just these two or three rooms that seem to have become our personal ones. I want to call them our 'return rooms."' She smiled at him looking at her, knowing he hadn't a clue about what she was talking about. 'I think you understand that life's not all go-ahead. Returning is just as important.'

'That's fine. Suit yourself about them. And while we're talking about mechanics, are you clear about Amuz's trips to Amos and having your correspondence sent on to Mal?' Amuz was her Parthian male servant.

'Yes.'

'If you need money, just ask Quintus. He'll give you whatever you need.'

'Needs and wants are two different things. I want to become pregnant.'

'Don't see Quintus about that. We only have tonight.'

'Will you promise me one thing while you're away?'

'Yes.'

'I want you to think long and hard about this spiritually.'

He smiled. 'Don't worry. That comes naturally. See!'

Seven days after he left, and when she was sitting alone at her dressing table, it struck her: why was he doing this? She understood his explanation of wanting to teach Marc - indeed, that was part of the original purpose for marrying him and moving here. But what else drove him to risk his life on such a journey? Surely, there was something more than the money. More than its material aspects. There must be. She picked up her comb and ran it through her hair. Am I afraid to know? He's been a good husband and father; and we're rich. What more is there?

Indeed, what more is there? She thought about her life. She never told him about her letters to and from Vologases; or what her life had been like, or what was now expected of her. Give, give, give had been drummed into her ever since she could remember. Men are warriors; please them and they'll protect you. But more importantly, remember that life is social; you can never find yourself in isolation, only through others. Giving yourself to others is the ath to the true light, the light beyond passion. She remembered Vardanes and thought he did. But she was so young then. Does Ti? She put her comb down. Not in the same way. He's different. He thinks all the time. About worldly things. Is he thinking about me now? Or Hero?

And why is he anxious all the time! Why should he be? Doesn't he know himself? Is that it? That he's unhappy with himself? Or is about something? How can I help him? To find peace. Maybe that's what he's doing: exhausting himself in the pursuit of material life to curb his anxiety. Does he know what makes him anxious?

PART TWO

REVELATIONS

12

THE man in white had been talking for a while now and observing the people sitting listening to him. He tried to see their faces and refer to his notes as little as possible; he wanted to be as personal and meaningful as he could. Sometimes it worked.

Each was different from the others but there were growing numbers of them and it was hard work. Families and individuals, men, women and children; each one precious. And here was this odd looking man sitting in front of him. Red streaked hair; emaciated face; arms hugging his knees and rocking back and forth on his haunches. God, he stinks from camels! Another casualty of the pain and suffering in the world. 'That's why I urge you to love your neighbor,' the man in white continued. 'Because that's what love is: friendship in its deepest sense. Deeper than any worldly gain – he paused – yes, deeper, even, than sex.' That got their attention as he knew it would. Even haunch rocker's.

Afterwards, when people milled about the food table while his helpers moved among them, talking and trying to be helpful, he saw Peter offer some bread to camel stink and went over to them.

'I've known Jesus for years,' he heard Peter say, 'and he's the most trustworthy person I've ever met.' Then Peter saw me over his shoulder, coming up-wind behind camel stink and said, 'Jesus, this is Judas. It's his first time here.'

'Welcome, friend,' I said as Judas turned around, his left hand covering his mouth as he choked and swallowed. Finally, he garbled, 'I resonated with what you said. You speak with more understanding than anyone I've ever known.'

Resonated? I thought. As in echo? What a peculiar way to put it! I immediately felt he was interesting. Worth knowing better.

*

I never forgot that first meeting with Jesus. About the same height as I was, but a few years older, his eyes looked into mine for the longest time without blinking, appraising or judging. Restful. Peaceful. Unquestioning. I remember feeling at ease for the first time in months. But Peter! I'm sure he thought I hadn't eaten in a week because of the way I was wolfing the bread down. And he was right.

I was twenty two and suddenly realized I smelled from camel. Peter was as tall as I but full bearded and a few years older. He said he was the only married man among Jesus' helpers, and had two children. The others were single men like me but much younger. In their teens and still naïve, I remember thinking, and with little experience of the world. I had already had enough for any ten of them of them. I asked Jesus 'how do I hear more about what you have to say about life?'

'Live with us for awhile,' he replied. 'We only ask you to help with the work. Peter or James will tell you what we need.' Then he looked more directly at me. 'You're not a Galilean.'

'No,' I answered.

Both of them stared at me for a long moment until Jesus finally said, 'welcome' and walked away.

*

That's how it began. I joined about fifty men, women and children who followed, listened and watched him. It was a fluid group, many dropping out and new ones replacing them; but no one seemed bothered by it. We moved out from Capernaum where I first met him to village after village and sometimes towns around the northern rim of the Sea of Galilee. Jesus spoke at the Sabbath services and outside when the crowds were too big to fit into the assembly halls. Only large towns like Capernaum had real synagogues but after a while they were closed to us.

He was most effective in the countryside where he would stand on a little hill, his back to the wind, and talk to hundreds of people gathered in a semicircle around him. We slept in the fields and walked on, people running ahead of us to announce our coming.

I joined the other helpers to drive, tether and feed the animals. I baked bread and served it; fished, cooked and served it. I guided other people who came to listen to him and talked with them about what he taught us. And I played with the children. It all felt so right; and I became less anxious and distracted, less bothered by my terrible nightmares. And I noticed my clothes felt tighter.

Jesus seemed to have known a few of his disciples from years past. But he was easy to talk to. So was a big bearded, more diffident young man named Matthew. He and Peter were really Levi and Simon; Jesus had renamed them but not himself. Renaming them seemed odd to me so I stayed Judas.

*

'You don't seem as anxious as you did when we first met,' Jesus said to me one day as I walked beside him. We were returning home to Capernaum from one of our tours.

'I'm not. You've made me think about a lot of things in my life. But especially to live it according to purpose.'

'Then you know your next step is to live it.' He said this as an afterthought while looking up at the sky. 'But you're not ready yet, are you?' When I told him no he said, 'taking the next step in life is more about being sure of yourself than it is knowing the next step to take.' He stopped talking and looked at me. 'Our numbers are reaching the point where we need someone to act as treasurer. Want the job? You seem to know about keeping accounts.'

'Yes,' I replied, little knowing what lay ahead of me. Or what Matthew would think about it.

'See what I mean?' he said.

This time I stared at him: how did he know that?

*

Jesus - I learned in bits and pieces - wasn't from Capernaum but Nazareth and was the eldest son of a farming family. His father was a carpenter by trade who disappeared when Jesus was about fourteen, leaving his wife with seven live children, four sons and three daughters, and two dead ones lying in little graves in an outcropping they called a farm.

But Jesus - who looked seven or eight years older than I was - didn't work at the carpentry trade, had never married and apparently didn't like farm work anymore than his father did. He had moved to Capernaum after joining the hordes baptized by John in the Jordan river. I had heard stories from other vanners about John; most of whom called him a wild-eyed incarnation of the old prophet, Elijah.

'Why did he come to Capernaum?' I asked Peter one time.

'Because he remembered visiting his cousins John and James there when he was a boy. He still loves to skip stones on the water.'

I didn't connect much of the information until I met Salome and Zebedee, his aunt and uncle; a warm woman and capable, gentleman. Both were very friendly to me as James their eldest son was, and completely the opposite of their son John.

Peter was also new to Capernaum. A fisherman like Zebedee, he had moved his family from the tiny village of Bethsaida on the north shore nearly five years ago and lived next door to James and John. Peter and James were like two peas in the same pod: big, active and outdoorsy. Jesus and I were not as big and John was the runt. He had been sick a lot as a child, Peter told me, and spent his time indoors reading rather than outdoors wrestling. He knew a lot; but from scrolls rather than life, which is how I accounted for his dislike of me.

Andrew, Peter's younger brother, was different. Something was wrong with him. He was dreamy and lost in his own world most of the time. And he was quick to take offense at what he thought about instead of what anyone actually said or did; so Peter tried to never leave him alone.

Eventually, Jesus chose them, a few others and me to become his special followers; his disciples as representatives of the twelve tribes of Israel, he said. He also said he would teach us things that not everyone knew. I didn't ask him where he learned them; but the longer I knew the others the more I believed the only thing we had in common was Jesus.

13

'**But** I thought *we* were the opposition!' The large man with the big beard was easy and out-going, and when you first met him you would think he was a natural-born leader: until you discovered he wasn't very smart. I don't mean scroll learning: he had just been around fish too long and they're as dumb as you can get. We usually had these kinds of discussions around the campfire after dinner and the topic tonight was about who opposed us and why.

'That's from their point of view,' Jesus replied. 'But our problem is that few people understand anything. Most don't and worse, don't want to. Very few want to understand--'

'But they're the ones we're trying to reach!' John interrupted. He was sixteen and ignorant about life which was excusable; his bad manners were not.

I think people become what – not who - they think they are and I confess that I thought Peter felt comfortable playing the 'poor dumb me' role because he had done it successfully for a long time. But I practiced charity by chalking it up to his being ill-educated and not having the opportunity to become imaginatively creative like John. Besides, he was married to a woman smarter than he is and - thank God, I thought - both were smart enough to know it. Everyone said character, not intellect, is his strength and that's why - as he frequently says - 'he's not afraid of opposition because he's had to deal with it all his life.' Well, haven't we all? Just different variations of it but we usually don't talk about it. Later, I learned that he had been forced to after his father died when he was eleven and his mother never remarried. But whatever the reasons, Peter never learned to fight with his mind like John does; that's why he doesn't see the invisible.

'We should think of opposition as temptation,' Jesus said, looking around. 'As a temptation to be overcome. Think of what you're after, what you want to achieve as your goals. Good ones, of course.' That made sense to several of us and to Peter which I was glad for because I knew he would ask Hannah about it when he went home.

But I thought about his observation and said, 'I don't fear either one as much as I find temptation to be personal and opposition to be social.' I felt John stare at me in an appraising way. He's probably thinking I'm six or seven years older than he but not sure why I'm different from the others. Probably thinks it's my Idumean heritage or experiences in the caravan trade. 'You seem to be taking your message to people as individuals rather than calling them forth as a social movement,' I continued. 'Re-forming people as individuals rather than our society. Is that what you're really after?' I said it partly to provoke Simon the Zealot and glanced at him. As usual, his face didn't reveal what he thought.

Jesus smiled in the silence.

I know what he's thinking, I said to myself: that there are sheep and goats and Thomas and I are the goats.

But finally he said, 'you can't have society without people, Judas. I'm not Moses leading the people to a new mountain.'

'But you're like him and Elijah and many of the old prophets. They all talked to God too!'

'The question you should ask is whether and how anyone in the world can ever go back.'

'To when? Before Eden?'

Jesus smiled again. At least he doesn't think I'm a fool, I thought.

'Yes, to before.'

James, John's older brother but even

slower in the brains department than Peter, suddenly stood up, which signaled - I had come to learn - that he had had enough abstract conversation.

'But before we all retire,' Jesus said quickly, 'I want to say that we'll be home by late afternoon tomorrow and I want us to meet at my house the following morning--'

'Third hour?'

'Yes. The third hour. I think this tour could have been more successful and I want us to think about what we could do better about our tours like this one. I'd like each of you to think of one thing we can do to improve the way we do things. And Judas, I'd like you to begin our discussion and I'll expect everyone else to join in the conversation.'

*

'Tents,' I said the morning after.

'What?'

'Tents,' I answered. 'That's the answer for us. That's how our ancestors did it. They kept the weather at bay and could stay anywhere for long periods of time as long as water was near.'

Andrew started clapping and laughing and rocking back and forth. His brother reached over and steadied him.

Jesus smiled and nodded.

Perfect, I thought. Just the kind of thing he probably expected from me.

Peter, householder and animal keeper, looked as though an idea was forming in his brain: you know that scrunched up face look? With a tongue tip showing? 'Then we could take a few animals with us and stay longer in one place!'

'It would be like camping out!' Thad enthused. By this time, I was over the shock of his being older than John.

'Why don't we just become Bedouins!' Thomas seemed disgusted but looked at me and winked, and said, 'it says a lot about how citified we've become, don't you think?

'Why don't you expand on your point.' Jesus said to me.

I smiled. This was fun. They seemed like such babes in the woods. 'Let's start with the synagogues. You all know how few and far between they are. Only towns the size of Capernaum or larger have one. The smaller ones have only assembly halls and--'

'So we could have one tent dedicated to setting up synagogue services!'

John's bright, I thought; I must remember that. 'That's right,' I replied. 'But let's go a step further and set up our tents in those villages that don't even have assembly halls!'

John was impressed and said so, and Peter and James were already planning how they would keep the animals. I caught Jesus' eye and pressed the tip of my index finger to the tip of my thumb. He smiled.

*

The trouble with tents is that they keep the rain out but not rocks. When it rained rocks in the middle of one night I knew some of our opposition had crossed the border between peace and violence. But by the time we were all roused and ready to go in the direction they came from, the rain stopped and we knew they were gone.

'What do you make of it?' Jesus asked me.

What was strange was that the instant he asked me that I understood he knew more about me than I thought he did. How did he? 'I think it comes back to what you said about opposition the other night,' I replied. 'Only the ones who fear us brought their hate into this.' I stopped and looked at him. They really fear change.' He nodded but continued looking back at me. 'I've never understood that. Fearing change.'

'But you still don't understood truth.'

That caught me up short and I stared at him. 'I won't argue with you about that. How can I understand something that doesn't include me?'

'You sound like Peter but you're really like Thomas, aren't you?' Jesus said in his dreamy voice and looked away. 'You fear the unknown and haven't found God's presence within you.'

'No, and I don't need to, to guess that this kind of violent opposition will just increase.'

'Maybe that's merely the way of the world that we also don't understand.' His reply surprised me.

'So, we're only trying to reach the ones who want to change? But how do we protect ourselves in the meantime?'

He wasn't listening. 'I've had three dreams about you.'

I looked at him, expecting – and hoping - him to elaborate.

'One time with a young girl. Veil-less. Another time you were with a Nabatean man.' Jesus looked up into the now starry night sky.

'And the third?' I asked.

He looked back into my eyes. His were looking into a different place. 'You were covered in blood.'

I shuddered and thought how could he possibly know? 'Perhaps I was involved in a sacrifice,' I replied. 'You know how bloody they can be.'

'No, I think that if you're not careful, Judas, you will be the sacrifice.' Then he shook himself, turned and walked away.

I felt fearful, creepy: it was the first time I felt a reality beyond my senses and I was afraid.

*

Judas woke with a start and bathed in sweat after spending most of the night twisting and turning. The girl's face was larger than life and focused in front of him. Young, innocent, sweet: but unsmiling; eyes blank; looking like she was pleading with him; her throat cut and blood all down the front of her. He panted and blinked several times, rubbed his eyes and sat up. As the image slowly dissolved in his mind he thought: it isn't going to be a good day.

And he was right. Nathaniel told Jesus and the rest of gathered around him the bad news. A little girl, looking for sticks for her family's fire in a small clump of scrubs had found Bartholemew and Thaddeus, horribly mangled and mutilated. After helping them as much as he could, her father had gone into town and told Absalom, ruler of Capernaum's syngogue, about it. He sent a messenger to Herod's court in Tiberias and brought several of the elders to our camp. That was decent of him, given his banishing of us from attending his synagogue.

We were camped five miles away on the road to Bethsaida; the elders and several of us took the two wounded back to Capernaum to their parents homes. They were delirious and nonsensical; none of us could do much for them.

Herod's soldiers arrived later that afternoon, leaving their medicus to tend them. Then they began their investigation.

That's when I noticed Simon the Zealot was no longer with us.

*

Bad as it was, the episode caused us all to think about the other side: the hidden and unseen part of the world we lived in. Even Peter recognized our problem: 'how can we fight what we can't see?' he asked our unhappy campfire that night. John said we should pay more attention to what we don't know than what we do. And Thomas - glum, serious and usually thinking God knows what - shook his head and priestacized how the depths of evil in our souls never ceased to amaze him. Few liked him but more and more I found myself agreeing with him. Matthew just shook his head but I didn't know what our most traditional Jew really thought about it.

I said to Jesus sitting on the other side of the fire: 'after all our talk about God, about living a better, more humane life, how can something like this happen?'

'It's the world,' he shrugged and replied. 'A ceaseless war exists between living a good life and evil. Never forget evil is real and is live spelled backwards. But most people don't want to believe that because they experience moments of goodness-'

'Which are only temporary!' I interrupted. 'Why don't people understand that? Or is it that they don't want to?'

'Both. Because everyone's different. Attitude plays the greatest role in it,' he looked at John. 'Which is even greater and deeper than understanding.'

'But how do we deal with it? With all this secrecy!' Peter asked.

Jesus looked at him. 'We try to learn as much as we can--'

'But it's their actions that we want to counter, not their thoughts, isn't it?' I interrupted again and he looked at me in rebuke. So I said, 'I'm sorry.'

He smiled. 'It's all right. And you're right.' He turned to Peter. 'We can never eradicate evil in the world--'

'But we can minimize it! Contain and control it!' interrupted John, very animatedly.

'<u>Torah</u>'s told us that for a thousand years!' I said, scoffing at his idea. 'We don't need to revise it.' I said to vehemently and shouldn't have. I instantly felt John would hate me forever.

'What would you do then?' Jesus asked me.

'Reform ourselves from within. Change that attitude that you mentioned.'

Jesus and Thomas smiled and Jesus said, 'the Kingdom of God will change everything.'

14

I'VE always read a lot though not as much as John I'm sure. But even if I read for truth, I'm aware it's man's truth. My eyes and brain, but another person's words. And God? It's always someone writing *about* him. Even Moses did. And then there's the tactile side of life: *I* hold the scroll in *my* hand. Sometimes, it's copied by a person from a source written by another person. So, whatever I was reading was written by humans for humans! My God! Where does humanity stop and God begin? For that matter, where does body and mind stop and spirit begin? Some Jews said thought was everything. All right! I'm a bad Jew; but not as bad as Thomas is!

One time, I discussed failure with John while we were walking home from Nazareth where Jesus' family – led by his younger brother James - had organized his community's opposition to us. That confounded most of us. Blood – kinship - was the Jewish and Idumean way; but I suspected this wasn't the first time they opposed him and why he pitched his message at individuals: to escape the blood connection. We commiserated with him, of course, and tried to tell him he should never have rejected his family first, the time they came to Capernaum when he denied them and told them *we* were his brothers and sisters. Even I found that hard to believe; which was why, a days later, when he told us that he meant to teach us spirit was more important than blood I didn't really believe him. What did interest me was the indifference of Simon, the understanding of my skepticism by Matthew and the hostility of John to my point of view.

'I don't understand why people don't understand!' John said on that occasion. 'They listen. They have the chance to ask questions. I ask them if they have questions and they're either silent or say they don't. But they don't follow. Why not? Isn't truth truth?' Indifference shocked John more than the rest of us. What do people hear but not follow? The others tried to explain it to the kid:

Peter: they have their own lives and interests;

Thomas: they have inner lives as well as outer ones;

Matthew: one person can't account for another's motives or behavior;

Philip: people are different from you and different from one another;

James (John's brother): it's like fishing, bro, either the net gets them or it doesn't; it's that simple.

Simon: maybe they simply don't care. Why do you care so much for this abstract thing called truth anyway?

Even Jesus said, 'some people hate us and some believe us; but I think the majority are simply indifferent. We make no difference in their lives but that's our problem: how can we make it meaningful to them?'

'So then we failed?' I asked. 'Whom did we fail? Them, God or us?'

'All three,' he replied. 'We can't make them take an interest in their own life. If we could, there'd be no individual responsibility for anything because everything would be done for them. Imagine living where your most important choice is what to wear?'

'But that's what most people do. Run from the hard choices into diversions,' Thomas answered. 'They really don't know how to live.'

'Because they're sheep who don't recognize their shepherd's voice.,' John said.
'But I look around here and count eleven or twelve of us who are interested in their lives.
Yes, I'm including you, Thomas. So we know our lives have more than six senses.'

So John's read Aristotle, I thought.

'What all of you say is true enough,' Jesus replied, 'but let me put it this way to try to clarify things. We have a message and the message is always the same. It doesn't change; so, obviously, it's the people. The differences among them--'

'You're saying that it's how people receive the message that's important. That we have to tailor it to their individual situations,' I said.

'But that's what I'm getting at,' John said. 'Why should we focus on our differences? God's truth is the truth! That's what's objective to all of us and the standard! We can't have every man his own church!'

Jesus glanced at me and I couldn't help myself: I mouthed 'priest ism.'

*

I understood our failure to communicate was due to the limitations of most men's minds. The appeal of the Gospel didn't lay in its truth or untruth in some Greek logical way; it had to awaken the core of man's being deeper than mind-knowledge; it must delve deeper through his mind into his very being. I almost stopped walking; it was the first time that I realized my mind is not my total being; so I paced my steps to think more about it but was interrupted by a recollection:

'I was just doing what any guard normally does. I was checking the animals and moving along from tent to tent.'

He nodded. 'Then what happened.'

'I came the tents where the caravan owner stayed. With his family I mean, and--'

'And the girl was his daughter?'

'That's right. But there she was - I mean, this was the middle of the night. 'What was she doing out there?' I asked myself.'

'But you say she wasn't alone?'

'No. There were two men with her. One was holding her--'

'Go on.'

'The other was pawing her and--'

'Did you recognize them?'

'Of course. They were guards of the van same as me.'

'So, then what?'

'The one pawing her started to rip--'

'Is that when you yelled out?'

'Yes. I yelled 'STOP!' And he did and they both looked at me. That's when the girl squirmed away from them and ran off.'

'Did they come at you?'

'No, they ran off in different directions. But I knew them. And that's when Aretas came out of his tent followed by the others.'

'And you told him what had happened.'

'No. I explained to him what I had seen and told him who the men were. He had his servants search the camp for them but they were gone.'

'And his daughter?'

'I found her hiding among the camels and took her back to Aretas' tent while the others searched for the men. He made me repeat what I had seen in front of her and kept pressing me to describe it in detail.'

'And she wasn't hurt.'

'No. I didn't think so.'

Jesus didn't say anything then. He just stared into the distance over my shoulder. Finally, he asked, 'but you didn't see her again until the next day. Did you hear them talking? Arguing?'

'Yes. The whole camp could. You know how voices carry in the night.'

'What were they arguing about?

'About what she was doing out there in the middle of the night. And in public without her veil.' Judas paused. He had the sudden thought Jesus might know something about father and daughter relations but not about Nabateans. 'Nabateans aren't like us.'

'I know.'

'I grew up with them. That's why I know their language. But he was saying - no, accusing her – of encouraging them. Making eyes – flirting - with them. That she made them want to--'

'Was that your impression when you first saw the three of them?'

'Oh, no! She was resisting them. Definitely resisting.' He looked wide-eyed at Jesus. 'But of course I don't know what went on before.' Jesus remained silent and just looking at me. 'But Aretas insisted she was to blame. That she was of that age--'

'She was fourteen?'

'Yes. That's what I was told. But Aretas kept saying that. That she was to blame and he slapped her. Several times; and she was crying.' I paused. 'Then he left her there and went into his tent and I moved over near the animals.'

'But you saw her again?'

'In the morning. When we were leaving. She was lying in a small ditch face up. Her throat had been cut and you could see the blood was fresh. They didn't even bother to bury her.'

'And you're sure he did it? Aretas?'

'Yes. He's the only one who could have. He was her father. They're fierce about those things, you know.' I stopped and stared at the horizon.

'Yes, I know,' he said.

'I heard later that his men caught the two guards who were with her and cut off their heads. . . after they did other things to them. That's how they right wrongs. Harsh climate; harsh people.'

Jesus stared at me. I thought he understood me better now because he said, 'you shouldn't blame yourself. You did what's right.'

But that made me realize he didn't. 'It's not me that's my concern. I told you this because that's why I don't believe you can just tell people things and expect them to follow it. They're going to do whatever it is they want to do. So you're better off finding that out first and tell them to do it. Why spend all that effort trying to change them?'

He just stared at me.

*

'Dear brother Joseph,
    Thank you very much for the money. Yes, I'm feeling much better now. It's amazing how outdoor living, good food and sleep restores one's spirits.

Speaking of that, not as many are flocking to Jesus' call, so-to-speak, as they did before. So, we find ourselves going further out, into areas we never did before.

Tomorrow, we leave to set up between Magdala and Arbela, and expect to spend a week or two there. +I explained our tenting operation in my last to you. It's been working pretty well so far. But we're starting to get resistance from rulers in the villages now about our tent synagogue services. They feel threatened, I'm sure. It's the old story. I don't think we'll go to Jerusalem this year. But if we do I'll be sure to tell you so that we can get together and you can meet Jesus. He's really well-intentioned and gentle. Not at all a screamer and yeller like people say that bug-eyed, locust-eating Baptizer was. Jesus doesn't baptize (we do) or eat locusts.

I'll stay in touch.
Your brother,
Judas'

*

Our time in Magdala wasn't as much a failure as it was a disaster and portent of what might come. We sailed from Capernaum down to Magdala in about half a day thanks to strong at our back from the north. The little town has become a center for the salted fish industry since Herod built his new capitol at Tiberias, and Peter knew it well. We carried our gear up the market street to the assembly hall they used as a synagogue and then turned left on the road to Arbela. We went about a mile and pitched our tents on a grassy and fairly level knoll. Then Jesus sent us in pairs into Magdala and Arbela to announce where we were and that we would be holding a service there all day on the Sabbath. Every pair returned with the curious and those having nothing else to do. I met Mary on the third day. She came to us but said she would speak only to Jesus. That wasn't unusual; what was, was that she stayed. And stayed. I mean with him in his tent. That was unusual. Peter didn't like it and certainly didn't like her. Three days later, John, James and Andrew didn't like it either. 'Favoritism,' is what Matthew said. I remember Thomas and I looking at one another as if we agreed about something; but I didn't know what and still don't.

She followed Jesus around like dogs do people. Listened to him talk to us and to him preaching to the different crowds. She observed everything. Like a spy would. She didn't speak much but on two different occasions, I looked up to see her watching me. Both times she turned away; the second time more slowly than the first. Hostile? No. Shy? I didn't think so. Wounded, I thought; and searching for healing. As we all were. But I didn't know that then.

Someone said she was sixteen - the same age as John; dark brown almost black eyes, slender and pretty with long black hair that hung down to her waist. Her voice was melodious; and she had been a prostitute in Magdala. But one of the common ones, unconnected with any of the temples. I heard the others talk about her and that's when I learned that a woman's position in traditional Hebrew society was only a notch above the Arabs. No wonder our people hated the Hebrews. Wives had a tiny bit of authority and freedom; unmarried women didn't: they remained under the authority of some male. That was her real sin: she wasn't under the authority of any man. Ironically, it was John – the sixteen year old kid – who told me that it was the Mary's of the world who threatened Hannah's status as Peter's wife; and that why he opposed her. It reminded me of 'behind every good man there's a --.'

Four days later, I was cleaning the goat pen when a voice started me: 'you're not a kid or naive like most of them, so why don't you have a woman? You look experienced in life.'

Mary's steadiness – certitude, really - confused me. 'So?' I replied.

'So, I expected you to proposition me by now.'

'You want me to?'

'No. I'm just curious and wondering whether I'm losing it.' She smiled. Provocatively.

It? I asked myself. I stopped forking the feed into the animal's basket and looked into her eyes. "You haven't. I've been with Jesus for a few months now and when I arrived I didn't know what I was looking for. But now I think I do. I suspect you're here for the same reason and I don't want to take advantage of you. It's that simple.'

She didn't reply immediately; but then said, 'what were you looking for?'

'Healing.'

She stared at me for a moment. 'You're being quite honest, aren't you? It's unusual. Are you sure you don't want to take the next step and show me what a man you are?'

'Yes, I'm sure. I'm not looking for anything. I just want – no, I need - to be alone for awhile.'

'To be what?'

'Alone. With no one but God. What we call that something we sense outside ourselves. I used to strive for things but I'm trying to get over that.'

'But I thought everyone wanted something; including being a different person?'

'In that case,shhhh. Don't tell anyone my secret.'

She smiled and walked off. And deliberately swayed her hips, I thought. Provocatively.

*

They attacked that night and burned us out. And carried clubs and whips to injure us, not swords or knives to kill us. They were Herod's soldiers who wanted to remind us that they made and enforced the law: to teach us that lesson. But thanks to a few converts in the town who warned us, we left just before they arrived, with most of our gear; got down to the boats and pushed off, sailing at night back to Capernaum. Thank God fishermen fish at night; I couldn't see a thing.

    I didn't believe the King was at the root of it; and he wasn't: it was Samuel bar Joab, the ruler of Magdala's assembly hall synogogue and one of Mary's former and regular customers. He had contacted the other rulers of nearby synagogues after discovering where Mary went and together they sailed the twenty five miles further south to Herod's court in Tiberias to complain about how we were disrupting the social order: 'enticing apprentices, stable boys and even prostitutes to leave their employment and join Jesus! Why, the entire social fabric was being torn apart!' they argued, and 'you must stop it! How are masters and employers to maintain order?' That's when I discovered the only one who hated that order more than me was Simon; but I didn't know enough to think Jesus may have hated it most of all.

    But that episode put us on the path of opposition to secular as well as religious law; and, because of it, I began learning how close the relationship between politics and religion really is.

15

'THE rumor at court is that he wants you dead,' said the older of the two Pharisees. They had just arrived by boat at Jesus' tiny house this morning, a week after we returned to Capernaum. The speaker's name was Blastus; and both hoped for a gratuity (the first time I heard the word).

'They say Herod thinks you're dangerous, like the Baptist,' said the younger one. Josias was darker and leaner. And learning as I was.

'He thinks you're stirring his people up, like the Baptist did.' Blastus paused looking at Jesus, 'and maybe even intending to lead a rebellion.'

'He thinks I'm a Zealot?' Jesus asked. But I figured he knew as I suspected that they were only trying to feather their own nests.

'Not only do you sound like one but you harbor one as a member of your chosen disciples,' Blastus answered.

Jesus smiled; a small one that Blastus took as a smirk and spoke up: 'I assure you it's not a laughing matter.'

'I wasn't thinking what you're thinking. I was thinking that if Herod sends his soldiers against us we will offer no resistance to him.' Jesus said, and then looked at the two of them. 'Do I seem dangerous to you?'

The younger one looked down. Blastus glared at him. Somehow, things had gone wrong from what he had planned and he hadn't achieved the friendly compromise he hoped he would. Maybe he should have been friendlier. 'Let's just say you've been warned,' he said. 'We've done our sacred duty.'

Sacred! I thought. So Herod decides where the sacred differs from the profane?

Jesus turned to me. 'And that's exactly what happened when Solomon centralized Judaism by building his Temple. Prophecy was changed forever.' Then he turned back to Blastus and said, 'thank you. Now you're duty is done.'

The two men left. With purses as empty as themselves and I knew I would ask Jesus later about why <u>Torah's</u> last book differed so much from Exodus.

*

'It's all right for you to talk about fleeing! You have nothing to lose but the coat and cloak you're wearing! But I have a wife, two children and a business! I'll lose everything!' Peter was worried. As he should be. Verbal opposition - name calling and shouting - was one thing but violence quite another.

'Calm down,' Jesus replied. 'No one's running away. This is why we're here. To talk about what we should do in a calm and reasonable way.' It was true. Jesus asked his disciples to meet here in his tiny house to discuss what they should do next. It was three mornings after we returned from Magdala in the middle of the night and we were sitting around the walls of his front room that still had the hole in the roof.

'Maybe we could just go as a group as usual but to another part of the country for awhile,' suggested Philip. 'We could go west or along the coast.' A couple of heads nodded in agreement.

'What's your opinion, Judas?' Jesus asked.

I had been listening carefully and hearing something I couldn't account for. He really wasn't considering flight because he was frightened but because of something else which I didn't know about. Then it flashed through my mind: he was simply indecisive. And perhaps confused. But why? I couldn't ask him now, but resolved to later. Anyway, I had a premonition that he was going to ask me for my opinion so I was ready.

'I've found it best to keep a balanced perspective on things,' I said. 'Yes, flight does seem to be an immediate answer, but I think we should try to find positive elements in it. Meaning preaching opportunities. So I think we should go north, where Herod's power is weaker and opportunities still exist to spread your message.'

'But that's bandit territory!' exclaimed John fearfully.

'Zealot country!' Andrew sing-songed in. Everyone knew they were his bogey-men and that he probably wasn't even aware of Simon sitting across the room from him, having rejoined us yesterday.

I forgot how many feared the Zealots. But their reaction gave me time to think. 'Let's think about what we could gain from this,' I said. 'Suppose we go beyond them, further north. To Tyre and Sidon--.'

'But that's Phoenicia!'

'Wait!' I said, holding my left palm up. 'Hear me out. Herod can't touch us there. Or, if you prefer, we could go east from there into Philip's territory.'

After a silence, John said, 'I like the idea of going to a mix of Gentiles and Jews.'

'And Tyre is Jerusalem's main seaport,' Philip added.

'What do you think, Peter?' I asked.

He scratched his beard. 'The only thing about it is that it's far away. It'll be the furthest we've ever gone.'

'What does that matter!' James gushed. 'I like the idea.'

'Judas,' Jesus asked, 'why don't you show us on the map the routes you think you think we could follow.'

He usually kept his papers on a small table in the center of the room, but had moved it over against the west wall after the first rains so I got up, went over to it, put the map we most generally used on top, and studied it. James was sitting to its left, his back against the wall. 'Help me move the table more into the center of the room, would you?' I asked him. After we did that, I said to everyone, 'let's gather around and I'll trace the general directions I have in mind.' They did; except for Jesus who stayed where he was, his back against the east wall. 'Suppose we take this main van road just west of Lake Huleh up north of Gischala and then cut west toward Tyre. We could then go up to Sidon--'

'How far is that?' Thomas asked.

'About twenty miles.' A day's walk.

'We'll stand out in Gentile country, you know. Will we be safe? I mean dressed as we are?'

Thomas had a point. 'I think we'll be safe because there's so many of us. And if we mix in with the caravans we'll be even less noticeable. People will think we're part of that van coming up from Egypt.'

When no one said anything I continued. 'Whether we go to Sidon or not, from Tyre we can take a road going due east to Caesarea Philippi. That's where Philip keeps his court.'

Jesus stood up, came over and looked at the map. 'Are there roads that go down along the eastern side of Lake Huleh?'

'Yes,' I replied and traced one that I remembered with my finger.

'Down the eastern side of the Sea?'

'Yes. But it goes through Decapolis.' I showed them with my finger again and said, 'we could to Raphana, then south to Abila and to Gadara in the Decapolis. We'll be south of the sea but we can sail home. Can't we, Peter?'

'Yes, but it will be a long trip,' Peter said.

'It looks like a giant circle!' John said.

I didn't say anything, wanting to hear their reactions.

'How long do you think it will it take?' Jesus asked me.

I had been calculating our tenting as I traced the route with my finger, estimating how long from rest stop to another. 'I would estimate two and half to three months. We have most of our gear and know how to use it. We can improvise as we go along.'

Peter let out a long breath.

John pursed his lips and finally said, 'I think we should go.' After several heads nodded, he added, 'Herod has other things to think about besides us.'

I looked at Jesus. He had that dreamy, far off look in his eye. But he suddenly nodded and said, 'yes, let's go.' Then he looked at me and said, 'plan it in greater detail' and as he moved away from the table said, 'let's leave two weeks from today.'

*

One week before we left on our northern tour, a group of men met in a house in Gischala, a tell atop a small mountain in northern Galilee which Jesus' group would pass but couldn't see.

'They're going north to Tyre and Sidon? Into Gentile country, Simon!'

'Yes, I know! I tried to talk them out of it but Jesus was adamant about it!'

'What good will they do for us up there?' Eleazar, leader of the north Galilee cell asked.

'And then they're going to come back into Antipas' territory?' Another interrupted.

'I think Jesus wants to test how receptive the Gentiles are to his Gospel and when they think Herod's no longer looking for them they'll return to Capernaum.'

Eleazar, head of the group, seemed to be minutely interested in his right thumb as he listened and then said, 'this was probably Judas' idea. He's a good head for strategy and thinks Herod will become less concerned about them the longer they're gone.' He put his hand down and looked at Simon. 'How long does he expect you to be gone?'

'He estimates two to three months depending on weather and what may happen.' Simon stopped and narrowed his brow. 'I don't have to go if you think I can be of more use here.'

'No. You go. Your reports are quite valuable. Do you need money?'

'I don't think so. Judas expects bountiful days in the Gentile cities.'

'He's right. But Gentiles!' He shuddered. 'Will you have to speak Greek?' Zealots refused to speak Greek.

'Probably.'

'Well, keep your mouth shut as much as possible.' He chuckled. 'Let Judas do the talking.'

Three weeks later, and two weeks after Jesus' group left Capernaum, a similar event occurred in the Procurator's office in Caesarea Maritima where the smell of pig fat, used to grease metal and leather overwhelmed everyone and offended orthodox Jews who first entered the office. But Roman soldiers were used to it, of course, as they were used to everything that smelled from the dead.

Having read Cornelius' report of a fairly large group of people moving into the Zealot part of Galilee, the Governor summoned Captain Lucius Quintus who was in charge of that province and told him the substance of the centurion's report. 'What I want to know is whether we can expect another attempt from them to capture the arsenal at Sebaste.'

'I doubt it, sir. The Zealots are now more of a cultural force with a political agenda and far weaker than the Sanhedrin. My opinion is that they're watching to see how powerful this Jesus movement will become and whether it can be useful to them. The Zealots are strongest there in northern Galilee but don't have as many supporters as they used to have. Also, they're not centrally organized like the Sanhedrin. They're more a loose collection of individual bands who exist for one purpose: to eliminate us from Judea.'

'No priests?'

'Not like the Sanhedrin's. They have a few holy men who live separately from them. But they're committed to war with us and all Hellenists.'

'They're extreme Sanhedrinists?'

'More rivals to them. They think Jerusalem's in the grip of devils.'

Pilate had been procurator for three years and was most concerned with Jerusalem. 'So, they have no political status. That means it's no holds barred with them?'

'That's right. We treat them as we do any bandits, brigands and seditionists.'

'I see. Have we infiltrated them?'

'We have a man in their Gischala headquarters. Absolom. Simon's their man with the Jesus people and reports to Eleazar.'

'So, we can follow this Jesus then?'

'Yes, sir. As contact is made.'

'And you think this Jesus may join them? He seems more religious than political.'

'The other way around, sir. They hope his movement grows so they can then support him against Jerusalem. He talks their language and was raised in their culture.'

'What does that mean?'

'He grew up four miles down the road from where the Zealots were first organized and I'm sure he knows all the stories about the two thousand we crucified there when he was a child.'

'Why haven't I heard about this until now?'

'Because it hasn't been a problem before.'

'So, you're saying this Jesus may eventually lead them?' Pilate's eyes narrowed.

'No, sir. It's more a case of him becoming their puppet. They're the murderers and bandits.'

'That's very helpful, Quintus.' The Governor thought a moment. 'I think we should just carry on as you have been.'

'Yes, sir. That's the wisest policy for now.'

Lucius Quintus liked his commander, Pontius Pilate, because he proved himself a realist so many times during the past three years. He understood his job was to dominate the Jews; make them feel that Rome's power would crush them if they got out of line. And while both Herod and the High Priest owed their positions to Rome, it was to a Rome thousands of miles away. Rome was the Governor here, two feet away from himself.

*

At virtually the same time as Pilate's talk with Quintus, the High Priest met with his inner circle, the chief priests, the leading Pharisees and scribes, and Joseph Iscariot, the leading secular lawyer in Jerusalem in the official residence of the High Priest. Annas called the meeting after hearing the report of the two Essenes – Ner and Zedekiah – he had sent to gather information about the Jesus group's departure from Capernaum. He wanted his advisors to now hear their report.

As soon as their wine was poured, Annas asked, the group, 'what did you learn about Jesus' group and their intentions? Are they Zealots?'

Zedekiah, the older of the two Essenes present, spoke first. 'We don't find any connection with the Zealots. It's more a matter of the Zealots watching and waiting to make overtures to them if their movement becomes large enough. But for now there is no connection because Jesus doesn't seem to want any.'

'But he hasn't rejected them outright!' Annas thrust his jaw out. 'What are they like? Jesus' followers, I mean. Are they dangerous?'

'Not at all, sir. Nearly all of them are younger than Ner, the younger Essene. But they're peasants. Ignorant, unsophisticated and naive. And unemployable. They don't seem skilled at anything.'

'Definitely unemployable,' Ner nodded.

'Yes, you're right, thank you,' Zedekiah said in a tone of condescension while turning slightly to Ner. Then he turned back to Annas and said, 'only two looked a little older. I would say about Jesus' age.'

'Any of them married with families?'

'Only this Peter. Oh, and here's something strange. Peter's real name is Simon and Matthew's is Levi. This Jesus likes to rename certain Jews with Greek names. But no one knows why he does that.'

'And Peter's one of the older ones, you say.'

'Yes. The other one is Joseph's brother.' He nodded to the secular lawyer sitting in the third chair to Annas' left.

'Did you talk with this Peter?'

'Only briefly but enough to tell you that he's not terribly bright. In fact, most of Jesus' people are misfits. Some are ner-do-well sons of rich parents and others are just confused about everything starting with their own identities. This Peter is among the latter. The others seem to be searching for daddy or mommy.'

Annas thought for a moment and then said, 'well, gentlemen, I thank you for your report. Are you returning to Qumran in the morning?'

'Yes, sir.'

'Well please take this purse and tell Daniel how delighted we are with you report. Well done!'

Chief Priest Ezra handed a small money bag to Zedekiah as they left the room.

After they had left, Annas said, 'well, Ezzy, they seem peaceable enough. Those nigh-hysterical letters we first received from Zedekiah must be read with a pinch of salt. It sounds to me like Jesus' group is quite harmless.'

Ezra smiled. 'Like the Essenes themselves?'

Annas smiled. He loved the practical Ezra. 'Yes. Unreal in a similar way. But peasants. Even more stupid.'

*

After returning to Tyre from Sidon we took the road east toward Caesarea Philippi and were nearing the slopes of Mount Hermon when I suddenly realized I hadn't been paying much attention to the buzz of conversations around me. I had heard so many of my comrade's stories and was thinking about setting up camp for two or three days where we could rest before starting the southeastern and last leg of our trip home. Jesus was telling them about how he felt his powers come and go and asking James and Peter if they remembered the woman who broke through their defensive ring to touch the hem of his cloak.

'Pouff!' He said it so abruptly it startled me. 'My powers disappeared.' They were amazed. I'm sure they thought, ahhh, so he really is like us on occasion! We all walked on in silence until he suddenly asked: 'Who do people say the Son of Man is?'

That nailed my attention.

They replied using the usual weasel words 'some' and 'others' as they replied, 'some say John the Baptist; others say Elijah--.'

I hated that and thought he did too because he then asked them more sharply, 'but who do you yourselves say I am?'

My God! I thought. Are they all having an identity crisis! Genuine people don't use weasel words and surely Jesus knows who he is. But Peter - God bless him! - blurted out, 'you are the Christ, the son of the living God.'

But Jesus suddenly stopped walking. And we all did too. But since I was walking in front I had to turn around. It was like a revelation to him! (How could Jesus have a revelation? I wondered. Why, he's older than I am!) But the look on his face was incredible! It was like some sort of confirmation; and then he went on and on about how it was Peter who had the revelation and therefore it was Peter on whom he was going to build his church and on whom he was going to give the keys to the kingdom of heaven and -- well, I could see John and his brother didn't like it one bit. But there it was. Matthew, Philip, Thomas, and even spacey Andrew heard it too though they didn't show their disappointment as the two brothers did. But this I know: Jesus seemed like a different person for the rest of the trip; he seemed transformed and his new attitude changed the entire direction of what we did. What was most strange to me was that he couldn't wait to get back home.

I knew I would definitely mention this in my next letter to my brother.

16

A month later we were back in Capernaum and two mornings after that John showed up at the door of my room which I rented from Philip and his family. It had its own outside entrance and this was one of those times I wish didn't.

'He wants to see you. Right meow!' John was young, always in a hurry and like doing stupid cat noises. But I discovered something else about him: nothing mattered to him once he decided it didn't. I knew he meant Jesus and didn't invite him in. But for some reason I forgot where my stylus and wax tablet were and had to look for them. His impatience grew. 'I don't know why the rest of us are always excluded from your meetings,' he said, meaning himself.

'I have no idea what he wants to talk with me about,' I replied, picking the two items up from under a nightshirt thrown over a bench and turning to go with him.

That's when I saw him grimace. 'He always treats you as his favorite. The rest of us don't like it.' He meant he didn't.

'I'm ready to go,' I replied.

He just glared at me, turned and we left.

'I know now what I must do.'

I suspected Jesus had something on his mind I told myself on my way over; and he did; but it wasn't what I thought. In fact, it was a turning point in our relationship.

'So, why now instead of before?' I asked after he told me.

'Because before didn't work.'

'You mean because we didn't attract enough followers?'

'That was only part of the reason. You have to appreciate I didn't understand any of this then. But now that I do why they didn't follow us makes no difference. It's never about them! It's about me!'

'You mean what you told John is right? That the reception of the message is everything?' I couldn't believe he had changed his mind about this. 'Now, I don't understand.'

'You see, Judas, I've been trying to make people understand with my mind instead of with my being.'

I took a deep breath. 'What are you talking about? Make?'

'We're born into a world in a specific culture. In a specific time and place. All people are. They understand their world through their culture. It's neither logical nor reasonable.'

'That's not helpful.'

'Let me put it this way, what's always been the heart of our culture?'

'Reverencing God.'

'Yes, but how? How through all the ages since Abraham?'

'Sacrifice?'

He smiled and sat back and I felt I was back in yeshiva.

'That's it. Sacrifice. Even before we centralized and ritualized it in Solomon's Temple. But now, tell me, have you ever seen me sacrifice?'

I thought for a brief moment. 'No, but then you're not a priest.'

'That's right. But the more important reason is that I am to be the sacrifice.'

I stared at him. And finally asked 'what do you mean?' half afraid of his answer.

'I must be sacrificed if we're to restore ourselves as God's chosen people.'

'You mean as we were before the Temple that we talked about.

'Yes.' -Before the monarchy.'

I sat back, as if greater distance would help me understand. He appeared to be the same Jesus I had known and it was too early for wine; but he was different now; more resolute. On the inside. I could see he had decided something and this was first time he was sharing it. 'How do you mean, 'sacrifice?' I asked.

'I mean I must sacrifice myself, my being, for our people. That's what they'll understand. I've been relying too much on merely the mind's understanding instead of the heart's.

'You're saying doing something - in this case, terminating your being (is what I said; suicide is what I thought) - will have a greater impact on people than thoughtful explanations or reasoned argument?'

'Yes. Especially if it'll be the classic way. Stoned after being thrown off the top of the Temple wall. And especially on the day before Passover, when Jerusalem has the largest crowds because of the festival.'

Oh, my God! I thought! But I'm afraid I treated it too lightly and laughed. 'What makes you think people will remember or even care? They'll forget your death just as they've ignored what you've been saying. You know how people think life just goes on like a river!'

But he was serious. Dead serious. 'You're wrong, Judas. They'll remember me.' He stared at me now, as if gauging whether to continue. Finally, he said, 'But that's not why I asked to see you. I need your help.'

I thought he was carrying this a bit far and tried shock and humor. 'My help? To commit suicide?'

'If that's what you want to call it. But I still need your help.' He remained serious.

I'm afraid I was still thinking this was a joke. 'You want me to help them push you off? Or be the one who casts the first stone? Or the last one?' I smiled.

But he didn't. In fact, he looked away and I realized he expected this. 'I'm serious, Judas. I'm asking for your help as my friend, not as my disciple. I think you have a great capacity for friendship.'

Now, I stopped thinking of this as a joke. 'All right. I'm sorry.' I realized that was what all those questions were about when we were near Mount Hermon. And I remembered how he seemed a different person when he came down from that mountain with Peter, James and John. He had made up his mind. 'How can I help?'

He leaned forward again and looked into my eyes. 'It's simple really. I want you to help by preventing me from betraying myself. By preventing my human nature from backing away from what I must do. Once I start down this road I must not betray my purpose. I must complete it. If I don't it, people will see it as a joke and never believe in the Kingdom of God. My credibility and authenticity depend on it. Can you understand that?'

'Yes.' It made perfect sense to me.

He looked down and said, almost ashamed, 'I'm afraid to put all my trust in my human nature.'

'So, I'm your backup, so to speak. Mr Outside to your Mr Inside.'

'Yes. You know how the Romans have their servants and slaves kill them. Well, I'm not asking you to do that. Just help me. Out of your friendship and love of me. And because I have great faith in you.' He looked steadily at me now. 'And I want you to understand what you're getting into because you must never tell anyone about this.' He stopped and sat back. 'I'm asking you to have as great a faith in me as I do in my spiritual self.' I was transfixed by his eyes and could barely nod. 'And make no mistake about it: you'll be hated by my followers for betraying me though you'll receive the riches of the world.'

I thought: hated for betraying you in the name of friendship and love? 'Followers. You said followers. You mean after you're dead. Who will they be?'

'You know I've asked Peter to head my church. But you also know one person can never be another in this world. So, it will be his – and probably many others – church. That's already in place,' he replied. But then he said a strange thing. 'I don't know how else to thank and pray you'll never forget me.'

'I could never forget you, Jesus,' I replied. 'When we first met, I loved you for helping me. But now I love you for who and what you are.'

'I know.'

Walking back to Philip's house, I thought about all that he said and felt strange. I felt he knew all our futures: his, mine, and everyone's. I wondered whether, once having taken this giant step of involving me, he would be sorry that he couldn't go back because that 'couldn't' was me. Would he blame me?

And then I began wondering about what a momentous decision it would be for me. I wanted to live; I felt I had so much more to live for now; but I feared everything about it; and yet was supremely proud to be part of what he wanted. I wanted to give him back something he wanted. I knew the stories about Socrates, but never personally knew anyone who consciously decided on such a course of action, knowing its result beforehand. I admired his planning it for the chief festival at which hundreds of thousands would attend. Was he right? That people would remember him forever? Surely he knew they would be from the Diaspora? Not residents of Israel?

And what would they know of me? Or think? And how important is it to me? To be remembered as his helper? Or should they even know? No, I decided. I was happy enough to obey his wishes. To perform this ultimate request of friendship. After all, men like Jesus are such a rarity in this world.

.

*

We spent the next two weeks preparing for our final assault (Jesus sometimes called it his final solution in our private conversations) on Jerusalem. I had been put in charge of erecting a small dais about two hundred yards toward the sea and upwind from the animal pens just west of Capernaum. Jesus' was preaching this morning pretty much the same things he had for several mornings now to whip up enthusiasm for our march on Jerusalem. Although we had set up those benches for the sea breezes to blow the animal smells further west, it was only semi-successful because the wind constantly shifted direction.

This morning, I had taken a break and stood behind the benches listening to the new, resolute Jesus giving his new purpose-driven speech but hearing only snatches of it depending on the force and direction of the wind.

'I have come to turn a man against his father, a daughter against her mother, a daughter-in-law against her mother-in-law--

I knew, of course, that he no longer sought to change the world through peace and humility but through shock: by turning the world's truth upside down.

'And I say to you that a man's enemies will be the members of his own household--' I looked left and saw Peter shudder and James and John flinch but they hadn't read Deuteronomy as much as I had so it didn't bother me as much as it did them.

Suddenly, a deep, male voice said behind me, 'you must be Judas.'

I turned right and looked down into a pair of beady eyes and swarthy, sweaty face I never saw before.

'Yes,' I answered. Have you come to go with us?'

The impassive face turned to look at Jesus. 'I like his fire but it's misdirected.' Then it turned back to me. 'But that's Jesus. He's always been off target. Too diffuse.' He paused. 'No, I can't go but I brought men who will. Who do we see about it?'

I saw Simon and James sauntering toward the animals and Peter near the packing area.

'See Peter over there? The one packing?' I said, pointing. 'In that dirty brown mantle with the torn tassels? Talk to him!'

He nodded and went off with many hard looking men. I counted them and thanked God.

But when Eleazar saw that Simon recognized him on his way over to Peter, he put his finger to his lips and said in a loud voice. 'Hello Simon! I'm Eleazar. I've brought some men to go with you. What can we do to help?'

Simon saw that Peter was within ear shot so he replied in a loud voice, 'start by packing these bags on those mules.' But when Eleazar came closer, Simon whispered, 'what are you doing here?' Then, he saw the men up close. 'I thought Barabbas was coming.'

'Don't worry. You'll find him. He's necessary to the final plan.'

'Does Judas know?'

'No, and don't tell him. Now listen, when you camp at Jericho, Judas will explain how everyone is to enter Jerusalem. But make sure to talk with Barabbas before you get there. He'll explain everything in greater detail.' Eleazar looked at Simon as he would his son going on a dangerous mission and squeezed his arm. 'Be careful. Don't get caught in Jesus' dream.'

'You mean you're not going?'

'No. If things go well with you the Romans will attack us and you know what I have to do.'

'Simon!' A high-pitched voice suddenly interrupted him. 'Do you want the goats herded behind or in front of the pack animals?'

'In front, Andrew. And make sure each one's tethered!

When Simon turned back Eleazar was gone.

*

Spies and their runners moved constantly from one hill to another along the roads Jesus' followers took from Capernaum toward Jerusalem. Their job was to keep the High Priest's people informed of their progress.

'How many are there? Are they alone? Are the Zealots with them?'

'No,' Ezra smiled. You know what a purist Jesus is even if his bastardy makes him unacceptable to many of the Essenes. So now he's trying to get the support of the Diaspora since they won't acknowledge him in Judea. As if his truth will free you from the world.'

Caiaphas shook his head. 'I almost feel sorry for them. How stupid and romantic they are. They're like <u>Tobit</u> only don't know he wrote an historical novel.'

'It's their peasant mentality!' Joseph said.

'Yes, that's what I meant when I called them peasants!' Annas replied. 'Idealists bent on destroying themselves. Real people won't support such dreamers.'

Ezra prided himself that he didn't become a chief priest because he was a fool. 'But since some do, we would be foolish to think we can prevent the Diasporists from supporting them.'

Annas and Joseph looked at him. They respected his hard-headedness: a wolf in priest's clothing. 'What do you mean?' Annas asked solicitously.

Ezra didn't disappoint them: 'we should attack them where they are most vulnerable.'

Annas and Joseph now smiled their understanding. 'That's brilliant!' Annas exclaimed. 'We must have faith in the goodness of man. That good men will do exactly that, pursue the good. Trust them to be unrealistic.'

Joseph the lawyer asked,, 'and how shall we do that?'

'I think I have the answer.' Ezra said. 'Counting money is part of my priestly duties. Jesus has no use for money and is always saying rich people can't get into his kingdom until they shed their wealth.'

The other two nodded.

'But let's take that a notch higher. He despises our Temple faith for using it.'

'You mean our tithing system?'

'No, I mean our Temple tax. Torah's half-shekel requirement. So far, he hasn't objected to people paying their tithes to their local synagogues or even the synagogues paying their tithes to the Temple. Ask yourselves why not. I think it's because we accept anyone's coinage - Herod's or even the Romans for that.'

Caiaphas sat up, more alert. 'I think I see what you're getting at, but please continue.'

'We don't allow any money to be used here in the Temple except the half-shekel in Tyrian standard coin. So peasants like Jesus' people have to exchange their Roman, even Herodian coins here. He'll attack us at this point.'

'Because the purity of the Temple would otherwise be violated.' Caiaphas said almost to himself and nodding his head.

'That's how we view it but they don't because they have to pay the exchange differential--'

'Which we benefit from, of course.' Annas smiled.

'Of course.'

'So that's why they'll attack us there?' Caiaphas said.

'Yes, ' Ezra replied. 'I think he'll physically attack the money exchangers in the Court of the Gentiles.'

Joseph looked from one to the other and smiled. 'That'll work especially if we have some of our spies with them whine about having to pay the Temple tax!'

Annas smiled and stood up. 'More wine for anyone?' When he finished pouring he said, 'I propose a toast. 'May their violence be their path to sedition."

They sipped. And Ezra added. 'You know, we can also solve our dilemma if this should happen.'

The others looked at him. As if to ask, what dilemma?

*

When the campfires were barely smoldering embers in the middle of the night Simon crept over to one of the bodies sleeping on the ground and whispered, 'Barabbas.'

He had just reached his right hand out to shake the body when Barabbas suddenly rolled over to him, his knife blade ready to strike. 'Don't ever sneak up on me like that! What do you want?' He whispered.

And I thought I had crept over here so silently! Flashed through Simon's mind but a voice from deep inside told him that's how you survive in this business. 'Eleazar said to ask you about your plans for Jerusalem,' he whispered.

Barabbas whispered back after looking around and putting his knife away: 'Jesus, Peter and James intend to break up the money changers court. That will cause a big ruckus and lots of noise which should bring the Temple guards and Romans. But we're going to riot in the lower city just before they do it. It'll divert those guards and Romans before Jesus' breaks up the court.'

Simon studied his face while hearing this. No, Eleazar had not told him about this; but that's how Zealots were. Only the top leaders knew completely what any plan was. But he didn't like that in this situation because things could easily get out of control - and Simon was as deeply involved as you could get. 'Should I help you?'

'No. Stay with the others. But don't help Jesus break up the money changers' court. Stay away from him and away from us. We need you to continue with them until it's all over. Understand?'

No, Simon thought but said 'yes' and thought he heard a 'whew' in his mind.

Then Barabbas said 'good night, then' and rolled over.

Simon crept out backwards marveling at how calm Barabbas was. A truly professional Zealot, just falling asleep like that. Killing out of passion was easy. But it was ever more difficult to kill in cold blood because you had to control your emotions. And that required careful planning. A calmness of mind and detachment of feeling. Thank God I share that. He grimaced and remembered what his mother always told him about Phinehas and how the Romans just let his father hang on that little tree, strangling in his own blood as the priests and Pharisees spit on him.

*

Jonathan ben Annas wasn't very bright; even for being the last son of old Annas. Annas told his friends he thought of Jonathan as his cross to bear, but softened it by explaining that God planned it that way: all his older brothers were smart , his son--in-law, Joseph Caiaphas, was, and Annas was the brightest of them all. They would 'advise' him. Caiaphas was currently serving as High Priest, and Annas tried to rotate the office within his family because it was so lucrative. So, he schemed and maneuvered sometimes up close and other times more distantly depending on who served in the chair. Besides, he liked to have his sons and sons-in-law to know that he was always there as the real power behind the chair. But Annas knew enough to also surround himself with bright outsiders like Ezra, the Temple's senior chief priest.

Another was Joseph Iscariot, a secular lawyer and that rarity in Jerusalem: a self-made man. Called Issy by his intimate friends and people he wanted to impress, he was very bright with an eye on the main chance; and he had maneuvered his way into Annas' inner coterie by dint of complete subservience to Annas' interests - and by displaying the most subtle, non-priestly mind Annas ever found. And Issy made sure his non-priestly status was beneficial to him because - as Annas frequently said – it was a refreshing perspective to the usual priestly claptrap he heard.

Four months previously, after learning that Jesus and his followers had returned to Capernaum from the north, Annas invited Ezra and Joseph to dinner and everyone knew why. After sending Jonathan out of the room on a fool's errand, Annas leaned closer to Issy to hear more about his assessment of Jesus' and his followers coming for what Jesus was calling a 'showdown.' 'That's what I think it is given his new aggressive speeches,' he explained.

'I'm sure he'll target the Diaspora for support,' Joseph replied. 'They have the numbers and I hear he's getting the support of those Zealot idiots' (everyone at the table knew this came from his brother Judas' letters to him). 'My brother thinks he'll come at Passover when he'll have access to the largest number of them.' He knew Annas thrived on placing the details he heard into a bigger picture. 'You know what it's like then: a couple of hundred thousand pilgrims. He could never get that many people together anywhere else or at any other time.'

'So he's coming in April. We'll have to prepare a proper reception for him,' Annas smiled.

'Yes. I'm sure we can think of some things.'

Annas sipped his wine. 'You know, Issy, I love the way your mind works. It's so incisive, so focused and practical. It's made you what you are today.' He smiled at him and then asked, in a solicitous tone, 'by the way, how's your wife?' He was so engrossed in their conversation that he had completely forgotten about her. 'I know she's been ailing recently.' Annas still had two young daughters and the oldest would be twelve next year - the scripturally perfect age - and he would dearly love to have Issy as his son-in-law. (Further under his thumb, he meant; a goal Issy wouldn't mind; and he thought of his wife's refusing to die on cue as one more thwarting of his career.) Everyone – even Romans - knew expanding families was the secret to success, But Annas was a true Jew: a stickler for observing that everything be done scripturally; something the Romans weren't concerned about.

'Thank you for asking, Annas,' Issy replied, 'but she seems to be no better and the physicians still don't know what is wrong with her. I wish things were settled.' (He had been administering a slow-acting poison to her for a two months now and couldn't understand the slowness of its effects.)

'Oh, yes! It would be such a comfort to your mind.' Again he smiled as he reached over and patted Joe's hand. 'I hope so too. That would be happy for all concerned.' There, I was sufficiently general for any future event, he thought. 'Now, about Jesus. Passover's three months away. Let's assume his peasants will accompany him and make their play. They'll probably stay east in Bethphage or Bethany where all the Galileans usually do. That means they'll be using the Temple's eastern gates and coming up from the Kidron valley into the city. I'll alert the Temple guards to that.'

'Since they don't have their own synagogue out there, they'll probably use Solomon's Porch and then return to their lodgings each night--'

'You know, I was thinking,' Annas interrupted Ezra, 'since Jesus' decision for this showdown probably resulted from his success in Tyre and Sidon, maybe we should watch the synagogue of the freedmen and the others who cater--'

'To those Goddamned Hellenized Jews!' Ezra interrupted again. But then he calmed down. 'But that would cut down on the number of synagogues we have to watch. It's a good idea.'

Annas nodded and said, 'and maybe we should talk with their rulers and some of the elders to see where their sympathies lie. That's a good job for Malchus.'

'Yes. He's superb for that.'

After a brief silence, Annas asked Issy, 'how's your brother doing? Is he still happy with our arrangement?'

'Yes. Quite happy, I think. We can count on his keeping us informed of what the Jesus people are doing. Most of them haven't a brain in their head. Clueless to how the real world works.'

'But you haven't told him how we're using his information?'

'Oh, no! You've read his letters same as I do! I told him to write me just about what he's doing and how he's coming along. Touristy kinds of things in reply to mine which show a brotherly interest. I don't want him to suspect anything. And I send him a little money each month to keep him going. I'm sure he has no idea how helpful his information is.'

'That's wonderful! I mean how he trusts you! That's what older brothers are for! Perpetuating trust in the family.' He paused. 'I hear this Peter is a real dunderhead. Do you think that Jesus really wanted to build his church think on him?'

'What they mean is their congregation. And yes, it's true. Ridiculous, but true.' Ezra grimaced.

Annas suddenly smiled. 'Would Judas be interested? He offers so many more possibilities!'

Joseph cocked his head to think about this for a moment and the others understood he was carefully formulating his reply. 'I think we should consider Judas's help as temporary. He's always been nomadic about his life and we can't know what's going to happen in the future--'

'Until what happens, happens.' Annas sighed and sat back, realizing how different the two brothers were. Joseph always knew what he wanted – stability - and went after it. Annas could count on it; indeed, he relied on it because experience taught him that predictable people were easy to manipulate.

'That's right.' Joseph smiled, feeling off the hook. 'We're all historians, aren't we? Living off the past and waiting for what happens. But I suspect Judas doesn't plan on staying here in the future. Although we're brothers by blood we're very different spirits. I like settled and routine. He's more of a rolling stone. He knows all kinds of weird languages and has different skills. But don't mistake him for the penniless, stupid drifters who follow Jesus. He'll settle somewhere until he's accomplished whatever it is that he settled there for, and then move on. I know this sounds strange to us but he's not all that interested in money or power . They're just a means to ends with him.'

'So, you don't know what drives him?'

'No. But I can tell from his letters that he's getting ready to move on from Jesus.'

'That's interesting,' Annas said but thought, I should alert Caiaphas to that.

17

WHEN his runners told him Jesus' people were coming from Bethphage, Annas invited his closest friends and advisors in the Sanhedrin to watch Jesus' 'parade'- as he called it - to Jerusalem from the top of the Temple wall nearly twenty feet high where they usually threw a person off whom they intended to stone. The priests wore their shiniest ephods to better reflect the sun.

'Look at that! A jackass riding on a donkey!'

'And they brought their monkeys!'

They watched the rag-tags and Jesus mingling with hundreds of pilgrims making their way from the Mount of Olives westward down the eastern slope Kidron Valley and back up the slope and through the city wall beneearth them into - as the Sanhedrin called it - their city. Jesus' people were among the last of the group.

On this first day of the week before Passover Annas had been told that Jesus and his followers had arrived in Bethany yesterday and that he and his closest disciples were staying with Simon the Leper. Joseph had already ordered the house watched since last Friday.

Suddenly, a mish-mash of trumpets, timbrels, cymbals and dulcimers sounded.

'Look at those people throwing their cloaks in front of the donkeys!' Jonathan shouted, clapped and pointed. 'They walk over them and pick them up and run to the front and throw them down again! Now, that's synchronization of donkey dung!' He was having a grand time.

I must remember that things like that catch Jon's eye, Issy thought. He always planned for the future and never observed Jonathan's behavior at parades before; he likes drama; maybe I should gesticulate more. 'Look, Annas! Look at that banner!' Issy put his right hand on Annas' shoulder and pointed with his left arm. The wind caused the banner to wave and droop but you could clearly read: 'King of the Jews.' 'Can you believe that?'

'Shhh. Shhh.' Said Ezra. 'Listen to what they're singing!'

'Hosanna to the Son of David
Blessed is he comes in
The name of the Lord.
Hosanna to the highest!'

'My God!,' Ezra said, 'they're actually claiming he's of royal descent! That should motivate Herod against him!'

Issy smiled: 'when push comes to shove, my friends, we could certainly bring him up on that charge!' When he saw Annas smile, he added, 'the trouble is that it'll be difficult to make them stick. Let's wait to see what he says in the Temple tomorrow.'

Annas thought for awhile. Issy's right. Better to be cautious. We'll do that. But it does seem stupid and ludicrous to portray the king of the Jews riding into town on an ass?

'Help! Guards! Help! Jesus and his men are breaking up the money changers! They're knocking the tables over and burning the accounts!'
'Where's the guard? Call the guard!'
Jesus, Peter and James were knocking the tables over and tearing up the scrolls! Coins and papers flew through the air and boards serving as tables on make-shift horses were knocked over with ink and quills spilling.
'Have you called the guard?'
'I did but they had to go to the riot.'
'What riot?'
'The one in the Lower City and they're fighting with the rioters!'
'Call the Romans then!'
'I did but they've gone to the riot because the guard can't handle them.'
'Have they murdered any of the merchants?'
'No. Only their accounts.'

*

Returning to the High Priest's house at the end of the day, Annas, Caiaphas, Jonathan, Joseph, and Ezra, together with several of his chief priests who had been present with them, settled down with glasses of wine and nibbles to discuss matters.

'Well, Annas, what did you think of that performance? He's clearly not going to negotiate.'

'No, he isn't but--'

'Let's kill him!'

Caiaphas caught the disgusted look on Annas' face as he said, 'wait, Jonathan. You must learn that patience and thought will take you further in life than emotional outbursts.'

'But Jonathan does have a point, Annas. May I make a suggestion?'

Annas looked at him and everyone could almost see his mind shifting from his youngest son to Issy. 'Of course!' You could almost hear the relief in his voice.

'That's what he expects us to do.

'To kill him?'

"Yes. That will give us a little more time to see what may develop and will allow us to calculate more carefully the right moment.' He paused. 'More importantly, it will give us the right reason to move against him.' He looked directly into Annas' eyes. 'Jesus is far easier to deal with than Herod because his danger is intellectual and long term; it's not about immediate power like Herod has.'

Annas knew Issy had something up his sleeve and sat back. 'You obviously have something in mind.'

'Let's offer him a bribe. One which he will probably refuse, but one that his peasant disciples would benefit from enormously.'

'A sort of divide and conquer bribe.' Annas said deliciously, licking his fat lips. They were his favorite bribes.

'Yes. It might be that we'll discover divisions among them we never knew about. But however it turns out, it will give us more time to plot his death in greater detail.'

'And possibly the bribe will make the second plan unnecessary if it's done right. I can understand that. But why you think we might be able to exploit divisions among them?'

Issy smiled. 'What educated, middle class, mature man is going to support Jesus' call to become anti-family and anti-worldly. I mean, my God! What else is there in this life? His message is aimed at male adolescent dreamers who don't know who they are or where they're going in life! We've moved far beyond Deuternomy!'

Annas leaned back in his chair and thought, God, there are so many lost souls in every generation! We can be in business forever! And thank God he made them a minority! Society wouldn't survive if they weren't! 'This sounds very practical. Let's work on the bribe and I'll create another committee to work on the plot. We have only a few days left if we're going to make it before Passover.'

*

Peter, Judas, Jesus, John and James sat in the front room of Simon the Leper's house in Bethany to discuss the High Priest's proposal. Peter was even more excited than when he thought he was going to walk on water. 'This is a helluva deal, Jesus! You would be the High Priest of Galilee and the rest of us your chief priests! And all paid for by Jerusalem's Sanhedrin until revenues come in to make us self-supporting! Boy! Would that take care of our financial problems!'

Judas knew that and that probably everyone heard his voice in their minds instead of Peter's, thanks to John. But Judas smiled: Peter probably even thought about a fleet of fishing boats!

In fact, Peter couldn't stop himself: 'you mean all we have to do is preserve the Hebrew traditions? And enforce the Law in Galilee which gives us religious protection against Herod's secular law?'

But I knew they received it differently from how Peter the innocent meant it. The look on John and Jesus' faces especially told me so. And when Jesus looked at me, I knew he was going to be charitable.

'You must realize,' he said, 'that the losers would be those poor Pharisees many of whom I attack but a few of whom genuinely believe in reform. You can't blame them for going to Herod when they couldn't get the Sadducees to change. And now the Sadds want to give us religious authority over them! To drag them back into the fold! You see how they're trying to divide and conquer us?'

We all felt Peter's shame when he hung his head and said, 'I'm sorry. I lost our plot.'

I turned to Jesus. 'You once said that we live in a moral slum and this just proves it. Herod cares nothing except for preserving his power which means staying in Rome's good graces. And the Sanhedrin represents - well, everything you've always talked about.'

'It would be wrong of us to benefit from the misfortune of others,' he replied. Then he paced around the room – twice.

When no one said anything, I asked, 'is it necessary to ask what the others think?'

Jesus looked at Peter but said to me, 'say what you mean.'

'Since when is morality decided by a vote of people who need it?'

'You know the answer as well as I do,' he replied. 'This is a spiritual issue that they've disguised as a worldly one.'

I looked up at him. 'My point is that they addressed this offer to you.'

'But it affects all of you as well. That's why I wanted all of you to know about it.' He looked around at us. 'All of you have a stake in it. After all, a chief priest--'

'But there's no truth in it!' I'm afraid I let friendship and emotions cloud my judgment because I didn't understand how we could even talk about this. Nor did I realize how my anguished look revealed what I thought.

Peter, James and John still didn't say anything and Jesus started pacing again, this time looking down and carefully putting one foot in front of the other. Finally, he said, 'I need some time with my Father. Will you return when you see my candle lit?'

'Of course.'

*

We returned to Jesus' room when we saw his candle light.

'Have you given any more thought to their offer?' he asked.

But I understood it was really directed to me so I replied, 'of course! And you?'

'Yes. But you first.'

I remembered my promise. Our secret. 'Reject it,' I replied. 'It insults you, God and us as God's children.' I knew Jesus expected to hear this from me but the others didn't.

Jesus looked steadily at me and said, 'you know what this means?'

'I know. Flight or fight. I'll fulfill my promise but ultimately it's your decision.'

The others looked at one another; we both knew they didn't know what we were talking about. So I said, 'it comes down to our personal authority. Or responsibility, or whatever we call it. What we do must come from where our authority comes from; and our authority as men come either from God or the world.' When he didn't say anything I said, 'remember we're in this boat together.'

We stared at one another while the others stared from one of us to the other.

'Then you'll help me in these next few days?' Jesus said, his eyes burning into mine but his voice calm and even.

I stared back and tried to say just as evenly, 'We'll help one another. But it's--.' I suddenly tossed my hand in the air and looked more intently at him. 'I was going to say, your decision. But now that we're talking about it this way, it's our decision isn't it?' To throw off the others I turned to them and said, 'it's all of ours.'

He nodded and some of the others did too. I didn't say anything more. Instead, I looked at the others and felt bad because of my deception. Their faces said they didn't fully understand; and John's face reflected hate because he just wanted to know the BIG TRUTH OF LIFE.

I just wanted to leave. As soon as possible.

*

We couldn't know everything the Sanhedrin plotted, of course, nor could we know about the factions and their little plots within the group. If it weren't for brother Joseph we wouldn't even have known about Annas, Caiaphas, my brother and Ezra who constituted one particular little group. We knew about the others but that was all: we knew *of* or *about* them. We were outsiders to what they thought and did.

Once we rejected their bribe offer, we put Jesus' intended plan into operation. He stepped up his fierce denunciation of them in various places in the Temple before various Diaspora groups and I went to my brother and agreed to lead their servants and Temple Guards to Jesus. I took their money and kept my word. To make sure everything went according to plan, I even went to the High Priest's house with Jesus and took Peter with me. I insisted he go because the others had run away and I wanted at least one witness to the proceedings.

But I should have suspected something was wrong at that point, once he had surrendered to them, because they insisted on his going bound, as a felon, when we expected just Jesus and myself to go peaceably to just to talk with the High Priest and his inner circle. But it was after leaving Peter in the courtyard and going upstairs with Jesus to Annas' office that I knew we had been betrayed. Annas told me to get out or get what they were going to give Jesus. I was puzzled but fear and ignorance drove me to return to Peter to tell him we should leave and that we would return in the morning.

But it was too late. First, Peter had disappeared from Bethany and the other disciples never returned after running off. I looked for them but never found them; so I returned to the High Priest's house and learned from one of the Temple guards that Jesus had been taken to Herod Antipas but that the King was saying he wouldn't press charges against Jesus for claiming to be King of the Jews. That he wanted to pass off responsibility for killing him onto the Romans. 'The Romans? What do they have to do with it?' That's when he said Jesus was at the praetorium being examined by Pilate.

That shocked me. Jesus and I hadn't talked about the Romans being involved because our quarrel was with the High Priest and Sanhedrin. It was obviously a religious matter and Jesus never claimed to be 'King of the Jews' as the Zealots well knew. But the High Priest was now saying that Jesus' destruction of the money changer's court was a public riot and fell under Roman jurisdiction. He was in their custody now and the High Priest and his inner circle were was pressing for his execution and stacking the growing crowd with their own men.

Who else but a lawyer - my brother - would think of that?

That's when I realized it had been a double plot all along! And that my brother betrayed me as much as the High Priest and his cronies did Jesus! I was furious but powerless because not one other disciple was present. Jesus was going to be judicially executed and I couldn't do anything about it! Worst of all, I knew what Roman soldiers did to Jewish male prisoners in the barracks before their crucifixion. And it wasn't just scourging them!

The horror of what was happening to him - and my own brother's betrayal - made me realize how irreligious, how bankrupt, how evil our Judaism had become, and how our High Priest was no different from Aretas!

I ran blindly through the streets, never wanting to have part of it again! Jesus had been right all along: Judaism was dead; it had become evil; but I realized it too late.

Intuitively, I headed for the Damascus gate; but one thought kept nagging at me: why didn't Jesus simply disappear as he had done several times before? He hadn't really needed me!

Or did he?

PART THREE

FRUITS

18

So, here I am twenty years and a meaningless fortune later, going to India carrying all this baggage from my past and present with me.

After contracting with Manga to receive and distribute our India goods as well as our JC textiles throughout the eastern region of the Great Sea except for Rome, we returned home where we did the same with Grupa for Rome and the western part of the Great Sea. Then we prepared to leave for living two years in India.

But not before I told Tay I wanted to take Marcus with me.

'I know you'll worry, but he's nearly sixteen and I'll watch him like a hawk,' I told her anguish-ridden face. 'He's my love as well as yours, Tay. And he's my future now as well as yours, and I don't want him raised uselessly like so many of boys his age are.' I paused. 'It's for his benefit because he'll have to make his own way eventually and I've learned the world responds to those who act responsibly.'

But of course she expressed her concerns – the long time we'd be gone, the dangers on voyage and unknown ones when we got there; but eventually agreed - three days later. That's when we left.

When Hellas, Marcus and I returned to Manga's Alexandria warehouse two weeks later, I found the letter from Fulgentius, the *aedile* at Aden waiting for us at Manga's office: he had secured passage for the four of us aboard the <u>Calliscrates</u>, captained by Arcas who had sailed several times to India with Hippalus. His competence was as safe as it gets, Fulgentius wrote. So, we picked up Thomas and made our way from Portus Magnus via the canal toward Lake Mareotis and then toward the head of the Red Sea where a fast sailer was booked to take us to Aden, a trip estimated to take four or five days depending on the strength and direction of the winds. At Aden, Fulgentius told us he had already written to Fabius, the *aedile* at Muzius to expect us and further assured me of his competence as a merchant.

Leaving Aden and bound for the unknown must have unsettled Thomas because he changed toward me; he became more reminiscent and personal, as if he wanted to confess something. One day after I joined him at the rail, he said out of the blue, 'it bothered many of us, you know. We didn't make the decision hastily or unanimously.'

I looked at him quizzically. 'What decision?'

'About sacrificing one of our own as the traitor to Jesus. All of us understood that's how most Jews would understand it.'

'Matthew told me all about it.' I could see he was embarrassed and had struggled to tell me this.

'Did he tell you about me?'

'No.'

'I didn't want any part of it and told them so. In fact, I thought what they were doing was all a lie and that's why I left.' He turned to face me. 'They invented the church for themselves.'

'For themselves? You can't be serious!'

He looked at me with -his steady black eyes I remembered. 'Oh, but I am. I mean they were serious and knew what they were doing. They understood that Jesus' failure meant their failure if they didn't do something about it and no one wanted to go back to that old life in Galilee. They thought everything out very carefully because they knew they had to succeed if they were to have any future in Jerusalem. Success defined what they did and it worked as you know.'

'Yes. I know and accept what's been done,' I replied but felt doubt for the first time.

Pain crossed his face. 'I never wanted to condemn you! But they had their minds made up and wouldn't listen to me! And you were only a part of their grand plan! And look at what happened! Peter took the spirit to the Gentiles but then substituted blood for spirit when he supported James to be head of the church because he was Jesus' brother! That's when I realized they intended to abandon Jerusalem to the Jews and go after the Gentiles! And that's why I left!' He stopped and drew a large breath. 'I think Peter intended to abandon Israel from the beginning!'

I looked at him, not knowing what to say. 'Matthias even told me that a few years later!'
'The Essene? The one who replaced me?'
'Yes. And even he broke with them when he saw what direction they were going in.

'But Thomas, their Council has just sent Matt to set up their church in Antioch! Isn't he to minister to the Jews?'

Thomas looked back at the sea over the rail and then shocked me: 'yes. And that's why he's the real heir to Jesus' teaching. Not Peter.'

I remembering facing out over the sea as well, not knowing what to say. I had abandoned it all so long ago and didn't want to think about it anymore. I was Titianus now.

The remainder of the voyage was uneventful. I chalked it up to Fulgentius' having told us that pirates attack the west bound ships laden with India goods instead of the east bound ones which they know are going to get the goods they wanted. It made good business sense to me and I asked Hellas to make a note of it for when we prepare to return. It also turned out that the winds were favorable but while Hellas, I and Marcus had good sea legs Thomas didn't. Only he suffered and kept repeating that God meant him to die on land.

A month and a half later we anchored off southern India, between the mouth of a small river and Malankara, a small island a little further offshore. I was surprised that the small seaport without docks was Muzius. People and goods got from ship to town and vice versa by lighters. Thomas didn't come with us the first time. He immediately had rowers take him to the island where he fell on the ground and thanked God. The next day, he erected a cross and altar there.

*

I remember four particular things about our early days there. First was the heat: it never went away. Second, was the smell of dung fires in the morning which gave an aroma of incense to the outdoors – as well as indoors. Third, the town and countryside was even more crowded than Rome but horizontally: without the huge and towering – many in Rome said tottering – *insulae* or blocks of apartments. And throngs of small-sized, straight-haired, dark-brown skinned people who looked like Manga and Grupa everywhere; all watching us. The fourth thing was the jungle. Noises – strange, constant and full of other lives who kept coming closer if you didn't cut the growth back weekly.

I had to hurry because we were staying only two years; but on top of that, we had an immediate problem: Arcas and our ship, the <u>Calliscrates</u>, was going on to Taprobane, the big island around the tip of this land further south, but would return in a month or so before returning to Aden. We had to assemble our first shipment in a hurry if we wanted to catch *his* passage. That's where Fabius, the *aedile*, helped us enormously. He was also a merchant who came out on a ten-year plan and knew the ins and outs of the trade.

First, we settled ourselves. We found an abandoned merchant's house to stay in and our first purchase was insect netting and raised cots. Then we learned to eat the local way: which was meatless and bizarre by every previous experience I ever had (imagine eating slimy, runny, unknown things on a palm leaf). The last things we addressed were what we were going to export to Rome – which were the first things we thought about in Rome.

I took Marcus to every meeting because it was education for life. Everything must be accounted for, I explained. We ship goods to Manga or Grupa - with whom Fabius also did business – who credits us with two-thirds of its Alexandria value as our 'draw' - as he called it - or credit that we can use as cash. We then use that draw for purchasing and shipping goods to us in care of Manga on the return, or we can authorize another party or parties to draw on him for an amount we assign them. It was too late to do this now, I told him, but in the future we'll buy commodities in Taprobane and pay for them by authorizing the selling merchant in Taprobane to draw on Manga for our purchase price. That selling merchant could take it in manufactured goods - or money. But since Roman money was of little use in India the draw - the authorization itself - was really the 'money.' The day when Marcus said 'so, everything really is accounting!' I knew he understood and had a feel for it.

'Ship black gold first,' Fabius advised us. 'It's fetching fifteen denarii a pound in Alexandria.' I looked at him knowing wages there were one denarii a day and didn't want to know how they diluted it or with what to make it saleable. All merchants in the west sent lists of India's commodity prices in their ports to us so we could calculate our draws. Marc's eyes widened when he understood that one pound of pepper equaled a man's daily wage for TWO weeks. 'Oh, my God!', he exclaimed, 'no wonder black pepper is called black gold.'

'But send a variety of goods if you can,' Fulgentius replied. 'Because the prices of each one fluctuates from week to week and have no relationship to one another. Pearls, gems – diamonds and amethysts in particular, and silver jewelry as well as cinnamon, cardamom, and ginger. And especially rock crystal. Silks as well; though they are not so plentiful. It all depends on supplies, of course.' Yes, I understood that perfectly; and now Marc did too. We set up an account in his name; and he watched it every day even though I told him it would be months before we would make another entry in it. I couldn't be prouder.

*

Our first hint that a serious problem could develop came three months later when King Chenkudduvan made his annual visit to Muziris to collect his taxes. His retinue included several elephants, a small army of retainers - warriors, musicians and servants of different kinds - and his hareem. When I asked Centurion Tanusius, commander of our Roman garrison, about them, he replied they could overwhelm us any time; but don't tell them. It turned out that paying the King's annual ten percent tax wasn't the problem; Thomas was.

Rome's imperial power rested on the people's annual acknowledgement of the godly status of the emperor ever since the first one, and Temples of Augustus were everywhere Romans were, even in Muziris. This wasn't a problem until after our first Saturnalia when the acknowledgement was usually made but Thomas refused to do so. I couldn't believe it; I remembered him doubting reality before, but this was business! Life! I talked to Cerco, Rome's chief priest there, and explained that Thomas was a Jew (a half-truth - he was a Gentile Jew like Philip and I didn't want to explain the difference between Jews and Jesus Jews) and a monotheist and blah, blah about all that one-God business. Cerco had never encountered Jews before; didn't know what or why they were; and so he let it go - but only in a grumbling sort of way after Hellas, Marcus and I made our acknowledgements – and gratuities. I then reminded Thomas of what Jesus said about paying Caesar's dues but I could see that he no longer believed it. That's when I began to worry about him. It was bad enough living the life I did, but to try living a belief that was separate from this world was too confusing.

If not impossible.

That's when I realized how deeply those Buddhists in Alexandria had changed him: and wrongly. They had intensified his drive to experience the divine within him far more than he had believed possible before. This was the real reason why he came to India: to find Buddhists who were doing this very thing and it didn't matter to him that they were doing it for a different reason. How they did it fascinated him; the result didn't matter while he was in the west. But I could see the context here was very different and Manga's warning came back to me: there were no Buddhists in Muziris; the Indians here were merely unenlightened believers in nature gods and in the person of the King. If Thomas was disappointed in this, he didn't voice it or that he even understood his problem. It wasn't the King's fault: he made it clear that he didn't want anyone denying his godly nature anymore than the Roman emperors did - his treasurer explained it to us when we passed our annual taxes over to him – and we had no problem with that. But Thomas did: perhaps because he didn't participate in our greed, ignored it or forgot it. But he definitely did not obey Jesus' injunction to pay the tax.

*

India isn't Rome in many ways and employing people is one of them. If you hire a servant or helper in Muzirus, you've hired his or her family as well. Patma was a helper-laborer. A packager, hauler and fetcher. Soon his wife was helping him; then his children; then his brother; then his extended family; and soon we were feeding and supporting seventeen when I thought we had hired one. But they worked cheap, seemed harmless and the seventeen did the work of about nine men for the price of one. That was the just the way it works, Fabius explained and sighed when I complained about them to him.

But theft was another story. When some jewels - very specifically, a strand of beautiful pearls that I had earmarked for Tay - went missing from our inventory for the next shipment, I asked Fabius and then Tanusius for advice. All the Indians we employed denied having anything to do with it or knowing anything about it. At first, we said nothing about it because we understood that such things in the possession of any native made him or her, ipso facto, the guilty party. I suppose it was the heat, or the insects, or the food: but my exacerbation boiled over one day two weeks later and I reported the theft to the King's representative and gave him a minute description of the missing necklace. Two weeks after that, he took Patma into custody and to Chera where the King's court was.

From that moment on, his family - including his brother's family - proclaimed his innocence and beseeched – plagued is more what it was like - us to intercede on his behalf. After the King's representatives and his helpers searched through Patma's families possessions, I noticed Patma's eldest daughter, Champi, began talking with Marcus almost daily. Then flirting with him.

Two weeks later, one of the King's representatives announced that Patma was dead. They had cut off his right hand but couldn't stop the flow of blood. Or didn't want to. Marcus, Hellas and I felt very bad about it; but it wrought a different effect on Thomas who said, 'I thought they needed Jesus but now I know they do.'

The pearls were never recovered, at least during the remainder of the time that I remained there, but Marcus' relationship with Champi grew closer and, much as I didn't want to have these conversations with him about sex, love and marriage, I knew I had to. He was nearly eighteen.

'Marriage is a public acknowledgement that the woman you live with is the mother of your children,' I told him, 'it legitimates having sex with her and no one will question your paternity of her children. But you have no idea how strangely fixated the Roman's are on paternity. It's part of their legal culture. Take your wife, for example. Few will condemn her if she has an affair but they will think something's wrong with you. And if she does and it can be proved you knew about it, then the law says you are presumed to pimp for her and can be prosecuted. That's if you are married to a Roman. What do you think they will think or how will they behave if she's Indian?' I looked at him trying to avoid my eyes. 'Your mother and I expect you to marry a Roman girl. From a proper family.'

Now he looked at me. 'You mean from an upper class one.'

'I know I should have had this conversation with you in Rome but later is better than never. You do know that sex shouldn't be confused with love don't you?'

'I know. Champi and I know we're not going to marry.'

'But are you being fair to her? Honesty isn't necessarily fairness but she is a person after all.' I hesitated. 'Does she understand the risks and still consents?'

'Yes. We've talked things over. We know what we're doing.'

I stood up, plucked my sweat-drenched tunic away from chest and said, 'but she's only fourteen. I know you think she's grown up but she isn't. My first wife was fourteen when we married and I didn't realize how much of a child she still was. She died, a child having a child. And never saw her seventeenth birthday. You have.'

'So you feel guilty about it and want to warn me?'

'No. I'm talking about honesty. With yourself and others. I wasn't fair to her because I didn't think about it before marrying her. I wasn't honest with myself because I was ignorant about myself. I never asked myself, 'what if she becomes pregnant?' That's the question, not whether you're married or not.'

'These people don't worry about being married or not.'

'I'm not talking about 'these people,' Marc. I'm talking about you. What is your responsibility? How responsible are you? And to whom? I'm telling you my sad experience because I hadn't thought about myself in relation to others other than in business terms. '

'I never thought about it that way.'

'Well, you should start now. Nothing is more important than knowing who you're responsible to, and that should be a first step in your life.' I swept my left arm in an arc. 'All the rest of this is just the froth of life.'

'Like sex?'

'That's right. Don't misunderstand. Sex is an important part of life but like everything else it's only a part of it.'

Whew! I thought. That duty's over.!

*

The King's second annual visit for collecting his taxes came after the *kalends* of January and he brought a sterner warning to Thomas: stop proselytizing my people. Stop telling them I am not divine.

I saw Thomas' look: hard and unforgiving and defiant. 'Look,' I said later to him, 'Hellas is staying on here to run our business but Marcus and I are leaving before the King's visit next year. I think you should return with us.'

But Thomas seemed more determined than ever. He had attracted two followers whom he called disciples and together, they built a small building housing an altar very much like a native temple, but where they worshipped Jesus - really Thomas' version of Jesus - and lived there with a horde of monkeys, snakes and things I warned Hellas and Marcus not to eat or even think about. I wouldn't go near it and also warned them not to go near it because monkeys bite and carry all sorts of diseases. Thomas didn't even sleep with insect netting anymore. 'He's gone native,' Hellas commented. 'That's what soldiers do but not merchants.' I thought that was rather astute of a citified man and it made me think about myself. Is that what I was doing in Rome? Sleeping with monkeys?

We planned to leave for Aden in mid-December when the prevailing winds shifted around to blow westward. This was before the King's next visit and I started pleading more regularly with Thomas to join us. I even proposed paying for set him up in Alexandria. But he refused. Even my 'live to evangelize another day' speech didn't convince him. Although he agreed that 'dead evangelists like Jesus 'don't evangelize I was beginning to see what impression Peter's church had on him. He was already depending on others now.

I knew it was a mistake but felt helpless. How can you help someone who won't help themselves? The second morning after we were stowing the last of our supplies aboard ship, Fabius sent us word that Thomas was found stabbed to death over his altar. His two followers had disappeared and only some monkeys, snakes and insects remained. It was theirs now, I thought as Marcus and Hellas helped me bury him.

'I knew someone once, a very close friend, who preferred death to life,' I told Fabius the next morning, 'but I don't understand it. I was taught that God wants us to lead a happy and prosperous life but these people apparently missed that lesson.'

'Don't you think he knew this might happen?' Fabius asked.

I shrugged and answered, 'I suspect he did. I warned him this might happen months ago when I told him we were returning to Alexandria but he refused to go with us.'

'He looked old enough to know better.'

'I should say so. Since I'm forty five he must have been around forty-seven or forty eight. Right minded men know themselves well enough by then.'

Fabius just shook his head.

'You've been very quiet since we left,' Marcus said the day after we weighed anchor and drifted out to sea. 'Is it because of what happened to Thomas?'

I nodded and looked at him instead of the receding shore line. 'It reminds me of when Jesus decided to make his final stand in Jerusalem. I've never understood people who choose death when their situation indicates it might happen. They lack purpose in their lives. I don't think God wants us to think the purpose of our life is death. If it was God wouldn't have created me. I can understand why Peter and the others want people to think my death will serve as some kind of horrible example of how not to live because it suits their own purposes.'

'But I always thought your life is so intensely personal to you.'

'Oh, it is! Between me and God who gave it to me!' I stopped and gazed out to sea without seeing it. 'Live your own life, Marc, as fully as God wants you to. And never be afraid to take responsibility for it because God gave that to you too.'

'But doesn't life change all the time? Forcing us to made decisions all the time? And don't some of which contradict what we thought or how we lived before?'

'Of course. But never fear change; embrace it. Change isn't the essence of life only its chief characteristic.' I looked at him and smiled. 'And I've had enough experience to know there's no escape from it.'

He was nineteen when we returned and no Roman father was prouder of his son than I was.

19

Five weeks after Ti and Marcus left, Tay's period began which forced her to think about what she didn't want to: I may never see them again and may never have a child with Ti. What will happen to me then? So, she began thinking about her choices and the more she thought the more she felt alone and fearful with the son of a man she hadn't had enough time to understand that well. But then Vologases' letter arrived and changed everything.

She felt his concern for her but knew he was primarily interested in Vardanes (Marcus). Yes, you're alone with *his* son, not yours, he wrote; (how did he know? she thought). But think about this as only temporary and never give in to fear. Take responsibility for your own life as your husband does. I realize you're in a foreign world and that's why I urge you to look and learn. The best way is to write me, tell me about Rome's commercial culture since it's so different from our own. You'll find you're able to understand it – and him - better. Hire whomever you need to help your achieve your goals and don't be afraid to assert yourself. Your hareem life is over. Start with what Roman's think is their ideal Roman matron; and live like one. Find your new self through actively pursuing Roman life; but always remember your foundations will be here. As his are in Judea.

Take responsibility for my own life? Assert myself? Such phrases struck her dimly but forcefully. Yes, she thought, the old hareem life is gone. I *have* entered a world where I make my own choices! Maybe that's what makes Ti so restless! Trying to decide which ones to make! Volo once said as an afterthought, 'what makes Ti run?' He's right. What does? All these choices? Maybe I can't conceive because he can't give. If he were more accepting of being Roman maybe-- But don't lose sight of our common goal. Our marriage is a merger, a means and they involve more than an end. What does 'common' really mean?

'I'm sorry to disturb you, mistress, but there's a little girl here who's been hurt and says she lives next door.'

The maid's announcement pulled Tay back into the present. 'You mean in the domus next door?"
'Yes, dom.'
'Where is she?'
'In the kitchen. Cook's washing her face.'
"I'll come right down.'
The girl looked about six years old, had a bloody nose and bruises but no cuts on her face. Her name was Valeria and lived in the bigger - and nearest - house. Tay examined her, helped Sophie and two other maids clean her up and asked what happened.
'Servius said to go away.'
'Who's Servius? A servant?'
'My brother.'
'Come with me. I'll take you home.' Tay called to one female and three male servants to accompany them.

The big house was nearly twice the size of Tay's with a maleness about it, as if no female cared for it, and when she arrived in the front courtyard several attendants were unloading its occupant, a man wearing a white toga with a purple stripe with a crippled right leg and right arm. When he turned, she saw the right side of his face was disfigured.

That was when he saw Tay talking with the house slaves at the front gate, his daughter standing next to her. He was about to send his chief attendant to ask her what she wanted, when the little girl ran up to him. He motioned for help from his attendents to go inside and told her to invite her friend in.

Once inside, settled, and served refreshments he heard their story. 'Thaxtos,' he called when they had finished, 'take Servius to his room and give him exactly what he did to Valeria. No more and no less. Do you understand?' Thaxtos nodded, bowed and left. Tay saw the pre-teenager smirk and thought this wasn't the first time this happened.

Senator Publix Vipsanius Agrippa looked about fifty but his injuries did not extend to his mind. On the contrary, he had already observed how Tay and her female attendant were dressed, how her male servants were more physically fit than his, and carried concealed weapons beneath their cloaks. He told his chief attendant to take her servants to the kitchen for refreshments while he talked to Tay. His daughter stood to the left of his chair, watching them while twisting strands of her hair.

So, he thought, her husband was a merchant in the eastern and spice trades and was in India with their eldest son while she's here with the younger one. But no daughter. And they are all Roman citizens as freedmen and live next door in Lentullus' old domus that Caligula had confiscated and sold to them. His mind raced ahead: rich, new to Rome and going to be richer. Good people to know.

He looked at her more closely under is lidded left eye and thought: beautiful in an exotic way, young and no doubt wants a daughter. Could pass as Italian but her dress and mannerisms reveal she isn't.

'From Parthia!' he blurted out – nearly spewing his sip of wine - which surprised even himself and made him blush with social shame. He apologized. Parthia was fabulously rich. Next on Rome's list if the Senate had any say in it. 'So few of you live in Rome!' Though Roman to the core, his tastes ran to the exotic and he began thinking how he could use all this when his daughter suddenly turned from staring at Tay and pulled on his sleeve. He leaned over.

'I like her,' she whispered in his left ear.

'Then we'll have to see more of her, won't we?' he whispered back. He turned to Tay, 'I hope you can join us for lunch the second day next week. Valeria is having a few of her friends in and it would be an honor for me to help repay you in a small way.'

Tay tried not to show how taken aback she was. She had little sense of Roman etiquette or the innuendos traded in its polite society, let alone in its political side. Besides, invitations to married women on their own just wasn't done in Parthia; and – oh my God – her husband wasn't and couldn't be present. But she would see Valeria again and she looked so. . . so wistfully neglected.

He sensed it. 'I should tell you that my wife and I were in a carriage accident two years ago. Furia was killed and I was . . .well, made to look like this. So the party is a girl's one and I'm afraid I've been out of practice a very long time. I would me most grateful if you could come.'

'What about the other mothers?'

He looked at her. How refreshing! He thought. 'I can see you don't really know Rome. Please come and perhaps you'll learn something about it.'

She said yes and left. Not knowing Roman mothers didn't go to their children's parties. Especially their daughters.

The arrangement began that way; then one occasion turned into another and it was all very polite and social. But then Publix discovered two things about Tay: she didn't gossip the way most Roman women did and didn't constantly importune things for their husbands, sons or lovers; and most delightfully, she was genuinely interested in business, in how to make money not just spend it.. The latter was why he invited her to help him host a meeting of his business friends. Once their raised eyebrows fell, they discovered how refreshing it was to talk with a female version of themselves and he invited her to help him host other meetings of his business friends. They were delighted with her as well; and wondered about her relationship with Publix - who lived the meaning of discretion.

So was Publix. But what really convinced him of her qualities was her refusal - her 'no, thank you' - to the proposition of handsome and much experienced Senator Felix Caverna, who was so taken aback by her refusal that he told his friends about it: it had never happened to him before.

So, a month after they met, Publix decided to propose his plan to her. But he was too late: she proposed her own.

'I've thought this over, Publix. It's obvious you love to socialize and my husband taught me that business is social. We're soon be coming into the social season so I'm going to suggest an arrangement with you. I'll manage all your engagements. All you have to do is tell me what you want to do, who you want to invite and what suggestions you have about.what you would like to do. You can take full credit for everything. I'm happy to work behind the scenes, so to speak. I'll learn from this, of course. You can merely tell people you choose to introduce me to that I am as your neighbor, a wife and mother who's waiting for her husband and eldest son to return from India. We'll both benefit from the arrangement and I expect to pay my share of it.' She looked at him as he raised his hand to protest. 'No, we're not poor.' He was about to agree when she added, 'But one more thing. There won't be any sex involved.' She looked into his eyes. 'with you or any of your friends. I'm married and committed to it.' She looked up over his head, 'and we have unfinished business between us.'

'Can I give you my answer tomorrow?'
'Of course.'

Publix thought about his situation for the rest of the day and into the evening and next morning: Valeria likes her and needs mothering, he thought. My two sons are useless ne're-do-wells; I'm fifty-three, she doesn't look thirty; and we'll be the talk of the town. She's beautiful, exotic, mysterious, rumored to be related to Parthian royalty with a husband in India. People will assume we're having an affair; do I want that? He smiled. Of course, you old goat! And it will be fun to rub some noses in it! Then a more sobering thought occurred to him: I can go out now more often as well as socialize at home! Something I haven't been able to do very well for a long time.

Tay read his note later that next morning:
> 'Yes. I would like to plan a dinner party for next month on the Ides. Perhaps we can begin our arrangement with that. Hope to hear from you soon.
> P.'

She called Quintus. 'We're going to be busy for the next month helping Publix. I may need your help on some extra things. Do you think your wife might have time to help me?'

While you have your time in India, she thought, I'll have mine in Rome.

*

Ti's first born had grown into a more serious young man than most boys his age were. Few of them were concerned with how their feelings, thoughts and ideas originated, let alone how they developed. But he knew he asked because he wondered where his revulsion, horror and disgust at Roman culture and society came from. He thought it started when he was seven and his parents moved to Rome. Its way of life - the harsh treatment of one another, its brutal treatment of slavery, and the overweening obeisance to materialism and lip-service to the spiritual side of life fixed a lasting hatred of them on him. Nothing about them made sense; and now, at age thirteen, with his father and older brother in India and his grandpa in Antioch, he began voicing his thoughts and feelings no matter how embarrassing they were. The first time he met Volumnus, for example, he said the word 'hypocrite' a bit too loudly and though he apologized and Volumnus laughed it off, he knew the man in black would hate him forever.

    Tay wasn't sure how to handle it. Reducing his exposure to Roman public life was an obvious choice but fraught with other consequences. She tried telling him about other ways of living; but she knew only Parthian ways in detail and they were so different from Rome's they seemed remote. Her cue was Hero's preface to them as 'once upon a time, long-ago-and-far-away.' He didn't say they seemed preposterous and unbelievable. The only stories he loved were those about Zorastrianism. Fighting on horseback didn't appeal to him.

*

The public baths and gymnasiums where his difference showed were the worst. Once naked ridicule was instant. 'Hey! Jew boy! Yes, you!' They made fun of him. Chased him, held him down and taunted him; and he couldn't do anything about it. They called him 'whiny' because he called for help from one of the servants - which only aggravated their attacks further. He hated them: the boys, the baths, the sports, the teachers and Roman ways of life in general.

*

So he wanted to know. 'Mother, did the emperor really order the Jews to leave the city because of the rioting about Chrestus?'

'Yes. I think so. Where did you hear about that?'

'The boys at the baths said it. They said I was still here only because father paid a lot of money.'

'No, Hero. That's not true. You're as much a Roman citizen as they are. We all are, darling.'

'Are father and Marc circumcised?'

She looked at him and wanted to cry at how fast innocence dissolved in this world. What things mothers of sons without fathers have to answer for! 'Marc isn't but your father is.'

'Father knew Chrestus, didn't he? Was Chrestus circumcised?'

'I'm sure he was. Jews circumcise their male babies eight days after they're born. That was true of you.'

'So, father and I are Jews but Marc isn't?'

'Marc and I were Parthians. We don't circumcise male babies.'

'You're like the Romans!'

'I never thought about it that way before, but yes. We are.' And this gave her a new idea beyond the commonly heard one of 'out of the mouths of babes—'

*

Hero liked the idea that he was circumcised like his father and was just getting used to it when the new emperor - who was younger than Marc and uncircumcised like him - said the Jews could return to Rome.

Then, three months later when it started to get warm again, a man called Peter appeared at their house. He said he was a friend of father's: but was big, bearded, and told Hero that other Jewish men looked like him. He also told him he liked children; that they were the future of the world. And he told him and mother that Chrestus had been his teacher as he had been father's.

Hero couldn't help it: 'are you circumcised too?'

'Hero!'

'It's all right,' Peter replied, laughing. 'Yes, I am. And your father is too.'

'I know.'

'So are people like Solomon and Volumnus.'

'Mother says you're important in spite of your poor appearance and because you talk about Chrstus in the synagogues and know all kinds of important things about him.'

Peter looked at Tay and smiled. 'That's very kind of her to say. But I would say Solomon and Volumnus are more important than I am.'

I didn't like him saying that. They were different. They always wore black and were colder and more distant. And formal; like most Romans. I didn't like them; no matter how many times mother took me to Peter's talks where they were present. They had shifty eyes and sudden smiles; they hesitated and whispered about 'interest' and 'money' I didn't trust them like I did Peter.

But in the spring, after a few of Peter's talks where I met other friends of his, father and Marc came home, browner and leaner. And Marc was more serious than he had ever been. And so much older! A man!

20

'THE nicest thing about long, good-weather sailing is that you have time to think and dream and talk,' Ti said to Marc as they were looking at the two islands which signaled their approaching Raphta on Arabia's southcoast.

'As long as you avoid the pirates!' Marcus joked.

Ti smiled. 'Apparently we have by now. The Romans patrol the sea lanes from here on in.' He looked at Marc. 'You know I'm grooming you to take over.'

'I thought that was part of the reason you wanted me to go on this trip.'

'Yes. I'm hoping that in years to come, you'll remember how we put together this second leg of our connection with the east when you were seventeen and eighteen. There's still a lot for you to learn in these next few years but it can't be done from India. Only from Rome.'

'You have some specifics in mind, then.'

'I try to plan long term as much as possible. According to what trends and directions the empire seems to be going in. But I've discovered it's like sailing and not let whatever prevailing wind throw you off course.'

'You need to rely on someone who's had some experience.'

'Yes. You've had this southern experience and I hope to teach about our northern one next.'

'Northern? I can learn that in Rome?'

'Yes. Plus learn about our Great Sea trade. Amos will be helpful about that.'

'What's west?'

'Not much. Some gold, a little silver but mainly low-priced raw materials and food stuffs. The real wealth is in the east.' Ti looked out at the Arabian Sea; maybe another four or five days to the Red one if this wind continues, he thought. 'You always want to remember the basics: supply and demand. And that profitability varies from market to market. Don't worry about final prices; they'll always fluctuate. Concentrate on profitability. Lower profits mean you have to go after greater volume--'

'And higher profits mean less volume?'

'That's the trick if you can make it do it. It's less work. And that's why you need to pay careful attention to who your market is. Everybody has to eat but not everyone wears diamond jewelry.'

'Except Tay.'

Ti looked at him. 'There's one more thing. You saw how India wasn't much of business society. Now compare Rome's when we get there. It matters there and lots of people know how to make profits. But you should hire those people and pay attention to the bigger picture.' He stopped for a moment. 'You never want to be confused about this. We're finished living as we did in Muziris. That was like existing on the ground floor while waiting to live upstairs which is literally built on top of us. The jewels and dresses Tay wears promotes others to buy--'

'But why don't we just limit them to buying from us?'

'For two reasons. Someone will always find an alternative and when that happens it lessons demand for ours. It's better to have seventy percent of a hundred than one hundred percent of five.' He saw Marcus didn't understand. 'Think of a pyramid upside down, resting on its tip. Be the tip; control the supply - or as much as you can - and you control everything up the legs of the rest of the triangle.'

'I see.'

'I want you to investigate the western empire. See what's there! I may well have overlooked things.' He thought for a moment. 'I want to say something else about the social side of our business. I'm not interested in its political side and I'm never going to be. But that's not to say that you may not. If you find it interesting that's fine with me. I'm just telling you that I'm not.'

'Any particular reason why you're not?'

'You probably don't think this, but I'm actually a very private person. I like to make the decisions that affect myself. Especially those that determine my life.' He raised his head to look directly into Marc's eyes. 'This includes you and Tay and Hero.'

'Thomas seemed to be that way.'

'You mean his decision to stay there. I can see how you would think that, but I actually think he stayed because he listened to something or somebody else instead of himself. You didn't know him twenty years ago as I did. We were much more alike then.' He paused for a long moment. 'But we went our separate ways. Perhaps that's what it's all about. I never thought about life the way he did when you knew him.'

'You mean going our own ways?'

'Yes. I can only tell you my experiences. You have to live your own.'

'So that's our uniqueness.'

'Yes, as individuals.'

*

We stayed in Alexandria only long enough to see Manga, describe our trip and what to expect from it, and tell him we were going on to Rome and would be glad to carry any letters he wanted to send there. He told us that Joseph of the JC line of textiles had died, but that his sons, Marc and Laban, had taken over. Yes, it was the old story among manufacturers, Marc was Mr. Inside, the administrator-manager, and Laban Mr. Outside, the marketing manager. I was amused at the old ring I heard about it in my head. I told Manga that we would go to meet them and pay our respects to their father, and Manga said he would have his correspondence ready when we were finished.

    I'm glad we went because for the first time I saw Marcus the young businessman with two others about his own age, and I could see that he was a bit of both. He had the accounting interests of Marc the manager and the marketing instincts of Laban. The three talked easily because Marcus was the bridge between them. We reaffirmed our interest in representing their line and told them that Marcus would be corresponding with them once we returned home and settled in.

*

We reached Ostia on the second day of the third week of April, 55, and walked into our home on the *kalends* of May. As soon as we had landed, runners had been sent ahead announcing our arrival to Tay and Hero who were waiting.

A week later Ti and Tay were in Tay's new 'return rooms' that she had constructed on the first floor over two of the dining rooms on the ground floor. They comprised a bedroom, a portico off it, a sitting room and a small bathing room. Tay sat at her dressing table, combing her hair. Ti was sitting up in bed when she said, 'Hero's been increasingly unhappy.'

'Because he went from eleven to thirteen?'

'No, silly. He's more intellectually sensitive than Marcus and the open conflict between our new emperor and his mother that everyone talks about bothers him.' She paused, holding the tortoise shell comb in mid-air. 'Nero's seventeen but his mother treats him as if he's twelve. The latest is that Agrippina has taken to wearing military blouses. Can you believe it? Everyone's calling her the she-general!'

'You're not the naïve Roman citizen that I left! What's changed you?

'Publix, our neighbor, and his friends. I've been attending some of his social gatherings.'

Ti went quiet.

She put her brush down and turned to face him. 'I know you've been gone a couple of years, Ti. But you should know I had these rooms redesigned for us. I expect you'll be making more trips for us in the future but these are our private rooms. Husband and wife rooms.   I'm completely committed to our marriage and our family. I would never - I repeat, never - have sex with someone else. Is that clear between us? I think we both know who we are and that this isn't some silly game.'

'Yes. And I never go a prostitute for sex.' Then he smiled. 'Shall I refer to these as our sex rooms?'

'Of course not,' she replied and turned back to brushing her hair so he couldn't see her smile.

'So, she's the she-general and Publix is a Senator?'

'And the biggest public contractor in Rome. He has his fingers in many different pies. He and his friends could be very helpful to us. You'll see for yourself.'

He didn't say anything for a moment. Then, he asked, 'how does this relate to Hero?'

Tay put her comb down and turned back to him. 'He's really taken up with your Judaism. The boys at the baths tease him about being circumcised and who knows what his grandfather said to him during those early years before you met me. His head is filled with all those old stories and he goes around saying how evil and corrupt Roman society is! Can you imagine? He'll be only fourteen next month!'

'What can I do about it? You know I've tried to be as Roman as I can these past six years!'

'Start involving him in the business. Maybe he can work with Marcus. He was even younger than Hero when you started with him.'

'All right.'

'Speaking of Marcus, how's he coming along?'

I deliberately waited for her to turn to me. When she did I met her eyes and said, 'I couldn't be more pleased and proud with how he turning out. He has a natural instinct for business and now it's just a matter of learning the mechanics and how to socialize. You should be very proud of him.'

She smiled and looked down in thought. Then she looked up, smiled at me this time, stood up, dropped her dress and walked over to me. 'Wouldn't it be nice to have a daughter?'

*

'I've waited to talk to you about this,' she said in the morning as we drank our coffee.

I knew it was serious. 'What?'

'Vologases is King now.'

'What happened to Bardanes?'

'He's dead. So's GoTayrzes.'

'Pacorus and Tiridates?'

'Both are alive and support Volo.'

'Was he behind it all?'

'I don't know and it doesn't matter.' She paused. 'The important thing is that Volo's on top now.'

I looked at her. She's no fool. 'There's more to it, isn't there?'

'Do you remember Volo's son, Vardanes?'

'Yes,' I replied, remembering a lad of fifteen or sixteen. 'A little older than Marcus then.'

'When Volo became king last year and made Tiridates king of Armenia, Vardanes revolted with the support of the Gevs.'

'Serious?'

'I didn't think so until I heard two days ago that our emperor and his mother reassigned Corbulo from the Germanies to Antioch.' Tay pushed her coffee cup to the middle of the small table between us. 'You've been away so you don't know. Corbulo is a brilliant general and has been very successful against the tribes up north. I'm sure he'll try to exploit this division in our family.'

I thought about it. This was serious and I didn't really want to go – but. 'should I go?'

He needs to rest, she thought. So, she said, 'why don't we wait a little while to see what happens in the next month or two. Corbulo will have to build up his army won't he?' She smiled, knowing he was thinking about those contracts. 'Why don't you write to Amos and tip him off to the possibilities?'

'I love you, you know.' And then he remembered: 'but I just told that ten minutes ago.'

'I never tire of hearing it, Ti. And you know I want to give you a daughter who will give you grandchildren. Let's try again.'

21

THE next to last man I ever expected to see again showed up three weeks later.

'A man called Peter is waiting to see you, sir,' the houseman said. 'He says you know him from "the old days," as he put it.'

'Send him in.'

I watched him shuffle along the portico surrounding the atrium toward the doorway to my office and thought: the quintessential old Jew. Yamachaed, fully bearded, dirty cloak with two missing tassels, and poorly shod. Yet, here's the man who successfully created what he calls Jesus' church in the name of his spirit and ruined my reputation forever. I never thought he was smart enough and he wasn't alone.. John and his brother must have had a hand in it. So must have Matthew. And they must have talked Paul into it. Now look at us all. How different our lives have become.

'Hello, Peter,' I said. 'You're next to the last man I ever expected to see!'

He looked up and smiled. 'Oh? And who's the last?'

'You know.'

We both smiled, knowing the answer. He entered my office and sat down in the chair opposite my desk. We talked about the old days (the pre-Jerusalem ones when we were disciples before he became an apostle) and then he told me why he came. 'Paul's in prison in Caesarea. The Sanhedrin's dominated by the ultra-orthos now and tried to kill him in Jerusalem. But the Romans arrested him when they learned he's a Roman citizen and moved him to Caesarea for his own protection. He's appealed to have his case heard in the imperial court here and now waits to hear whether they'll accept the appeal. Governor Festus wants his gratuity, of course, and you know how slow the courts here are. So that's my problem.'

'So, you've made peace with Paul.'

'We need him and his churches. He's helped our movement expand more than anyone else.'

Ti looked away. 'The dockets of all of Rome's courts are more than full. Even moving his case up won't save much time.'

'I know and I was hoping you might be able to speed things up a little. But getting him away from Judea as soon as possible is most important,' he replied.

'I think I can help on that issue. But once that's in motion he'll be under the jurisdiction of the praetorians, you understand. It ceases to be a civil matter and falls under imperial law.'

'Then you'll help?'

'Of course.'

'I'm returning to Caesarea so I'll pay Festus' gratuity.'

'You know Amos. Just draw on him for what you need.'

'Thank you, Judas,' he said but quickly looked up. 'I'm sorry. I forgot.'

'That's all right. I understand. It's sometimes difficult even for me to think of myself as Titianus.' I looked away; and then back. 'So, you're going back.'

He looked down. 'And for another reason. Hannah's very ill. She wants to die in Jerusalem.'

I nodded. Then we both were silent. 'I don't think you've spent much time there in recent years. I hear it's changed quite a bit since the Sionists have the upper hand.'

He grunted. 'We've become more like the pilgrims there when we go back. But it looks final this time. I don't know what I'll do after. . . afterward.'

Ti reached over and squeezed his forearm. 'We're old men now and our day in the sun is over. But I want you to know that I'll never forget you or Jesus. Or what you did for him.'

He looked steadily at me. 'It was John's idea, you know.'

I was startled because he caught me off guard. 'What was?'

'Creating the church to carry on Jesus' mission and brand you as his betrayer.'

I knew he was lying.

'All of the rest of us were reluctant. But the more he talked the more it made sense and you weren't around--'

It suddenly fell into place in Judas' mind: Peter had accepted the rich young man that Jesus wouldn't and renamed him Barnabas because he gave the church money and got his cousin Mary to lend the Upper Room of her house to them for their meetings!

'—but I know that Jesus would have wanted you to support what we did. Don't be miffed by us telling people you committed suicide out of guilt and remorse! After all, you're out of it now. You're Titianus, a rich Roman. No one knows you're Judas and we could never tell since we said you were dead and we need you as our devil. This suits both of our situations, doesn't it?' That's enough! Peter suddenly reminded himself. I don't want him knowing I want to use Hero as his blood tie to me. Remember everything Jesus said about money: and I can't trust Titianus' loyalty. So, he stood up to go. 'Thank you. I feel the same way about you.' He turned, took a step, and turned back and said, 'good-by old friend.'

*

'He actually told you that?'
'Yes. They're going to Caesarea where he wants to see Paul and then on to Jerusalem.'

Tay thought for a moment. 'Why don't you go with him and his wife? You'll be only a day's sail away from Antioch and you could take care of whatever business things you have to do and you could meet Corbulo--.   And why don't you take Hero? He likes Peter, and Peter and Hannah are so good with him. And you know Amos and Ruth would love to see him again. He's never been to Jerusalem and this is a perfect opportunity for him to see what it's really like in safety with those who know!'

I knew this was the real reason she wanted me to go; and it meshed with my own reasons. Great idea, I told her; but I have other concerns as well. For one thing, Amos was strongly hinting that he wanted to retire and I had no idea how difficult it would be to replace him and I didn't want it to be Marc. Well, maybe temporarily. Our business – the volume as well as the variety of goods – was expanding rapidly after our trip to India and I wanted him to watch over it with Quintus' help.

That's an excellent idea, I replied to her question. Quintus was spending more and more of his time at our warehouse office because of our expanded trade and that made me realize taking him with us made him more valuable than his accounting merely did. I had already decided to switch from his fixed salary to offering a percentage of the profits to him as an inducement to our further growth. But that meant minimizing his service as Marc's private secretary. Now, with the potential of new business with Corbulo and a potential new trip to Ctesiphon, Quintus' skills would be far more valuable in the business than as a private secretary.

'Yes,' I said to her. 'Let's hire a new a new private secretary for Marc. I'll look for someone older and familiar with business accounts. Hellas is managing well for us in India and Quintus has done well in our expanded trade here across the Great Sea.'

'What about you? Especially if you get anything from Corbulo or more from Ctesiphon?'

'Let's cross those bridges when we get there,' I replied.

We got to that bridge exactly three weeks later when Quintus burst into my office and said we must hire Albus.

I looked up at him. 'Who's Albus?'

'He's Marcus' age; comes from a good Roman and well-connected family; knows the etiquette of society; and did his military service on General Corbulo's staff.'

'But I don't need a field commander!'

'He's not. He knows the procurement procedures of the most brilliant general in the army and is well acquainted with the needs of the military.'

That's how Albus joined Hero and I, and Peter and Hannah aboard the ship bound for Caesarea three weeks later.

*

It hit me aboard ship. I've probably said this before, but I've always had the ability to stand outside myself and see myself in a particular situation. This was one of those Eureka moments as the Greeks call them.

Here I am, looking like a mature, Roman male aristocrat. The proper hair cut and dress down to my sandals and signet ring accompanied by an obviously Roman secretary. I'm sure I appear to others to be master of my destiny. So, what is he doing - I imagine people thinking - traveling with an old Jewish man and his wife with their heads covered and wearing dirty old clothes? They weren't even dressed as well as his secretary. Do you think he's a spy? I sighed: if life weren't so serious it would be a joke.

Peter filled me in on what had happened to them during the past decade after Barabbas rescued him from prison. John and James continued in Jerusalem; yes, he agreed that James was not well educated or smart and he seemed very homey in his interests; but Peter explained that John helped him in everything. Matthew had moved to Antioch where his son, Aaron, joined him and his friends in combating Samuel's attempts to separate the Jesus Jews from the traditionalists. Peter also told me about his work in Rome and Hannah told about their narrow escape from the lion when they first arrived in Puteoli. Finally, he described their grand council meeting nearly five years ago and Paul's work in proselytizing Gentiles and how this continued to cause dissension within James' Jerusalem church.

I expressed my surprise: 'even Jesus did that. Remember our northern tour?'

'Yes,' he replied. 'But it was the Sanhedrin's about-face in favor of Paul's work that made his success possible. But now their political shift threatens to undo everything.'

Then he told me about Solomon and Volumnus' efforts in Rome to encourage his own work.

Finally, he said they heard in Corinth about Thomas' death in India. I explained how much I thought Thomas had changed from when he was with us, and how I had practically begged him to come home with us months earlier; but he had refused to leave.

But the more I listened to him, the more I thought about how differently my life has departed from the disciples. They were called apostles now, he said, but when I asked him how that differed from disciple he simply said it was a step closer to acting as Jesus did. I told him I thought Jesus approved his success in founding the church. He asked me if my fortune was all that important to me and I told him no. And that was true; it never really mattered and I knew it never would. I said it was all too easy to make; it just seemed to flow in, as if angels – I didn't say Jesus because I still wanted to honor our relationship by keeping it between ourselves – directed it to me.

'And that's something I hope to pass on to Marc, Peter. That money is only part of life; it isn't life itself.'

'What do you want from life then?'

'I think my privacy. To stay out of public life, pursue my own interests and enjoy my family.'

'But where did you come from and where are you going? Remember how we used to talk about that with Jesus?'

Oh, boy! Here we are full circle, I thought. Back to fighting the same old battles.

I looked into his eyes. 'Our lives haven't changed much, have they?'

'Only outwardly,' he replied and turned to look across the sea.

That's when I saw the two of them more clearly than I ever did and suddenly realized that they have never changed; they hadn't grown or developed spiritually. They remain the immature Jesus Jews that we all were when we started, stuck at the emotional level of life and never maturing into the whole beings that Jesus talked about. It would be as if I maintained a particular view of the world. But life, all life - including its spiritual as well as physical aspects - change, and the spiritual should become more important and more profound than the physical. Or is that merely my yeshiva talking? I'm amazed that Peter doesn't seem to know that his physical world should follow from our spiritual one. Or is his stunted physical world the result of his stunted spiritual one?

I wonder what Paul will be like? I haven't seen him in seventeen or eighteen years.

*

A month later I found out.

I was sitting in the cool stillness of Governor Festus' (Porcius Festus had been Nero's replacement for Claudius' Antonius Felix in 60) office sharing a glass of wine with the governor where the only physical activity was the grappling of two minds trying to understand one another. Below, in the dirt of the courtyard were three middle aged Jews talking and gesticulating in the hot sun, one of them chained to a ring in the wall of the building I was in. Peter was taller and grayer than Paul, and John looked like an old child. I would have been with them, but I knew John and I would probably get into one of our usual arguments and saw no point in it. Moreover, I still hadn't gotten over the shock that Peter really believed he could just walk in here and interview the prisoner and didn't know a gratuity must be paid first! 'So, you've known those three for years! Well, I met a newer friend of yours two months ago.' He paused in a thought. 'Or maybe he said he was a friend of your son's.'

'Who was that, Governor?'

'A young man named Laban. From Alexandria. He had been traveling in Jerusalem and some of our other large cities and finally realized he would be better off conducting his business as a Roman citizen.'

'I hope you helped him out. He's very enterprising.'

'That's what I thought. He used your name.'

'I know him from Alexandria. We are handling a line of his textile products for Rome and its other cities.'

'I hope you didn't mind my telling him that Titianus is a trusted name in the silk trade.'

'Not at all, sir. I've found diversification very interesting.'

'Will you be going there next? To Alexandria, I mean?'

'No. To Antioch. I have some business with the Legate.'

'So, you know Quadratus?'

'I have for years. Before I went to India.'

Festus had heard about Ti's Indian connections and now learned he was a friend of administrative his superior. But he guessed that Titianus was really meeting with Corbulo - for military contracts. But why come here? And all the way from Rome? The general normally contracted locally. There must be a political angle to it. 'Laban said that Israel's become a far more dangerous place to trade. You haven't been involved here for years, have you?'

'No. I'm afraid I've been tied up with my new India venture.'

'That's by the new water route, isn't it?

Through Alexandria to the Southern Sea?'

Fishing for information. Something to use, Ti thought. 'Yes.'

The Governor got up and walked over to the sideboard. 'Another glass?'

'No, thank you. Has the King been helping you against the bandits? I'm curious because I don't remember him being here very long.' He didn't want to use words like naïve, inexperienced, enervated and incestuous.

'Not much. And banditry was far worse under my predecessor.' He looked at Ti. 'Our countryside is far more peaceable now.'

What a hypocrite and liar!, Ti thought. Angling to promote trade that's fallen off. 'I'm sure it is. But I'm going directly from here to Antioch.'

The Governor nodded. 'Well, be careful. A new group of Zealots have appeared in the cities. We call them sicarii because they murder with small curved daggers. They're not bandits like their rural counterparts, but assassins for hire. Which makes them even more dangerous.'

Ti put his empty glass on the table and stood up. 'How can anyone conduct business here?' he said in a disgusted tone.

'The increase in violence has followed the shift from peaceful politics to religious emotionalism. Fanatics. That's what they are! The Sanhedrin seem less and less able to control their own.' The Governor stood and added, 'please give my best regards to Quadratus.'

'I certainly shall, Governor, and I'll tell him what a very kind and generous host you've been.'

*

When Ti stepped out into the entry where Albus was waiting, Festus thought he recognized him and tried to remember where he had seen him. In Rome! Years ago. That's it! He was one of Corbulo's officers. So *that's* what he's up to!, he thought.

Albus tucked his shoulder bag a little closer tohim as he and Titianus rode in Ti's carriage toward Daphe after leaving his warehouse meeting with Amos. Ti was as Quintus said: business first, religion second. Or is it world first and spirit second? No matter. It's life first and everything else second.

The old Jew should retire, Albus thought. New blood will be needed if Rome's to pursue its eastward march. Corbulo's no fool; he knows he'll need the latest, most up-to-date weaponry most efficiently delivered. Titianus seems to have all the right connections but needs something to pull it all together. What could it be?

His future is Marcus. At least he knows that. And it's him; not his merely being the eldest son. Hero's a nice young man but Peter-like. I don't understand people like that: a fortune is given to him on a silver plate and he refuses it. He stopped himself from shuddering.

And I'm sure Corbulo doesn't either. It's a good thing Hero stayed in Jerusalem with Peter.

22

QUADRATUS was overjoyed with his gift: all the way from that fabled land of India. Of course, he couldn't be happier than to introduce him to Domitian Corbulo, he told him, but didn't add that Nero was intensely jealous of his famous general in the armies.

'He's a civilian who travels with his private secretary,' he told the general over dinner that evening. 'You may remember Albus. A very competent officer with you in the Germanies.'

Corbulo nodded but looked confused. 'And he's now his secretary?'

'I suspect that Nero may have put Albus up to Titianus. You know how jealous the emperor is of you.' Quadratus drummed his fingers on the table. 'Titianus may be innocent in this, but don't underestimate him. He has Parthian connections that are far more important politically than his business with them. Things are done differently there as you know, and the volume of his trade is simply too great to be purely civilian, if you know what I mean.' He nodded slightly. 'And he has trade connections through Parthia even further east. I should add that lately he's developed a trade with India following the Southern Sea. It's like a pincer movement around Judea.' Quadratus paused. 'You should also know that he's a close friend of Senator Publix whom you remember--'

'The public works contractor?'

'Yes,' Quadratus raised his eyebrows. 'You know him?'

'The biggest and most influential one in Rome,' he replied, nodding. 'Very well connected at court as well as in the Senate.' Then they suddenly looked at one another, Quadratus virtually certain and Corbulo guessing why Titianus was here.

'He could be helpful to you in many ways, general.'

Still, Corbulo was a little surprised the next morning when Quadratus introduced the tall man with streaks of red hair who said, after exchanging pleasantries, 'how can I help *you*?' The emphasis was on 'you;' Corbulo was used to 'me.'

'Do you know what the emperor sent me to do?'

'I've heard about your exploits in the Germanies, general, and neither of us got to where we are because we're fools. My friends and I help people in your positions. If we fail, it's my fault. If you fail, it's my fault. You can't lose. And I'm standing here because I'm good at what I do.' He looked directly into the shorter man's eyes and the general decided he would be useful. He also picked up on Ti's use of the plural: positions. It could mean so many things.

'Do you know Armenia?' the general asked.

'I've never been there but I've heard it's very mountainous.' He remembered the stories of Pilate's complaints about its mountain wilderness when he returned to Rome after spending years in Tyana as his penalty for his debacle in Judea.

'Why don't you come to my headquarters tomorrow morning where we'll talk in more detail.'

'It will be my pleasure, general.'

*

Corbulo had a slight physique for a military man but was balding as many commanders were. He remembered hearing Publix argue at great length in the Senate about the superiority of using specialized construction workers as auxiliaries to the army years ago.

'Keep the army as the killing machine it's trained for,' Publix told the other senators. 'Let the contractors smooth their way forward. Specialize and professionalize; plan and innovate; and stop all this amateur, jack-of-all-trades stupidity. Our imperial future lay in expansion and expansion depends on our military, and our military will flourish through specialization and innovation. We must fight to win - for territory and treasure – not for nobility. The glory days are over; the days of defense are over. Who among us opposes a strong Rome?' He remembered Publix looking around magisterially when he said that and no one raising their hand or standing up. He sat back down. An impressive performance; and, most importantly, the emperor led the clapping. The empire needed more men like him at home.

As a result – and after two years of working with Ti as his chief military supplier - Corbulo invaded Armenia, captured Artaxata, its capital, a year later and then its second greatest stronghold, Tigrancerta, the year after that. His success so astounded the imperial court that the twenty three year old emperor – who had celebrated his coming-of-age birthday two years ago by murdering his mother – was forced to publicly acknowledge his brilliance. And, as usual, he found a diversion: he was in lust – some said love - with the wife of his party-time friend, General Marcus Salvius Otho, a political-court general famous for his spindly legs and fondness for wearing dresses and other, unmentioned, effeminacies.

And in Antioch, everyone took Tigranes' arrival from Rome as the new King of Armenia, replacing Tiridates, as Nero's approval of Corbulo's command. That was our mistake: and we didn't learn the depth of Nero's jealousy of Corbulo until two years later when Lucius Caesennius Paetus was sent to 'assist' Corbulo.

News of Paetus' appointment decided me to take a course of action I had long thought about but dreaded. I went to Corbulo's headquarters after I heard the news and asked him, 'have I worked long enough with you for you to trust me more completely?'

He looked up at me and pursed his lips. 'What do you intend to do?'

'I want to get my son over here as fast as possible and take him east with me.'

Corbulo didn't say anything for a long moment. Then he said slowly, 'I'm not going to ask you what you intend to do but I don't think it would be wise of me to provide you with a military guard beyond Dura.'

'I understand. But I want to assure you that whatever I do, you will only benefit from it.' Corbolu didn't reply, so I said, 'by now, you know I do not pass on secrets or secret documents. All I ask from you are two passes to the Parthian lines.'

He nodded.

'Thank you,' I said and left.

The lumbering, overweight Paetus had proven his laziness and incapacity during the past few years as Legate of Cappadocia. But Nero, jealous of Corbulo's reputation and distracted by his new love, Poppea, as well as of everything Greek, let himself become impatient for 'results' in Armenia as he called them, and he finally accepted Paetus' repeated claims to be a better general than Corbulo. Publix' last letter through the military pouches had warned me that Corbulo's days were numbered so I knew we didn't have much time to preserve the peace so vital to our civilian trade.

That's how it was that almost a month from the day of my receiving the two passes from Corbulo, Marcus and I and ten others were heavily armed and riding as fast as we could on camels for Dura Europas where I hoped to find Parthians. Albus was left in Antioch to keep our business with Corbulo flowing.

'I'm getting too old for this,' I shouted to Marcus on our second day out.

'What?,' he replied, 'you're only fifty-three!' He smiled; as twenty-three year olds riding camels day after day do.

When we reached Dura we rested because I was tired, sore and because I recognized two of Vologases' court runners. I contacted them and sent a message saying we were coming to talk with him and requested that he ask General Monaeses to join us. I knew he wouldn't think our visit was about wanting more trade goods.

*

'I hope you understand and appreciate how Corbulo got rid of Vardanes' rebellion against you which allowed you to consolidate your position among the other noble families.'

'I do, but it cost us Armenia--'

'No, it hasn't and that's why I'm here!' I knew I was taking a chance interrupting the King but felt I must convey my sense of urgency to him. 'I couldn't write this in my message but I think it's only postponed things. That's all.' I turned to Tiridates. 'Don't worry. I think you'll be returned there as king. But I need to talk this all out to all of you,' I said, turning and nodding to General Monaeses. He nodded in return.

'Let me start with my work with Corbulo. I'm sure you all know I'm his chief supplier of military equipment; but I've gotten to know him and I'm telling you he's more than a careful and capable general. He's a reasonable man, not a military maniac. He understands the political realities beyond the battlefields. I trust his judgment and I'm here because I do. I don't have to tell you what a chance Marcus and I are taking.' I looked around at them but no one said anything.

'Now, here's what I know and think of Paetus. He's an armchair general. One of those braggerts who talks a good game but doesn't play it well. Not like Corbulo or you, General.' I nodded at Monaeses. 'He talks a fight more than doing it. The trouble is, he's convinced Nero that he's better than Corbulo and Nero's been jealous of Corbulo for a long time. So, now Paetus is going to have to prove it by marching against you.' I looked at Monaeses. 'I think he'll come next spring because -- .' And I went into his laziness. Then I described what I thought of Nero, the easily distracted, immature playboy, Hellenophile and armchair emperor. 'He has the teeth to bite everyone because he's emperor; but I don't think he'll bite Corbulo until he sees what happens with Paetus. If you defeat him,' I said to Monaeses' impassive face, 'you must do so overwhelmingly, utterly. You understand? This is a political not a military battle and they must be so shocked that Nero will be forced to look for a way out. But we don't want him to say 'oh, I was wrong about Corbulo' and just pick a replacement for Paetus. We want him to look for a quick, easy way out; and if there isn't any immediate one – which there isn't - he'll undoubtedly ask for Corbulo's opinion. That's how we'll get him to do what we want.'

'Because you have the ear of Corbulo.' Vologases said. The others looked at me so intently that I stopped and returned their looks.

'And this is your opinion?' Pacorus asked.

'Yes,' I replied. 'None of this is factual at this stage. And yes, I only think this will happen. But I've invested a lot of time, treasure and a lot of effort to come here to tell you this in person.' I paused. 'I think you all know I can't put any of this on paper.'

Then I turned to Tiridates. 'This is where you re-enter the picture. As soon as Marcus and I return, I'm going to suggest to Corbulo that he recommends accepting you as King of Armenia to Nero.'

They looked at one another, not knowing what to say so I turned to Volo and Pacorus. 'I think Nero will accept that providing he takes the credit - I mean he steal's Corbulo's suggestion for his own - for thinking up the idea that Tiri will serve as Rome's client-King over Armenia. I'll suggest that Corbulo also tell Nero that's the way policy has been and that it follows from how they've been treating the Germans, Gauls, and Britains. It's like shifting a policy that worked in the west to the east.' I turned back to Tiridates. 'That means that you'll probably have to come to Rome and accept the crown from Nero in some kind of ceremony. But don't worry. I can smooth over a lot of things about that.' I stopped for a bit. 'One last thing about all this. If everything works out this way, it will give you years of peace to build up your forces, your culture and do whatever you need to do. That's entirely your business.'

Now they looked at one another and smiled. But Pacorus asked me, 'why have you taken so much trouble to come here and tell us all this? For more trade?' Although he was the King's younger brother I understood Pacorus was trying to get a better sense of me.

'Because you've trusted me and been loyal to me,' I replied. 'And, yes, you've made me rich. But I want you to know that I am more than Tahirir's husband or Marcus' surrogate father; I am your friend and friendship means everything to me.'

They murmured and shot glances among themselves; but everyone seemed to understand the general propositions and directions that we would take, and there were minimal questions. So when we were ready to break up, Marcus left quickly to go to where I thought and I said, 'General, I'd like to speak to Marcus' uncles in private for a minute.'

After he left the room, I said them, 'I want you all to know I have no ambition to be king. King of anything. And I want you all to know that I've been training Marcus to think the same way, to stay away from public life and pursue a private one.' I looked at Volo. 'I'm sorry about what happened with Vardanes but you know we had nothing to do with that and were in India at the time.' Then I faced Pacorus, and Tiri and said, 'if anything should happen to Volo, God forbid, I want you to know that it's none of our business who succeeds him.' I turned back to Volo. 'I'm sorry to talk this way as if you're dead, but I want this understood perfectly among us. You have nothing to fear or worry about from us.'

Volo looked me in the eyes. 'And our sister? You know she's been corresponding with us.'

'Have you read her letters?' Pacorus quickly asked before I could answer.

'I never have and never will. I think of them as her private correspondence with her family. I ask only that you continue to allow our eastern goods to come through Mal.' I started to stand but thought of something else. 'I forgot to say one other thing. You see how Marcus is. This may be difficult for you to understand but I'm very proud of him and think you should be too. He's become very Roman, even more than I, and he understands their commercial culture better than I do. He's a true citizen of their world with all its freedoms. Feel free to talk with him without my being present.'

I'm not easily surprised but Vologases did by replying, 'we were all married when we were his age.'

'That's next, isn't it?' I replied.

'We know a few princesses.'

I looked directly at Volo and said. 'Tahirir has one in mind. In Rome. A commercial princess.'

'Her father must be greater than you, then.'

'That, gentlemen, is, as the Romans say, something you can bank on.'

They smiled their understanding.

*

Two years later, Tiridates' was crowned as Rome's new client-King of Armenia. Corbulo even sent Nero a congratulatory note on his brilliant solution for peace. Four months after that, when Marcus, I and Albus had returned to the routine of Rome, we received even more pleasant news. Marcus raced home from the warehouse offices one morning with Amos' letter about the autumn shipment that had just arrived in Antioch.

'Ti! Ti!' he shouted, 'Amos reports the autumn's silk shipment is nearly double what it had been!'

Tay rose from her chair and smiled. 'See,' she said, 'I told you you're not so old.'

23

BUT that's not how Marcus remembered the trip. What he remembered was how different, foreign, exotic and strange 'going home' had been; how different Ctesiphon was from the 'home' of his memory and from Rome. At first, he thought it was because he was older and now had Antioch and Rome and Alexandria and India to compare Ctesiphon to. The sights and smells, the clanging of armor - all those dim memories had scarcely changed. But most of the faces were different; and he surprised himself by realizing the depth of his feeling: he had changed and he now knew he could never go back, could never live there again – and, surprisingly, didn't want to.

He remembered the exact beginning of that change when he went on his favorite walk and met Vologases sitting in a glade beside a brook with his guards scattered under the trees. Later, he wondered how 'accidental' it was.

'It's good to see you again, Vardanes.' Marcus hadn't heard himself called that since he was a child. 'You've grown into a fine young man. I'm sure my sister is very proud of you.'

'Thank you.' He smiled and sat down next to him, recalling how he always felt at ease with uncle Volo. 'She tells me that frequently.'

'And Judas. He must think so too.'

'Yes. He's letting me take over more and more.'

'And Amos? What does he do?'

'He manages the Antioch warehouse and reports to us in Rome. But he's going to retire soon.'

'Splendid! We couldn't be more pleased and happy for you. We hoped this would happen. Are you pleased?'

Marcus thought his use of 'we' strange. Roman's didn't use that expression. 'Yes. There's always something to do, and new ways to improve yourself, to make life better. And there's so much to learn.'

'And your brother? Judas' other son?'

'He's very different from us. He's like Azasus.'

'Azasus?' Volo asked, looking surprised. 'Our scholar?'

'Yes. He reads and thinks all the time.' He smiled. 'He finds life in scrolls more interesting than what goes on outside them.'

'He wants to be a scholar?'

'More a priest, I think. He's interested mainly in religion.'

'Which god? There are so many in Rome I can't keep track of them all!'

'I can't either and it doesn't matter. But no, to answer your question. He's interested in the god of the Jews. The one Ti left behind.'

Vologases' eyes and brow narrowed. 'And what does Judas think of that?'

'He doesn't oppose it. I heard him tell mother one time that if he did, it would drive Hero to want it all the more. So he leaves him alone. I think he hopes he'll outgrow it.'

'Hero has no interest in your business?'

'No. Ti tries to get him interested but it only lasts an hour or so.' Marcus paused. 'The strange thing is that he's better at numbers than I am.'

'Well, listen to Judas about business. He has a gift from some god for it. And listen to me. Being good at numbers doesn't guarantee success at business. Our best fighters lose battles. You met General Monaeses. He knows winning a war sometimes doesn't depend on winning a battle. There's a lot more involved. He has a military gift just as Judas has a business one.'

Marcus laughed, remembering the sight of Ti bouncing on his camel and walking around rubbing his behind afterward. He told his uncle that story and he laughed too.

'And they haven't wanted to have more children?'

'Not because they don't try! I think the gods have said no.' Vologases raised his eyebrows so Marcus explained, 'I hear them try.' They both laughed.

*

But Marcus was surprised at his feelings throughout his visit. He liked Parthians and wanted to like Parthian society, to match his memory with reality, but he felt estranged - not alienated exactly – and didn't know why. Here I am, he told himself, related by blood to some of these people, but they still live in the old fashioned ways I did when I was a boy. Romans were coarse and brutal, but in mannered ways; these people are coarse and brutal in unmannered ones; yet they seem friendlier. People here deal with you personally, directly and simply, even matter-of-factly. Would they do the same for strangers? Would this be the case if they hadn't known I was Vardanes? Is this the case because the people live here much more physically than in Rome where personal ties are so tenuous?

Why does it seem so much more personal here? He spent a lot of time trying to understand why before it came to him: their life was not as abstract as it was in Rome and did not depend on money as much as Roman life did. Here, blood prevailed over money which made it seem so much more primitive. People's allegiances were tactile; those chain-mailed cataphracts who annihilated Roman armies did so because they were personally obligated to their commanders to kill you; they weren't paid. They feared for their lives as much at home as they did on the battlefield; perhaps even more.

The more he thought about living a life of personal obligations, of living according to trust and loyalty and friendship, the more he thought he understood Ti and Rome a little better. Ti rejected all this; he felt more comfortable in the more abstract Rome we live in.

And I do too! But I'm closer to it than he is because I've been raised in it earlier than he was.

Then he remembered how he felt in India. Everything was completely different there and he didn't feel related to anything.

His instincts didn't work in India as well as they did in Rome; now, what he thought was familiar here and relied on didn't work here. He would have to learn life all over again to live here. But why bother? I prefer living in Rome; so, why apologize for it?

How did Ti ever do it? Or is there more to Ti than . . . Ti?

*

'Now I know I'm old after seeing Mal after so many years,' Marcus remembered Ti saying to him later that evening while they walked together along the river. 'It's clear his son will take over soon.'

'He didn't look in good health.'

'I know. But he didn't complain about it.'

'I don't remember her.'

'Who? His wife? They didn't marry until a month or two after we left. Mal told us at the time that Zelia didn't want anything to detract from Tay's wedding. And she looks like she takes care of everyone.'

'She works in the business as well, I noticed.'

'That's a good thing for little Mal. He learns from her.'

'Did you ever want Tay to work in the business?' From Ti's hesitancy, he thought he touched on a sore point.

'I never did,' he finally answered. 'It doesn't occur to you until you're older that you carry a lot of baggage from your youth with you as you get older. You've touched on one of mine.'

'But how did she become so business-like? She wasn't that way here when I was a boy.'

Ti laughed. 'You could say she's more adaptable than I am. When we were India, she started learning about it. You know how pervasive it is in Rome. You practically breathe it.'

'From Publix! She learned it from him!'

'Yes. This may sound strange to you but Tay and I are a lot alike. Oh, we have different interests and personal values, of course, but we share an attitude and have a common purpose. I encourage you to look for that in a wife because you talk more than you. . . .'

'And your first wife didn't have any--.' I deliberately interrupted him but stopped when I realized this was probably too personal.

'Gentiles think Jews are all the same, but they're not. I grew up as an Idumean. In Jewish tradition, we were the Edomites, the descendents of Esau, Jacob's brother, and were supposed to hate those Jerusalem Sionists But many of us were originally Arabs. At least my family lived that way. 'Tent-dwellers;' 'towel-heads;' they called us. What's strange is how that background has played into my pulling away from my Jewish heritage. I never realized how much I wanted to replace it with Rome's at the time; to literally have as little to do with Judea as possible.

'So that's why you never insisted on my circumcision. You were ambivalent about me being Jewish.'

Judas picked up a small stone and tried skimming it across the river. Unsuccessfully. Then he turned to Marcus. 'All my life I've usually taken the flight instead of fight path when confronted by major decisions that I couldn't ignore. It's been easier and I've felt more comfortable doing it. At the time, I told myself that I wanted you to make that decision because it's irreversible and marks you as a Jew forever. I didn't feel that was my decision.' He kicked a small pebble. 'And now it's become one of those things from our past that crops up again and again in our lives.' He hesitated. 'Those Jerusalem Jews conquered my grandfather's generation, you see, and forcibly circumcised all the males. I think I always hated them for that, and didn't want to be like them.'

'But you had Hero circumcised.'

'That was a completely different situation. It was done a week after his birth to a Jewish mother.' He looked at the path they were walking on. Jewish family's follow the mother's family line you see. Not like the Parthian and Roman male lines. But I'm not making an excuse. I simply didn't know any different then. Can you see that I was different with you because I was different?'

'Yes,' Marcus replied and they walked on in silence for a moment. 'So, we can't change our identities as easily as our appearances. Is that why Hero's going in the direction that he is? He doesn't seem to be interested in what we do.'

'In part. But he's also had different experiences. Amos and Ruth are very traditional Jews who practically raised him for the first few years after his birth. But I think it was our move to Rome that really shocked him. I don't mean the physical changes as much as the immorality of it's everyday life. Did he ever talk to you about it?'

'Not in any deep way. Only about its degeneracy which I never understood as much as I do now. I think he had some bad experiences that turned him against living there.' He paused. 'Do you think he'll like living in Jerusalem better? I've never been there.'

'I can tell you that it's a small town of small minds that bicker constantly. You're not missing anything. You'd even be better off in Antioch and that's not saying much after you've been to Rome.'

'But you haven't answered my question.'

'I don't like Jerusalem and wouldn't wish it on anyone.' Ti stopped and plucked a handful of grass and let the blades slip through his fingers. 'And yes, I worry about him.'

'But you trust Peter and Hannah. That they'll take care of him, I mean.'

'Yes. I think Peter has his best interest at heart. I've known him for nearly thirty five years and I've always liked him.'

'That took a lot of nerve, to create Jesus' church the way he did.'

'I agree.' He paused and looked at Marcus. 'I don't know or pretend to understand what happened in Jerusalem that summer and don't want to. I accept what they did and don't have any problem with what they've said about me. It was Jesus that I made my pact with.' Ti walked on. 'But don't misunderstand me. Life is complicated and I want you to know that I think Peter's a good man. And being good is frequently worth more than being smart.'

'But why isn't he very smart if he started the church?'

'I didn't mean it in the sense of creating the church but in its worldly sense. His church has experienced many problems.' Ti stopped walking and put his hand on Marcus' arm. 'I want to tell you something. Peter may not be wise in the ways of the world but men like him are completely trustworthy and worth your last denarii. Never completely judge things - and people, in this case - by the world's standards.' Ti walked on.

'You mean he's a holy man?'

Ti didn't say anything until a few steps later: 'I gave up trying to figure out who was holy years ago. It's much easier to simply identify the good from the bad guys by their behavior.'

'You've compromised then.'

Ti looked at him. 'I ask myself here I am a Jew in Roman clothing in Parthia. Am I confused or are you?'

Marcus didn't reply and they walked the rest of the way home in silence; but he decided Ti's description of himself wasn't the whole truth; his waffling was for show. But why did he prefer to show instead of tell?

*

'So, what do you think about girls?' Marcus smiled at the memory of Ti asking him over a glass of wine their last night in Ctesiphon before leaving for Dura in the morning. 'I don't mean the prostitutes. There's more than enough of them around.'

'You mean am I getting ready to be married?'

'I mean having children. A family. That's why men marry. Otherwise, why bother? Have you thought seriously about any of this?'

'No, I admit. There's been so much to learn and do!' He hesitated. 'But I'm really glad you didn't send me to Athens to study. I now see how artificial it all is.'

'Marriage, wife, children, and social position aren't theoretical.'

'It seems like you and mom were made for each other. How did you do it?'

Ti thought for a moment. 'You raise an extremely important point. It's very complicated, but I want to explain it to you. Our story, at least.'

Marcus stood up and poured a little more wine in Ti's glass. He didn't pour more for himself.

'My first wife had a similar Jewish background that I had. We shared many assumptions about life and behavior. I was just poorer, that's all. But Tay and I come from very different backgrounds. I was still poorer but our identities were very different when we first met so we relied on one another's reasonableness and goodwill because we had faith in each other and wanted our marriage to work. We had purpose beyond mutual attractions. Don't ever be fooled by our coming together, separating, going our own ways, and coming together again. I would say we've grown closer together as a result of that and talking about our experiencing our lives together as one.' He looked into Marcus' eyes. 'You probably don't think so, but we talk more than have sex.

'So, how does that work, being apart from one another?'

'Perhaps I shouldn't have used the word separately because we've never been separate after marrying. Apart yes, but we've never been separate as I had been from my first wife even though we remained married. Do you follow?'

'Yes. So, it was Tay who came up with the 'return rooms' idea.'

'Precisely, and that's a perfect example of her reasonableness and goodwill in keeping our marriage alive. That was completely her idea and you know me, I'll support any idea that works.'

Ti seemed to drift into another thought so Marc, asked, 'did you--.'

'You never want to confuse sex and marriage,' Ti interrupted. 'Tay told me one time that marriage is a license to have as much sex as you want, but I want to tell you that I think sex is also an expression of a good marriage. Going to a prostitute for sex is pure selfishness. There's nothing greater there than sexual release. Satisfaction is another issue. No larger meaning to it. That's why you prostitute yourself as well.'

'But it's private.'

'Yes. And that's why marriage is public. Because marriage is social and that's what I'm trying to tell you. It tells the world that the woman you marry is part of you and establishes the legitimacy of children. In your case, I not only married your mother in both Ctsiphon and again in Antioch, but I also took out your Roman citizenship in my name so there's no doubt about who you, Tay and Hero are. It also tells the world that I'm not ashamed of you. But that wasn't the reason I did it.'

'And when I stamp a document with my smaller signet--.'

'That's exactly right. It tells whoever sees it that you're my son and will inherit everything that's mine.' He stopped and looked down. 'But I didn't mean to get off on this. I want you to know something else.' He paused. 'It's been a great disappointment to us - and to Tay especially - that we haven't had any children of our own. Don't ever say anything to her about this, but she feels this . . .this disappointment more keenly than I do because women give birth to our futures and she feels she's failed. But I tell her that's not how I think of it.'

'That she's failed to give you your shared future, you mean. But dad, she's only what – forty? There's still time yet.'

Ti thought about his reply. 'The thing you never want to forget about us - I mean about all people - is the mystery of conception. Think about your mother and me: each of us had a child by another spouse; there's no reason to think she couldn't or shouldn't have a child by me. But she hasn't.' He sipped his wine. 'I've often wondered why the source of my business ideas and success can't help me give her what both of us want.'

'You mean your Jewish God. But there's still time!'

'And so we live in hope and faith! But we're entering the danger zone - for her, I mean – in a few years.'

Marc looked at his father. 'You're laying a lot on me, you know.'

Ti laughed and sat back. 'I only want you to start thinking about it. You're only twenty-three. Think about the kind of marriage you want to have and who you think would be a good partner.' He smiled.

'You mean I have to think about that now?'

'Your uncles offered princesses.'

'I'd prefer Roman.'

Well, at least we got this far, Ti thought. 'Do you have any one in mind?'

'I like talking with Valeria.'

'You like talking with Valeria,' Ti thought to better understand it..

But Marcus heard him because Ti thought out loud and he smiled broadly. He must be in a state of shock to do that, Marcus thought.

That's aiming pretty high and she's not the prettiest, Ti thought with his mouth closed this time. 'You mean Senator Publix' daughter?' Marcus nodded, not understanding how his father could not know who she is. 'Well, we have plenty of time to think on it. We have to get home first.'

'And be richer.'

*

But so much for wishes. We didn't return directly to Rome; we spent a month in Antioch where Ti met with Corbulo several times and I with Amos about our business expectations. And then, as we were finally preparing for our trip to Rome, an invitation came to dine with Matthew and Aaron. Matthew invited me but made it clear he wanted to talk with Judas. I knew I would have to go though I didn't want to.

'I hope this won't be too disagreeable,' I said as we rode in the litter from Daphne to Matt's home over his synagogue in the city.

'Nowhere near as taxing as that trip,' Ti laughed and looked at me. He knew I didn't understand like this side of his relationships. 'I don't know if I can do that again. You might be on your own from here on.'

Actually, the news turned out to be much more important than the food eaten or the camaraderie between Ti and the others that I expected. It turned out that James, Jesus' brother and head of the church in Jerusalem had been murdered. Annas, grandson of the bad old Annas, the instigator of killing Jesus, and temporary High Priest, had managed to pin a stoning offense on James. So, Jude, his younger brother, now assumed the headship of the church and continued the bloodline.

'But what about John?' Judas asked.

'He's already moved to Ephesus. To pick up the pieces that Paul left,' Matthew replied. 'But that includes all the churches in the province so he'll have a lot of work to do.' He looked down at his folded hands. 'I can only think it was God's will that John moved there before James' stoning; and if it is, then it's one more sign that he wants us to evangelize the Gentiles.' He looked into Titianus' eyes. 'Our movement is falling to pieces. Do you have any ideas?'

No one said anything. Then Aaron mentioned that Hannah died, leaving Peter, and Hero to decide what to do. Mark had returned to Alexandria and Peter was under pressure from the Sanhedrin to return to Rome. Sol and Vol wanted him there to combat Paul who's case everyone thought would be decided shortly. But Hero didn't want to go with Peter. But Mark supported Peter, saying that Peter's work in Rome was more important and unfinished. But others in the church who didn't feel confident about Jude felt that Peter should remain in Jerusalem. He was the rock. All this was boring until they mentioned the latest news: Hero would like to join Matthew and Aaron here in Antioch if Peter goes to Rome.

I could tell Ti didn't know what to say because he diverted the conversation to the future direction of the church. Should Jerusalem remain its center or should it move to Antioch with Matthew? Matthew thought it should follow Peter, even move to Rome with him because Jesus clearly identified his church with him. 'The worst thing I can imagine is for Peter wanting to stay in Jerusalem.' Matthew said, and looked at Judas. 'Neither of us have been there in years,' he said to Judas, 'but the stories are that it's become very dangerous for us to live there. And the truth is that I think that's really behind the Sanhedrin's supporting Peter's move to Rome: they want to make their problem with him there disappear.'

The conversation went on like this and I felt almost bored to death so I asked Matthew how his work in Antioch was going.

'I know I shouldn't think much less say this but it's been flourishing since Samuel's assassination. His son isn't as committed to separating the Christians from the Jews as he was. But more importantly, Joshua simply isn't as clever as his father was. I don't think we much to worry about with him.'

I never heard about this! Assassination? Joshua?

But then Judas suggested that Jude might like to move the headquarters of the church to Antioch where he could perhaps use the services of Matthew and Aaron, and their rebuff shocked me.

'Oh, we could never do that!' Matthew said huffily. 'Jerusalem was where we began--' and he stopped, suddenly realizing that Judas was part of the end of Jesus but not of their new beginning.

I didn't understand why he stopped so I asked, 'what do you mean "where we began?"'

'Never mind that,' Judas interrupted curtly. 'I understand and you don't have to say it.'

An awkward silence followed and I didn't say anything.

But Matthew finally did: 'I think Peter should return to Rome. John should do all right in Ephesus because he knows their culture better than Peter and we' – he nodded to Aaron – 'have enough to do here. But I want you to know that if Hero really does insist on joining us here then he'll be welcome.'

Judas nodded. 'That's agreeable with me. You know you can count on my support through him.' He hesitated. 'From what you say, it would seem you've given up on Jerusalem.'

That fit with what I thought but I didn't really know about, so I still didn't understand the bigger picture.

Five days later, when we were finishing our packing, Ti received a short note from Hero:

> I heard from Aaron that you and Marc are returning to Rome. Please don't leave before I talk with you. I want to go with you. I'm leaving for Antioch immediately.
>
> Your loving son in Jesus,
> Hero

After he read it, Ti didn't say anything but handed the little scroll to me. Reading it made me feel more perplexed than ever and I lapsed back into thinking I don't want to know about this.

*

Later, when we were at sea on our way to Rome I asked Hero why his note had such urgency about it. This is how he described it.

'When I reached home they told me you were at the warehouse office with Amos and father was in the garden. When I saw him, I told him what John told me about him.'

'"Goddamn that Judas!" John had said.'

'"Who's Judas?" I asked.'

'John stared at me for the longest time and then said,, "you don't know? He's your father!"'

'So?' I said to Hero. 'What's so important about that?'

Hero looked at me as if I deserved death. 'For someone who's so smart you can be the dumbest person on earth at times!' he replied and took three steps backward, away from the rail. Then he took those same three steps forward. 'Don't you know that Judas told the Sanhedrin where Jesus and his disciples were hiding in the Gethsemane.'

I looked at him and said, 'but so what?'

'They hate him! They've built their entire following around what they call Judas' treachery.'

I must be dumb because I still didn't get the significance of this. It was all in the past anyway. History. Nothing that concerns us.

'Don't you see? They say shame drove him to change his name to Titianus and his identity from a Jew and Jesus follower to a Roman pagan scum! And he's never denied it!'

I could see how upset he was but didn't know what to say to comfort him.

He continued to stare at me with big bulging eyes. 'But why didn't he tell us, Marc? Does Tay know?'

'Why do you care about this so much? It isn't part of our life now!' I said.

'But it is to me! Don't you see, Jesus is the Son of God! And Judas helped kill him!'

My father turned God over to his murderers? I think I understood Hero for the first time; and decided I should talk with Ti; not Hero. He was too upset; and emotional people don't reason very well. I was more distant from his involvement and I didn't have to understand all the theology behind it. 'I'll speak with him,' I said. 'Why don't you stay here. Better yet, go over and sit on the deck against the hatch cover. Ti's on the upper deck with the captain and I'll come back and tell you what he said.' He nodded and I watched him lurch over and sit down. Then I went in search of Ti.

I found him on the upper deck looking at the islands off Asia's coast and told him about my conversation with Hero. 'Look,' I said, 'I'm trying to understand this so I can help him. He's very upset. Why didn't you tell us what you did when you were Judas?'

He looked at me. 'Because it was my old life,' he replied. 'I had walked away from it long before I came into your lives. I stopped being a Jew. I mean a practicing one. My God, Marc, you've seen me pay obeisance to Rome's gods a hundred times!'

'But were you the bad Jew, the betrayer of the Christ, that Hero says John and the others say you are?

'It didn't happen like that. We agreed that I would help him go through with it because he feared his weak human nature would betray him.'

'It? You mean his death? Hero asked, 'John warned me you would try to make Jesus wanting to commit suicide!'

'They're just stories. The truth is it wasn't suicide. We planned it that way but they double-crossed us. They took him into custody and then turned him over to the Romans because--'

'Then why did you run away?'

'We all did! Matthew, John, Peter, James--'

'But they returned! They spoke with him! I mean the resurrected Jesus! And received the spirit! Hero said you weren't even there!'

'I wasn't. But you don't understand. *They* said he appeared to them; *he* didn't appear to me! And creating Jesus' church after his death was Peter and John and Matthias ' idea! No, I wasn't part of it and never wanted to be! But I was part of what Jesus had planned and they weren't! They knew nothing about it! And I think were jealous when they heard about it. They were very competitive about who was the greatest of his disciples and I was never part of that!' He looked off again. 'You see, he wanted to sacrifice himself for all our people but was afraid he couldn't go through with it. So he asked me to help him! Out of my friendship and love for him. We expected to negotiate with the High Priest and his minions and Jesus just asked me to help keep his courage up! John doesn't know what he's talking about!' He jutted his chin out, the way he did when he had resolved something. 'I think they were all miffed about that. And my special relationship with Jesus.' He looked intently at Hero. 'John never forgave me for Jesus loving me more than him.'

'But I'm talking about betrayal, dad. First, you betrayed your friend and now us by not telling us about it! Don't you understand? We want nothing from you! Just honesty and integrity!'

A movement – someone approaching us from behind us – caught our attention. It was Hero who apparently followed me.

'No,' he said, 'I won't apprentice under Peter or Amos! I'm going to return to work with Matthew and Aaron. At least, they know who they are and are honest about it!' Then he turned and walked away.

24

HERO returned home with us after we arrived at Ostia, but said he still intended to return to Antioch and that it would be best if he explained his intentions to Tay and Val. He agreed, however, not to tell them why he was doing this; only that he wanted to help Matthew. Two weeks after arriving, he left and we couldn't persuade him otherwise.

That was in the early spring of 63 and the boy emperor was now his own man: proven by divorcing his first wife, then arranging to have her poisoned as well as that of his former tutor, Afranius Burr, general of the Praetorian Guard, and now made no secret about lusting (he called it 'being in love') after another man's wife. Now, I felt old: Nero would be twenty five this year; two years younger than I was.

But that's not what made Ti more aware of his own mortality and feel old at sixty two. My impression was that he was concerned with putting his house in order. How else was I to interpret his single-minded fixation on my sex life.

'I'm happy you haven't confused sex with marriage.'

It struck me like one of Jupiter's bolts: completely out of the blue. We were working in our warehouse office over the shops in the Emporium, discussing whether we should expand our trade in the wines from Massilia vertically by starting our own vineyards when all of sudden Ti comes out with this! Do all men who age become preoccupied with sex? I put my stylus down and looked across the room at Ti, wondering whether he would start frothing at the mouth.

'I understand it started with Champi but I'm also happy that you understand there can be consequences. What really pleases me is that you'll honor your obligations whatever they may be.' Ti thought: I better nail this home here. 'Tay and I have tried - often and intensely, I should add - to give you a blood brother or sister or several. But it's never happened, as you know.' God determined this, he thought and breathed deeply. 'But I want you to know that I've always gone to your mother for sex. No other woman.'

'Didn't we discuss this years ago?' I replied. I really didn't want to know the details about my parent's sex life?

'Yes. But it's becoming more important now.'

'Why?'

'Because you'll soon be twenty four. You know enough about the business to manage it. And you know who to ask for help when you don't. The next stage you should think about is how to expand –and I mean diversify - the business.'

Marcus smiled. 'And what does this have to do with sex and marriage?'

'I shocked you because I think it's time for you to think there's more to life than business--'

Marcus smiled. "I can think of lots of other things.'

'Ahhh, but are you keeping them in balance? That's what life is about: balancing its different aspects. And that same wise man told me that everything has its season. There's a time for duty, for enjoyment, for diversion, play, fun; and for family. You don't want to wind up like Thomas, do you?' He saw Marcus furrow his brow. 'You're wondering where this is leading?'

'Yes.'

'Family. It's getting time for you to have one. I married Tay when I was forty and I married Miriam when I was thirty four.' He looked down, as if having second thoughts. 'Frankly, I waited too long to marry Miriam and then I realized I shouldn't have.'

'Why did you?'

'Because I wasn't ready to marry until then. But you are now. Your situation is completely different from what mine was. I couldn't afford to support a wife and family until I was older but you can now.' He walked back to his desk and sat down. 'I knew then that love can't survive in a vacuum because it's a relationship. I should say relationships. Plural. It's much easier for a wife, family, and children to survive if the husband provides worldly support. I didn't have that until was ten years older than you are now! But what was true for me doesn't have to be true for you!'

'The first time I saw you, I was eight.'

Ti sighed. 'What I'm trying to tell you, Marc, is that you have your worldly support now. If you want to think of this as a race with me that you want to win, do so. I'm only saying that it's time you look at your life more as a whole--'

'Marriage.'

'Not just marriage! Think family! Marriage is only the first step. And it's both easy and difficult. You're young, rich, smart, and capable. But no, we're not an old, aristocratic family; we're nouveaus as the Gauls say. But thank Jesus money gives you choice in Rome! Money is the new aristocracy which makes you freer to marry who you want to than in every other place in the world that I know about.'

'I never thought about it this way.'

'No reason for you to until now. Look, all I'm saying is that the most important thing is for you to know what you want so you can marry someone who'll be compatible with you and can help you. You don't have to marry rich or old and titled or even educated. Those are the world's externals and can frequently change. Your starting point should be with you. That's what you should think about.'

'Yes. I think I understand.' Marcus thought for a minute. 'Mother gave you different things than Miriam did, and when you were ready for them.'

'That's right. I'm trying to save you making my mistake.' He hesitated. 'No, that's not quite right. I'm trying to save you from having my experience because you don't have to repeat it and smart people learn from life as well as from scrolls.'

'And you learned from mother?'

'Of course. Sure, she brought money and connections into our marriage. But what's made it a good one is that we share a basic outlook on life. We're not identical as you know. But we match one another – our personalities, I mean. And what I'm trying to tell you is that your uncles - live and dead - and your grandfather knew this about your mother and me. They knew what I wanted but more importantly was capable of.' He saw the question on Marcus' face. 'Yes, they knew me better then than your mother did. Even better than I did then. You could say they made our marriage possible and I'll be grateful to them for the rest of my life. You should be too; but that's your business. All I want you to know is that my relationship with your mother is priceless so to speak.' He put his stylus down while I stood up and went to look out over the river.

'But even that's not the important thing. It's the attitude we share about ourselves and our relationship to each other. We're more than a couple; we're a family; you and Hero are part of it. That's what's most important. Don't base marriage on what's external or only on sexual attraction. Base it on your internal, personal relationship, allow for it to grow by adding to it and you'll always stay in love.'

Marcus turned and realized he had his mouth open. He had never heard Ti speak so passionately or personally. So he closed his mouth and, not knowing what to say, said, 'so, you were lucky with my mother.'

Ti looked at him for a long moment. 'It's easy to think it's the things and people in this life that help or direct or influence us. But the older I get the more I think it was Jesus who directs my life.'

*

Tay thought something was bothering Ti since his return and it wasn't his success or increased wealth and she wanted to know not for herself but for their relationship and decided confrontation was the best way. So when he was seated in one of the chairs in their return room, she stood in front of him and asked, 'what's bothering you? You've been edgy and preoccupied since returning and I know it's not because of business. So what is it?'

'Marcus told me he likes Valeria. Says he feels comfortable with her.'

She smiled. A big one. 'My gods, you should be delighted!' When Ti didn't reply, her smile faded and she asked, 'what's the matter with you?' When he still didn't reply she turned, walked over to the chair in front of her dressing table, sat down, picked up her comb and said, over her shoulder, 'she's a smart, loving girl and they've known one another for years.' She looked back at him and said, 'and she likes and understands business. So, snap out of it.'

'But she's Publix' daughter,' he finally said. 'It doesn't get much higher in Roman society and this is about something far larger than being neighbors or having money. He's old aristocracy and at its very center. Nero's a nouveau in contrast.'

'But we've been friends for years!' She turned to her burnished Corinth bronze mirror and said in a far-off voice that he knew, 'this is far deeper than friendship, Ti.' Then she shook herself and stood up. 'I need to think about it for awhile.' And as she walked to the door she turned and said, 'don't say anything to anybody about this and don't encourage him. I have some things to do downstairs but I forgot about them after you said this.' Then she went downstairs.

And left him baffled by her response. He thought she would have been pleased. At least, more than he was. It seemed such a natural thing to him. He remembered living in tents and moving around as a boy. One day, a new boy showed up one day asking to see his sister and his father saying to his mother, 'it's all right. They'll only be here for a few months.' So sis went to stay in the boy's tent and in the morning the tent was gone. He never saw her again.

*

Ti didn't understand something else but had long feared to question it: something about Peter bothered him. He had known him for nearly thirty five years now but he couldn't understand how or why he hadn't changed. He seems stuck, Ti thought. Why? If he was so committed to Jesus and the Jews and Jerusalem – and so committed that he founded his church there - why would he now suddenly want to spend the rest of his life in Rome? That was so – well, Judas-like. So why does he want to do this?

More importantly, why does it bother me? Peter always gave me the impression that he understood me. But do I understand him? Even a little? Why am I not more tolerant of him? Surely, he understands I didn't attend Hannah's funeral because I didn't want to embarrass him or his Jerusalem friends? I even understood their need to create Jesus' church thirty some years ago by denigrating me! But how can Peter be happy about not changing over all this time? Isn't it natural for ideas to change as their circumstances do? And another thing: why doesn't he understand how important social appearance is? I have my reasons for choosing to act as Titianus instead of Judas and that's my business. After all, my behavior demonstrate faith in what I'm doing as much as it does what they do; but why don't they see that it's behavior *in this world* that we're talking about and it doesn't matter whether it's religious or business behavior. Surely, what Peter and the others did in creating their church proves my point!

Or am I confused? Just look at my sons: Marcus my worldly side, Hero my spiritual one. Peter confined his trust in the next generation to its spiritual side and sacrificed his son and daughter to the world in the process. He lived what Jesus preached, but how could he sanction the blood principal of accepting James and Jude as successive heads of his church just because they were Jesus' brothers? He seems like Abraham, willing to sacrifice his son for God, but Jesus never had to do that. So, who are you Peter? You're a bundle of contradictions: Jew and Jesus follower? Or a Christian, a Jesus separationist?

What added to his confusion about Peter was Peter's willingness to abandon Jerusalem for working with Sol and Vol in Rome. They had tried to break away from domination by Jerusalem's Sanhedrin in 44 when Peter first fled to Rome and Samuel started calling the Jesus Jews 'Christians.' Why didn't Peter object to those separatists? He must condone it! Even when emperor Claudius banished Jews from Rome to end the riots between the Jesus Jews and synagogue traditionalists and Sol and Vol aligned Rome's seven synagogues into a consortium to support Rome's empire under the banner of 'Jews for Rome,' Peter didn't object to it. He must have a larger and longer game he's playing than merely using Jesus to point the Jewish way to the Gentiles. What could it be? Ti shook his head, not wanting to admit the thought that was forming in his mind; it seemed such a contradiction but it mixed religion and politics. He stood up and rubbed the back of his neck. Poor Peter! And now they've cajoled Peter into preaching harmony among the rifts caused by the vigorous preaching of Paul. Calling Paul a rabble-rouser, a trouble-maker who went too far too in appealing to the Gentile, claiming it would strip Jesus of his Judaism. What have you gotten yourself into? Do you even know?

I'm glad Hero went back to Matthew. He's the real rock.

*

'So, what did you think of Servilia, Marcus? She certainly seemed interested in you! And she was the prettiest girl there!'

He couldn't help but smile. 'Stop trying to marry me off, mother! You make her seem like a carcass for sale at the meat market!'

'I'm trying to focus your sexual energy so I can become a grandmama, darling.'

He looked at her and sipped his wine. 'You always get right to the point, don't you? Yes, she's pretty and from a well-to-do family. Butdoesn't have a brain in her head and I'd be bored after a week of sex with her.'

She looked at her son, then at Ti and then thought: my blood. Smart as a whip. 'I'm glad you know the secret of sex: it's just a physical act and it can be boring. Especially when that's all there is between a couple --"

'And too frequent.'

Tay smiled. That's Ti talking. 'You've just made a valuable observation whether you know it or not.'

'What's that?'

'Sex without love can become boring. With love and purpose it never is.'

God!, Marcus thought, sex lessons from your mother during dinner! If people only knew what our family life is really like!

'The trick is to marry someone beyond sex.' she continued.

'Now you have my interest. What do you mean?'

'I mean you should relate to your wife through things you have in common beyond sex. You won't be spending more than a fraction of your time together making love.'

'You're sounding like dad,' Marcus said while thinking about all the times Ti was absent from Tay.

'Of course. What did you think? That only sex defines marriage?' She put her glass down and looked intently at him. 'I mean really married. Personally, not socially.' Ti cleared his throat. She looked at him; then back to Marcus. 'Do you remember when you returned from India?'

'Yes.'

'What's the first thing Ti and I did?'

'You took him with you up to your rooms and probably had sex until you couldn't anymore.'

'And then - only then - did I tell him about things that had happened here while you were gone. Because I knew he couldn't concentrate on the social things until after we finished what was important between us.' She looked at him. 'Do you understand the priorities? Personal first then business because we had just had the reverse.'

Marcus nodded. 'Everyone sees that you like one another -' he said it as if it was the most natural thing in the world to say and he was just thinking out loud - 'and I like Valeria.'

Here we go! Ti thought

'Publix' daughter!' Tay seemed to find the mural on the wall behind him intensely interesting. 'Isn't she a little. . .hmmm . . .plain?'

'Aren't you aiming rather high?' Ti followed, hoping to he was on cue.

'I'm just saying I like her. I like talking with her and being around her.'

'You feel comfortable.' Ti tried to understand. 'Maybe because you practically grew up with her. She's like the little sister you never had.'

'Yes, you may be right.' But he didn't understand that, beyond his mind, that is.

'What about Tullia? Or Galla? Or Porcia?' Tay tried to break out of thinking how she failed by mentioning other, prettier and more party-like, girls. 'Their fathers are Senators too.'

'I wasn't thinking about their fathers because I don't intend marrying them - or Publix. I was thinking about how I feel when I'm with the different girls.'

Tay and Ti glanced at one another as if asking one another, 'is the die cast?'

*

Three weeks later, in the month named after Caesar's family, Tay stood in the entrance to Publix' dining lounge: 'What's this?'

'I thought you'd be surprised! It's the latest fashion for eating. We sit at a table instead of reclining on couches!'

'But it's just a big table! Like workmen have!' Ti said.

'Yes, and we sit in chairs at it! But watch this!' Publix was so excited he pushed one of his canes away and hobbled along holding and sliding along the edge of the table. 'See these plates? We leave them in front of the chairs where we sit and eat our food off of them; then we pass the bowls of food along to one another! Isn't that interesting?' The look on his face virtually demanded that you agree with him; which they did. 'Now, Tay, you sit at that end of the table, Ti you on that side. Yes, there in the middle. And Marcus and Valeria, you sit over there, on that side. I'll sit at the opposite end from you, Tay.'

They all sat down and Publix said, 'see! Now we can face each other while we eat and don't have to roll around to talk to one another!'

He loves this, Tay thought. Like a little boy with a new toy. How could I ever think that Valeria or anyone would replace his wife as the woman of this house. He never wanted her to. 'This is so you, Publix!' she said. 'You keep up with fashions better than I do.'

Publix almost beamed. It was one of the few pleasures he got in life anymore. 'I'm sorry that Servius and Julius can't join us this evening. They had previous engagements.'

Probably with prostitutes and gamblers, Ti thought. The number of Publix's sons' 'previous commitments' seemed to be increasing. A bad sign. 'Well, their loss is our gain,' he said. 'We welcome every opportunity to be with you.' He said. He genuinely liked Publix. They did business together and advised one another about matters that one or the other was unsure about but knew the other was experienced in, and they flourished together as well as on their own. It was personal yet impersonal because both understood how to use polite formality to maintain the social distance between them: Publix, heir by blood and spirit to the aristocratic traditions of old pre-Augustan Rome and Ti representative of the new moneyed, international order. It never crossed his mind that Marc would feel 'comfortable' with Valeria. Her brothers, who should be her comfort, were too useless to feel 'comfortable' with.

'Now, what we do, Tay, is start with that bowl of olives in front of you. Take the bowl, put some on your plate and then pass the bowl to Val. That's it. We do that with the other bowls. Put some of the food from each bowl on your plate and pass the bowl to your left so we have a continuous flow. Couldn't be easier, could it?'

Tay smiled broadly at him. 'And we don't have to push our way up to the food table! It's brilliant!'

'See, how following fashion pays off!' he replied.

Valeria turned to Marcus. 'That reminds me, Marc, I think I know how you could increase sales of your JC line. I--'

Tay interrupted. 'Why don't you tell Marc about it later, Val. He'll be more attentive.' She caught Ti's eye and he responded with, 'and comfortable.' He understood social cues and Publix saw him smile.

When the dinner ended they adjourned into a more comfortable room where chairs and lounges were. Wine and minted figs were served and the talk turned to Publix' favorite topic - politics and gossip - which he knew kept men and women's interest; the young people excused themselves 'to talk about Valeria's ideas about the JC line,' she said.

Sure, Tay thought as Publix, she and Ti watched them leave. But Publix's sigh told her that he wished Valeria's two brothers were more business minded - so, maybe Marc had a chance after all.

*

Peter didn't go directly from Jerusalem to Rome after he agreed to the Sanhedrin's request; he went to Antioch first where he met Mark who had come from Alexandria and they stayed with Matthew to coordinate their next moves. All agreed that Jude was the best choice to succeed James in Jerusalem; he was more confrontational than James had been and would stop Simeon's bid to make the leadership of Jerusalem's church more popular.

But Peter's real purpose in the meeting was to discuss his plan with Mark and Matthew, the first stage of which was his intension to move his church to Rome.

'You mean split it?' Matthew asked.

'Yes and no,' Peter replied. 'I know this seems a shock to you, especially coming from me,' Peter replied, 'but you haven't lived there in years and haven't seen Jerusalem's descent into chaos. Life there has simply become too dangerous and chaotic for continuing to use it as the 'center' for the new world movement that our Christianity is becoming—'

'Worse than when we first started out?'

Peter thought for a moment. 'Yes. Because the Sanhedrin has split into factions and that's where the real war is. But I have no objection to keeping Jerusalem as our spiritual center.'

'What about the Sanhedrin's support for our evangelizing?' Mark asked.

'It's evaporating rapidly,' Peter replied. 'I think the only reason everyone supported my return to Rome was to buy time to sort themselves out. The body is dominated now by conservative ultra-orthodox men who are more focused on defining and defending Hebrewism as Judaism. And they're Sionists.' He looked at both men and, seeing no rebuttal, said, 'besides, I have the golden opportunity for using Titianus' financial support for my work Rome and. . . .'

'But Hero's returning here to work with us,' Matthew said.

'I know,' Peter replied. 'And that's a good thing for us in the long run. At first, I thought it may be just a mask for their real intention which is to have him work in Judas' office and take over from Amos. But I don't think so now. I think it relates to a larger dimension which Judas is quite aware of. Every year Antioch is strengthened as Rome's spear-point toward the east. That Corbulo business was just the latest installment of their steady interest. So, it's vital that you - he nodded to Matthew - remain here and work with Hero. We don't want to lose Judas' financial support.'

Matthew nodded. 'So, that'll be one of your priorities in Rome.'

'Yes, but if I've learned anything from Sol and Vol it's that the lynchpin to all this is Rome. I want to use their Jews for Rome organization as a stalking donkey for the future direction of our church. Just substitute the word Christians for Jews and continue emphasizing my role as their humble, prophetic leader. I know Sol and Vol are using me to counter wildman Paul, but I need them just as much to counter Paul's potential leadership among the Gentiles. We must not allow them to separate from us. That's why the first item on my list is to eliminate Paul from Rome.' He turned to Mark: 'I hope to achieve that with your help; that's why I want you to come to Rome with me.'

Peter, Mark and Aaron met with Matthew several more times over the course of week to flesh out Peter's ideas and when Hero arrived he joined them.

'You and your ministry here are vital to us, Matt,' Peter said when they were alone after Hero was settled in. 'And with Hero helping Aaron, you can push your agenda even further.'

'It sounds as though you have some ideas about that,' Matthew replied.

'I have one vague idea; let me sketch it out and perhaps you can improve it. I intend to give a series of sermons in Rome. Sol and Vol have already agreed to it and are letting me use the synagogues to deliver them in. I've asked Mark to take notes and afterward to write them up and circularize them as the Greeks do their books. It will save us a lot of time traveling around delivering Jesus' Gospel orally and will widen our coverage immensely. It will also give us the opportunity to begin defining Jesus' Way our way instead of Samuel's or his son's or Paul's.'

'Yes, and Paul's letters have certainly been making the rounds.'

'Yes, but they're letters. Epistles. And they reflect his experience with Jesus in the same way that he preaches his Gospel. But Paul never knew the man that we did. I intend to flesh him out so to speak and tell his the story of his life along with what he taught us. Paul can't do that!' Peter sat back. 'In case you don't know, these Greek biographies sell rather well and we could raise money for the church through it.'

'Brilliant!' Matt responded as he nodded, 'but will Sol and Vol allow you to do that?'

'I should think so. As long as I keep Jesus as the Jew you and I and others who knew him are still alive and not make him out to be some sort of Gentile god. Besides, I hope to use their contacts throughout the Diaspora to market it.'

Matthew nodded again. 'Yes, I can see how the truth should sell well as long as those who heard him and became his followers are alive and form our market base.'

Peter smiled. 'Once again the spirit breaks through history to remind us of the word.'

'Yes, the living word.' Matthew replied. 'In the present.'

*

'I want to show you something,' Ti said and stood up. They were in their bedroom upstairs two weeks after their dinner with Publix and she was sitting at her dressing table. He walked over from his chair in front of a corner table, carrying a little piece of parchment. He smoothed it down on the table in front of her.
I've been thinking about this since our dinner with Publix.'

'It looks like a chair on wheels!'

'That's what it is. I've been going over this with Telas, our delivery man, thinking to follow some of the little carts he uses but with only three wheels. A vertical shaft comes for this front wheel so you can turn it to go in different directions--'

'Do these two rear wheels turn?'

'No. We haven't figured that out yet.'

She suddenly put her left hand down; palm flat on the sketch. 'This is a chair for Publix!'

'Yes. But he'll need someone to push it.'

'That shouldn't be a problem,' she said. 'Could the wheels turn on grass? I was thinking about his cat cage.'

'I think so. Or he could put something down on top to prevent the wheels from sinking into the ground.' He saw her thinking about it. 'Why don't you take the sketch and discuss it with him. He must have a lot of people in the construction business who could build it for him.'

She looked at him. 'This is a great idea, Ti. I certainly will. I'm going there for lunch next week.'

25

'**W**AKE up! Wake up! Fire! Fire!' Albus shouted through the doorway to Ti and Tay's bedroom before running down the hallway to Marcus' room.

They heard Marcus grouse, 'not another one!'

'We better get up, Tay. I'll look outside.' Ti stepped outside onto their portico and saw the flames a short way to the southwest. 'It's those shops by Maximus and getting bigger!' he shouted, 'and the wind's coming in this direction!' He turned and went back into their bedroom. 'Get everyone to the boat!'

'All right!' Tay replied.

She was up and half dressed when Ti was in the hallway shouting, 'Marc! Marc!'

Marcus came out of his room, dressed. 'Should we go to the boat?'

'Yes. But wake Publix and everyone first! Make sure he and his family are up and tell them what we're going to do!' Marcus left.

'Quintus! Albus!' Ti yelled walking rapidly toward their room. 'Get everyone up! Then join me on the roof!' He turned, 'Tay! Come with me.'

They went up to the roof over their bedroom, three stories from the ground, and saw the fire getting larger and coming toward them. 'There's no point waiting!' Ti said. 'Quintus!' he commanded, 'help Marcus get Publix and his family to the boat. I'm staying here to monitor the fire! Once you're on the ground just yell up to me about Publix's family! Don't waste time climbing these stairways! Now, go!' He turned to Tay: 'assemble all our servants and pack as much food as you can! What? Yes, use the wagons and carriages!' She left and he saw Albus. 'Go to our warehouses and hire as many men as you can! Make sure everyone is armed! Get our people first; the biggest and strongest and tell Lucas he's in charge of them! Tell them I'll pay two denarii a day to guard our houses for the duration of the fire and send as many as you can to me and the houseboat! Terentius knows the boat. Stay with the rest and guard the warehouses. Make lists--'

'Should I help Grupa and his family?' Albus interrupted.

Ti stopped and blinked rapidly. 'Yes, make sure they know where to come. I'll stay--'

'Ti! Ti!' Marcus was shouting from the ground, his hands cupping his mouth. 'Only Publix and Valeria were home! Their servants are bringing them!'

'Who's helping Publix?'

'Quintus!'

'Get a couple of their menservants to do that and tell Quintus to come here! Tell Publix and Valeria they should go with us to our boat!' He thought for a second. 'And tell Tay about them!'

Ti looked at the fire and saw it was definitely coming in their direction. Then he heard his name being called. Looking down and left he saw a group of armed men and more coming. 'You there!,' he shouted to the biggest one, 'Lucas!'

'Yes, sir!' the big man with the big voice answered. He was firstman at Ti's warehouses.

'Organize the men here! Pick two or three to help you! The rest to guard each house! If you need more, get them! We want no thievery! Don't use you're weapons to fight the fire with! Understand?'

'Yes, sir! What about the *vigiles*?'

'Forget them! They're useless! Five d's to you and three to your helper firstmen. Understand?'

'Yes, sir!'

Ti turned to Marcus and Quintus who had returned and were standing a few feet away from Lucas. 'Quin! Stay here with Lucas!. You're my representative to guard both houses! Absolutely no pilfering and if anyone tries robbery stop them by whatever means! I'll be responsible! Understand?' He turned to Lucas below. 'Did you hear me?'

'Yes, sir!'

'You're to be Quintus' firstman.'

'Marcus, as soon as everyone downstairs is ready, get to the boat! If you need guards, hire them! If Publix wants to go on his boat do that first! Understand?'

'What will you do?' Marcus nodded and waved his arm.

'I'm going to stay here to monitor the fire! I'll join you on the boat as soon as I can!'

Publix and Valeria heard all this when Tay joined them.

'He seems to have control of things.' Publix said.

'I've always known him to,' she answered. 'Now, let's get you to the boat. Valeria, see Dorcas in the kitchens and make sure food and water's packed.'

When Valeria turned to leave, Tay took Publix' arm and noticed he was distracted and shaking. 'Don't worry about your sons, they're grown men now and can take care of themselves.'

He looked at her. 'It's not them. I had to leave their cage open! They were terrified by the smoke!'

*

Marc guided the servants – some of whom carried Publix most of the way, Valeria, Tay and their own, to the east bank of the Tiber above the Porticus Aemilia area where many houseboats were moored. Some of the others had already pulled away and everything seemed chaotic because of their desperate attempts to escape. Tay thought Publix and Valeria were better off with them and maybe, after they were rested, could go on their own. She had no idea how long they would have to spend on the river.

But then she surveyed the ones that had been launched: the people were treating the emergency like a party! Laughing, drinking, eating, calling to each another, telling where the best places to anchor were to watch the fire. Some of them were anchored while others rowed up and down the river to change views of the fire. On one, Tay saw Servius laughing and talking with Piso and other Senators; all obviously drunk. She felt horrified but said nothing to Publix or Valeria when they speculated about where his sons and her brothers were.

'Should we wait before casting off?' the boat master asked.

'Yes! But no more than an hour,' she replied.

Ti showed up in half that time after visiting his warehouse. Marcus remained with the boat party to help Publix and Valeria if needed. Later that afternoon, after Ti had come aboard, Publix, Valeria and Marcus moved with their servants aboard Publix' own boat for more room. After a week of socializing with people on the other boats, of rowing up and down the river and sometimes berthing to assess the progress of the fire and replenish their victuals, Ti announced their homes were high enough to avoid the fire and they all returned to them.

That's when he thought the fire may have been providential: but not all their neighbors were so lucky. Robbery, rape and looting escaped the fire and the woefully inadequate *vigiles*.

*

Ti didn't tell them this story until a month later. He had stopped by the Circus Maximus across from the row of shops where the fire was said to have started; and he was surprised to find it like every *castrum* in Rome's world: the tents in perfect right-angled rows; every fifth one a medical unit for the victims; every third one a kitchen, and latrines were dug along its' southern perimeter. Peter, Mark, Proteus, Linus, Clemens and their fellow Christians wore red ribbons around their upper left arms to identify themselves as helpers. People asked every conceivable question of them and they helped everyone, the burn victims receiving priority. The emperor visited the camp daily between his organizing the clean-up operations and the continuing fight to contain the now diminishing fire.

Two weeks after that - at the end of September – the praetorians reported the city devastated and a complete rebuilding program along more modern lines was required. The rumor began then, when he smiled. Soon, more and more people said that Nero started the fire.

'But why would he?' Marcus asked when Ti reported it to their families..

'Because he's crazy.' Publix' answer shocked everyone and they stared at him. No one said a word.. Everyone knew he didn't wear his heart on his sleeve, but this was treasonous. 'If there's any truth to it,' he continued, 'it will have severe repercussions.' He paused and looked at Ti before adding, 'I suggest you stay out of the picture as much as you can.'

Ti knew the remark was personally directed to him but didn't know what to make of it. His first thought was of the rumor he had heard - that Publix was growing increasingly eccentric. But he attributed a lot of what he didn't understand about him to his injuries getting worse.

And this, in turn, confused Publix. He had meant his remark to be friendly by Roman standards so he was surprised at Ti's reaction. Didn't he understand it as his way of trying to help him? Didn't Ti understand how his various roles brought him into contact with different kinds of people and especially how his connections as a Senator opened a dimension beyond Ti's understanding. But as he returned Ti's stare, he realized Ti couldn't understand them beyond their shared interests: which were not values and traditions.

He realized the gap between them for the first time and involved his emotions because the more they socialized the more he liked them. They were efficient, straight-forward and no-nonsense; and he was struck by their unselfish help after the fire broke out. Not the usual 'me-first' of his other neighbors which proved Ti's point about his preference for private over public life. A very un-Roman attitude. And what impressed him was how father and son worked together - as he and his sons did not. In fact, he felt bitter – dare I even admit abandoned? - about their disappearance at the time of the fire. They went gods-know-where leaving him and Valeria to cope on their own until Marc arrived. He finally said to Ti, in an effort to bridge the new gulf between them: 'have you heard from Hero recently?'

Valeria thought nothing of the question but Tay, Ti and Marcus looked at him as if the three were were one and thought, he must know something we don't.

Publix noted their collective attentiveness.

'He's been staying with Peter's group to help the victims,' Ti answered carefully. 'He was part of the group that Matthew sent over from Antioch. 'We don't expect to hear from him until they finish. Why?'

But Marcus interjected, 'I saw fewer tents there when I came home from our warehouse yesterday so they must be winding up. He'll probably come to see us when they're finished.'

'And before he goes back,' Tay added, uneasy about where Publix was taking the conversation.

Publix looked from one to the other and said, 'all I can tell you is that the emperor doesn't like the rumor that he started the fire. It's seditious, you know.'

The trio looked at him again. Publix never bantered about serious matters like his sons did.

'You mean Nero's looking for a scapegoat,' Marcus said, his eyes narrowing..

'And Jews have traditionally provided them with one. It's almost as if they are compelled to sacrifice something, even themselves.' Ti said. Fishing outloud.

Publix looked from father to son. 'I've heard that Peter and his helpers wear red ribbons on their arms for people to notice them. Like those whitewash signs on buildings advertising coming attractions at the games. I suggest you think about other things that such signs and symbols can be used for.'

Father, son, and mother looked at one another. Was Publix becoming senile?

What does eccentric really mean? Ti asked himself.

*

Senate meetings were presided over by the emperor, conducted in private and everyone was sworn to secrecy. In effect, Publix was acutely aware he had just violated his senatorial oath. Of course, he knew the three in front of him were not practicing Jews; but the emperor usually brought his own agenda with him to the meetings which had been hammered out between him and his sycophantic advisors, and it was decided to blame the fire on Jewish arsonists..

Publix hoped they would identify the traditional scapegoat that Nero had come up with - the Jews — as Ti had done, and that they would act accordingly. He even mentioned Peter by name. How much more pointed could it get? And everyone in Rome hated the Jews because of their privileged status. So he drew his line: he couldn't tell them what the emperor was about to.

26

WHICH was just as well because Publix hadn't reckoned on Sophonious Tigellinus. A former lover of Nero's mother and now sole general of the emperor's Praetorian Guard, whose rise from obscurity and poverty was guided by to his unscrupulous seizing of main chances, stood outwardly smiling and inwardly horrified. He stood first among Nero's many sycophants and openly told others he owed everything to him. But that was a lie; he didn't say he was deeply indebted to Rome's Jews who financed his various endeavors because he didn't want Nero to know that. So, when Nero started talking about how the Jews were the real arsonists, Tig rushed to Solomon and Volumnus, his leading creditors, with the news; and with the advice - so typical of the General, Solomon thought - that this must not be allowed to happen. Tall and magnificent in his uniform, he was reputedly the most handsome and corrupt military man in Rome. Solomon thought he was a birdbrain.

The answer was simple, Vol told him later that afternoon, after consulting with Sol. It wasn't the Jews; it was the Jesus Jews. Yes, those bastard Jews! We need to call the emperor's attention to his misinformation. But delicately, Soph. The followers of that long-dead prophet whom the Antiocheans had mistakenly labeled Christians twenty years ago really did it. Blame them, not our hard-working, God-loving Jews. In fact, our Jews will help you. They'll identify themselves by wearing a short black serapi with a gold pin in the shape of an R ('yes, for Rome, General,' Vol replied to his question smiling while thinking, God, you're dumb!) So your men can easily distinguish the emperor's good and faithful Jewish supporters from those licentious and disloyal Christians. Yes, the R will be pure gold. And yes, the serapis with their pins may be collected in the synagogues afterward by your brave soldiers. After the General left, Sol and Vol agreed: their slogan, 'Jews for Rome,' has many different virtues.

One and a half weeks later, Nero announced to the Senate that he had been misinformed; it was really the Jesus Jews – the ones who tried to disguise themselves as Christians to hide their identity – who were the real arsonists. As soon as he left the Senate building, Publix immediately told one of his trusted servants to run - not walk - and tell Titianus that the Jesus Jews were now officially charged as arsonists.

Publix worried about what he did while his litter was carried home; yes, he admitted, I feel guilty. He had now violated his oath completely; was he going to violate his Roman identity as well? Was he abandoning his Roman ideals and traditions for personal friendship? Why? Finally, after realizing he had no answer, he sighed and consoled himself with knowing it would soon be public information anyway.

*

As soon as Publix's servant left Ti, Simon the Zealot, Judas' old friend, stepped through the portico doorway into Ti's home study, knowing Ti was home and not at his office with Marcus

Not hearing him, Ti looked up from his desk in surprise and put his pen down. 'It's been a long time, Simon so this must be very important.' He stood up and shook Simon's hand.

'You always cut to the chase, don't you?'

'It's still good to see you,' Ti smiled and gestured to a chair. 'Please sit down. I'm sure you don't need me to tell you how dangerous it is for you here.'

'We're opening a second front and I'm quite busy.'

'A second front?' Ti looked baffled.

'You'll learn about the first one in due time. Right now, I want to tell you that what Publix' servant told you is true and that Nero will begin moving against the Christians immediately. You need to protect Hero now.'

Ti nodded. 'What about the others?'

'We're organizing their evacuations but I'm not going to tell you how because what you don't know may save your life.'

Ti stood up, walked over to a small chest, raised the lid and took out two bags. 'Here,' he said, tossing them to him. 'Use them how you think best.'

Simon caught the bags and said, 'I'll arrange Hero's flight. It's better that I do it and not you because they'll come looking for him and the others.' He stared steadily at Ti. 'Nero's crazy about this, Jud. He's ordered his praetorians to seal off all of Italy's seaports. And Hero's people should not try to get to Caesarea or Jerusalem. I'd suggest using Joppa but think it will be patrolled from Caesarea. Alerts have already been sent to the procurator in Caesarea so I suggest Antioch. Just keep your story straight about where Hero went and make it believable or everything will collapse. You understand?'

Ti nodded but said nothing.

'I can't get too involved in this because I have other things I must do. But I wanted to warn you and I've already told Peter. He'll tell the others. You know that Mark is with him, don't you?'

'Yes.'

Simon nodded. 'Mark will help Peter. I can't do anything for Paul and don't you try to interfere. We must play a waiting game about all this.'

'What do you mean about Paul?'

'He's already left Spain and may arrive in Ostia at the very time when Nero's prosecutions are in full swing. Notices are now sent to the ship captains after they arrive but before they land forbidding them to say anything about the persecutions.' He stared at Ti. 'I can't do anything about it. I'm sure they'll pick him up eventually. The guards in Ostia and Puteoli have already been notified and given his description.' He scooped up the two bags and stood up to go but then stopped and looked sideways at Ti. 'This is like it was with Jesus in Jerusalem, Jud. You couldn't stop them then either.' Then he left.

Ti got up, walked over and closed the lid of the chest, then walked through the doorway into the hall. 'Albus!' he called.

'Yes, sir,' Albus replied, appearing in the little doorway into his office.

'We may have some praetorian visitors this afternoon.'

*

'How did you know?'

'I can't tell you. Let's just say I felt it.'

Publix, in his wheeled chair, and Ti were sitting over wine in Publix's study. Valeria was with Marcus and Tay in the garden. Except for the arrival of the grains from Egypt and other foodstuffs from other parts of the empire, trade in civilian consumer goods had fallen off sharply since the great fire.

'And he's safe?'

'I assume so. He's disappeared with his friends from Antioch.'

'They took others with them, I hope!'

'Yes.'

'We can't assume anything these days. Nero's blood is up. Or I should say the Christians' blood.'

'How did the Jews ever manage to pull this off? I see the rabbis and rulers all wearing little black shawls and these goddamn R pins!'

'The Roman way, Ti. You should know how it works.'

'It all boils down to religious hatred, doesn't it?'

'And complicated because of their identification with Piso's conspiracy--'

'Is that what those soldiers around your house are for? Protection?'

Publix looked at each one of them for a long moment before saying, 'I'm deeply ashamed to tell you this. But they think Servius is part of the conspiracy.' He looked away. 'Even as a little boy he dreamed about past glories, the way things used to be. He was never much interested in the present or in business. Anyway, he's disappeared but they think he might return here.'

'So, you don't know when – or if - he'll be back.'

Publix sat back in his chair. 'I've resigned myself to his being gone – lost - forever. He's a marked man now.' He pushed himself back in his chair and looked into the distance. 'I'm just now coming to grips with the fact that I should have dealt with this ten or fifteen years ago but I was too busy pursuing my own things.' He was silent for a moment and then turned to Ti and Tay. 'How did you do it?'

'I think the tale of my two sons is straightforward. I married my first wife before I was ready for marriage and after she died, Hero was raised by her parents during his early years. Then I married Tay later, when men like me should marry, and you can see Marc is even passing me now. So I understand one better than the other but I love them both and support Hero in pursuing his own way.' Ti stopped and looked at him, but Publix saw he was looking into his own memory.

He was; but differently from what Publix imagined. Ti was thinking how much he shared as a father with Publix,, but that this ended Publix' male line. Three months ago, Julius had been arrested along with his 'friends' for looting shops and robbing the homes of wealthy people during the fire. Nero had them quickly executed as a slap in the face to Publix and other potential senatorial opponents. Every family, even Roman ones, have their tragedies, he thought as he sat up straighter. He suddenly shook himself and snapped out of his reverie: 'how can I help you?'

Publix rested his chin on his chest for a moment and then said, 'you've done so much for us already. More than you can know.' He paused and then looked up at the sky through the doorway. 'I think it's more social and economic than religious because that's the way we are. Nero's killing the poor, ignorant Christians instead of the wealthier, more educated Jews. People like Solomon and Volumnus will survive. They'll even become richer as I and my partners rebuild the city.' He sighed and shut his eyes. 'But what does it matter. Sometimes I think there's no justice in the world.' Then he opened them and said, 'I think you could be right. You're way is a smart one. Pursuing your private life instead of the public one. You're more free to yourself than I am; I'm enslaved to my public life. It's very difficult for me to admit that because my old identity between freedom and public life, the one my father and grandfather knew, is over: but I don't want to admit it.' He paused and Ti didn't know what to say. 'I'm having a difficult time accepting that.'

Tay said nothing to either man. She understood they were reaching out to one another as man to man.

'The dead hand of the past grips all of us. I've always tried to escape it by looking forward into the future.' Ti said, sipping his wine reflectively. 'Perhaps Rome's simply becoming more international than it's ever been and that change is what you sense.'

'And celebrity conscious,' Publix said quietly and then looked at him in a friendly way. 'Everyone wants to be one. To live more loosely and freely these days—'

'Which takes money.'

Publix looked at him. 'By the way, you should invest as much as you can with me in rebuilding the city. This maniac is opening up the aqueducts to the imperial treasury in ways I've never seen before.' He looked into a distant and added, almost foregetfully, 'millions will be made.'

'Thank you. I will. I'll talk with you tomorrow about it.' The word 'maniac' reverberated in both Ti and Tay's head: did Publix really say that?

Publix looked off in the distance again. 'I haven't mentioned the latest news, have I?'

'What's that?'

'You know Poppea was pregnant?'

Tay's ears perked up. Was? 'Why do you say 'was?'' she asked.

'Because he kicked her to death last night in one of his drunken rages.'

A deep gloom settled over her and Ti.

He really was a maniac, they both thought.

*

Two months later, Publix' eyes glittered as Ti's family never saw them before and it wasn't simply because of April's warm weather. He was also more animated than they had ever seen him. He started waving his hands and seemed unable to speak.

'Where did you ever get them? I've never seen them with blue eyes! And such short fur!'

Publix was so lost in studying their black markings, long tails and quick movements that he barely heard Tay's reply: 'they came in Ti's latest shipment from India. We've had to keep them quiet because they were so terrified by the trip.'

'I just can't believe it!' He kept repeating. 'Some of my friends have miniature lions but no one has anything like these! Did you call them India cats?'

'Yes, but they came from north of India,' Tay replied. 'Did you see them when you were there, Ti?'

'I saw a few but they weren't as distinctive as this, Pub. Grupa says these came from even further east. He says the people there believe they are the wisest in catdom, even wiser than the Egyptian ones. And they don't particularly care for humans.'

Pub's eyes never left the cats. He never even glanced at Tay or Ti after greeting and welcoming them into his home. After the servants carried the big box inside the walk-in cage, opened both ends, came back out, closed the cage door, the first head appeared and then a second one. Publix sat transfixed on his wheeled chair that Tay had pushed into the large outdoor cage, and sometimes put his chin on top of the back of his hand whose fingers curled around the handle of his cane.

Ti looked at the cats, looked at Tay, shook his head, shrugged his shoulders and said, 'I'm afraid I have to get back to Marc. He wanted to go over some accounts with me.'

Tay knew what he was up to: escape as soon as possible. So she said to Publix while looking at Ti with a twinkle in her eye, 'perhaps Valeria would like to see them before you go.'

Ti rolled his eyes and Pub didn't answer because he was remembering having to open the large cage door when he thought the fire would come up the hill. It was so horrible; but had to be done. So, she asked again.

'Oh yes, of course!' he replied this time. 'Jason, tell Hera to invite Valeria to see them.'

Ti sighed in surrender. He looked at Tay who turned to him and smiled. Both knew Valeria loved cats almost as much as her father did. Growing up with them, she had fonder cat memories than brotherly ones.

'Oh, how lovely!' Valeria said from the doorway. 'Look at their blue eyes! Where did they come from? They're so sleek! What kind are they?'

Not wanting to make gulping noises, Ti sipped steadily from his wine glass and tried to hide behind it. He had never been a cat person. Whoever heard of a Jewish cat? Just goddamn Egyptian ones.'

'--and they came in the latest shipment from India,' Tay said. 'But Grupa says they're from even further east.'

'And a pair! Male and female, I--'

'Of course!' Tay interrupted. 'We knew you may want to breed them. I thought about your poor empty cage for months!'

'Dad! They're so. . . just charming!'

Like father, like daughter. And Tay just encourages it! Ti thought. God! The things I do for the family! I hope you like cats, Marc!

27

VALERIA, Ti, Tay, and Marcus had to be careful over the winter of 65-66 not because Nero's persecutions extended to them but because June was the most popular month for marriages; and Roman society loved marriages as the occasion to reaffirm itself. But unlike other societies, Rome's vested a greater legal consciousness about it because legal status determined the 'who' of it, and that 'who' determined what one could do. Making contracts, initiating and participating in law suits and marrying, for example, were determined by one's legal status. This hadn't been true when Publix' grandfather, Marcus Vipsanius Agrippa, was born; but it was now the case because it was invented by the needs of empire. And yes, beginning with Augustus, the legal profession blossomed over the next three generations as it never had before.

The trouble was that a social consciousness had arisen of a pecking order, a hierarchy of position within the range of social groups. Everyone having a legal status above slave fell into one of two groups. The first - and the tiniest - class were the governors whose offices frequently became hereditary. The Senatorial class was at its top. Below them was the equestrian class - who provided such leaders as Pontius Pilate as well as future Senators from among the leading equite families. The bottom of this first group were the municipal office holders.

The second group were freedmen - the ordo libertinorum. If you've guessed where Publix and Ti were located you know why Ti, Tay, Marcus and Valeria had to be careful. Crossing Rome's social boundaries could be as dangerous as passing through Dura Europas – and in either direction. But for people with long visions--

*

Fortunately – and from the freedmen's of view - birth was less important than wealth. Men like Calpurnius Piso at the top viewed money as the democratizer, the leveler, even the destroyer of the old order. But men like Ti saw money as the Great Helper to upward mobility. By the decade of the 60s, one's occupation, residence and consumption advertised one's position as much as birth and civil governance continued to do so. And the fingerpost was clear: one could expand one's freedom (rise in society) through wealth. Getting rich was all the rage for these people. More and more, the question for all wannabe governors was 'how much wealth do you have' not your birth lineage. And as money democratized social bonds, so it personalized them as well. During Judas and Ti's lifetime, the wealthiest, most influential families, and the most sought-out-socially families - even by emperors – were found in this second group. In the winter of 65-66, Ti had known this for twenty years and – happily for Marcus - Publix was just discovering it.

Publix didn't like what was happening any more than Piso did; but he knew it was like disliking a volcanic eruption: it was greater than the individuals who were involved. And they were visible: domus' were no longer confined to the Palantine; they had spilled over to the new neighborhood around the Circus Flaminius, a part of the imperial accommodation of the traditional *flamines* (priests) by the 60s . Many among Publix' class bemoaned this leveling effect of money on the old aristocratic values of three generations ago – which many of his classmates called it 'corroding' because it tarnished the 'purity' of their society even more than it did their copper. And, of course, many of them were part of Piso's conspiracy last year (and of Vinicianus' this year). But Publix was more open minded; he accepted the long-term trend as inevitable. Who would you rather have conversation with, he asked himself, a man bristling with energy and ideas about improving life or someone who only talks about the good old days. Titianus was right, Publix decided, life was now and in the future. The past is for historians.

Marcus, he also decided, was new because he was untainted by his parent's past - Judas' Jewishness or Tay's Parthianess - and defined the new Roman wedding of imperialism to financial internationalism. Blood and 'old' was less important to this new future than spirit, talent and imagination. 'Life is show not tell,' Publix heard Ti tell him several times.

But what most amazed him was discovering Valeria was no different! She even told him, 'why, just look at what those old ways did to Servius and Julius! They couldn't compete with the new ways! And what they taught me was how important choice is! They didn't fail because they didn't embrace the new: they embraced the wrong ones!

So, one day in early March, Publix told her: 'I give up! I see the future! So what do you want to do!'

'Marc.'

'You mean marry?'

'I mean merge. He's a nice man and I can live with him for the rest of my life. But more importantly, I can live a new life with him every day.'

So Publix listed what he thought was everyone's wants:

Valeria wants to marry in June.

Marc doesn't care when; just jot it in his diary as far in advance as possible and minimize his social responsibilities.

I want a traditional Roman, old-fashioned wedding involving a series of religious ceremonies that my Senatorial friends would understand.

Tay wants them to be married and produce children she didn't from Ti.

Ti just wants it all to be over and to stop talking about it.

Hero wrote saying he couldn't come because of the refugees pouring into Antioch, but wished them his heartfelt best wishes and prayers for God's giving them a happy life together.

Ti scrunched up his face when he read it and muttered, 'what refugees?'

*

'You know,' Ti said to Tay after the marriage and the couple were housed in their own quarters – a self enclosed suite in an extension of their home along its west wall - 'I'm happy for Publix that the old guard honored them by recognizing their marriage. But I'm surprised at some of our merchant friends. I mean, I don't think I've seen such gaudy, grotesquely ugly gifts!'

Tay smiled – knowing the difference between the tastes of old and the new - but continued brushing her hair and replied, 'I know. And everything is so big! Did you size of Grupa's vase? It's as tall as I am!'

'What a difference from our marriage!' Ti replied, smiling.

She stopped brushing and looked at him. 'That was eighteen years ago!' After pausing she asked, 'Ti, when do Romans think women stop conceiving?'

'Most think around age forty.'

She put the brush down, stood up and slipped off her night dress and walked toward him. 'Maybe we can be parents before becoming grandparents.'

*

Most didn't know it was a wartime marriage. In the previous month, one faction of Jewish leaders in Jerusalem decided to stop the daily sacrifice to the emperor in the Temple. That signaled revolt; and three months after their marriage, the Governor of Syria – and the Procurator of Judea's superior - Cestius Gallus seized the opportunity to demonstrate his control of the matter to Nero. He marched with his legions from Antioch and appeared before Jerusalem's walls. But he was no Joshua; he was defeated and humiliatingly retreated through October and November after losing nearly fifty eight hundred men and the eagle of the *XII* legion, the *Fulminata*. Nero received reports about it between bouts at the Olympic games where he usually spent his winters, and where he heard the news of Corbulo's son-in-law supporting Piso's conspiracy. He decided to change everything in the east before Saturnalia. Corbulo was summoned to Corinth in October and committed suicide. Gallus was replaced by Licinius Mucianus, current Governor of Lycia and Pamphylia, and a friend of Ti's from his service under Corbulo in 58. And Mucianus' old enemy, Titus Vespasian, was appointed commander of an army to put down therebellion. That changed everything. At least, Ti thought so.

'Times could not be more auspicious for Valeria to announce her pregnancy, could they!' Marcus said in the warehouse office three days before the week-long Saturnalia began. He meant it merely as an offhand remark but was surprised by Ti's response.

Ti rose from his desk, walked over to the maps on the wall and said, 'our overland trade with the east and south will undoubtedly diminish.'

Marcus didn't know what to say but reminded himself he should have seen this coming: Ti had mentioned the rebellion it several times. 'We can't know how long this war will last. Two or three years, do you think?'

'I don't know. But I suspect you're right. At least two or three years.'

'Can we hold out that long? Maybe increase the India trade?'

'Thank God wars don't diminish demand for luxury goods as much as for other things--'

'Maybe we should get into staples. Grains?'

'Query Amos about that in your next letter.' Ti walked back to his desk. 'Maybe we should shift our strategy. Pursue entirely new things.'

Marcus knew he was thinking out loud. 'Such as?

'We know the geography quite well and I learned something about military requirements when working with Corbulo. I also know Mucianus from those days. Maybe we could do some contracting with him.'

'You're a better judge of that than I am.' Marcus replied. But Ti didn't reply; he was thinking; so Marcus asked: 'do you have a problem about our fighting the Jews?'

'No, I'm long past that and very different now.' He stopped and smiled, almost ruefully, Marchus thought. 'I really am,' he said. 'But the Romans have already lined up people who hate the Jews to support them. To tell the truth, I don't think the Jews have a chance and it's far too much of a risk for us.' He stopped, thinking about the logistics of this new enterprise. 'Even if I could do something through Mucianus we would need help here in Rome while I and maybe you did the leg work over there.' He paused, lost in thought.

'You mean someone with connections at court.'

'The problem is that everyone is so corrupt.'

'What about Publix? He's a Senator, has all kinds of construction contacts and you worked with him before.'

'Good idea! I'm sure Mucianus will remember me.'

Marcus smiled. 'And here I thought you were going to retire and play with your grandchildren!'

Ti chuckled. 'Oh, yes. I forgot. Congratulations!' He looked sheepish. 'What can I say? Never say never.'

*

'So, Pub, I propose an agreement between ourselves along these lines. We go fifty-fifty between us and I'll take care of Marc out of my end. I don't pretend to know your civilian contracting business as well as you and I'm not asking about it. But I'm quite sure it will diminish during the war the same as myoverland trade with the east will. So I think we should work together to get war contracts. I'm fifty eight and still in good health. I'll be the leg man. I know the geography quite well and have contacts in Alexandria, Caesarea and Antioch. I also know some of the people involved and Mucianus in particular. I would start with him. I'll do the footwork, proposing to supply them with various things. You remain here and get what we need. Since those seaports I mentioned will be the main contact points for the military, we can use their transports for communication--'

Publix smiled. 'So, I'll be Mr. Inside and you Mr. Outside?

'Something like that. My point is that you don't have to go anywhere and can continue dealing with the same people you've always dealt with. Maybe some new ones given the nature of the business. I'm thinking you know your sources for food, military gear, weaponry, but I may want to contract locally over there for horses, camels, and any immediate needs they might have. And I may want to use your name to get started.'

'You mean my credit. For fifty percent of all profits? On everything we do in our two names?'

'That's right. I've worked with many partners in the past so I'm comfortable working with you. I'll take Albus with me but Marc and Quintus can run the accounts here and Antioch and you can inspect them whenever you wish.' He stopped and thought for a few seconds. 'My idea is to minimize your efforts but I should tell you that I've only dabbled in military contracting before. Supplying Corbulo in Armenia was small stuff compared to what we may get into in this war, so I may need your advice as well. Marc can act as our go-between and for arranging the military transport. He can carry your dispatches if need be and I should think all the military commanders will know your seal. Mine will be addressed to you and go in the Senatorial pouches.'

Publix looked out over the Forum. 'What I like about your proposal is that you know the geography and people over there and I can continue dealing with the same people I've always dealt with and maybe even some new ones given the nature of the business.'

'Yes, and I've thought you know your sources best for food, military gear, weaponry and the like, but I may want to contract locally over there for horses, camels, and anything that may be needed immediately.'

Publix nodded and said, 'yes, I can see we could make good money from that. And I've always had a distant but good relationship with him.' He paused and looked out the window of his study again. 'And it would be a new learning experience for you and Marc.' *The son I wished I had!*

'I don't think I have to tell you that at my time of life what I do is really for Marc and Valeria and their family.'

'No, you don't. Besides, they're my family too.'

Ti sat back in his chair, thinking he's accepted it, so he decided to lay more of his cards on the table. 'Thank you for saying that. If I sounded too one-sided I didn't mean to. There's more at stake here than my little goals. Speaking as father-in-law to father-in-law, I think our growth in the future depends on ourgrowth as an overseas empire. The days are gone when Italy provided everything Rome needs and we should no longer think of the military in simply defensive terms. It's crucial to our future growth. Marc and I make a lot of money from our commodities trade but civilian markets wax and wane and decline in times like these. I think we should figure military contracting more into our future.' He hesitated. 'Like your aqueducts and grain docks. I want Marc to understand that – I mean understand the world that we but especially he will live in.'

Pub didn't reply; he just nodded his head indicating his - understanding? Or his agreement? Ti couldn't tell which.

*

But Ti's meeting with Mucianus in Antioch shocked him. Memories of friendship are one thing, he thought after he left their meeting, but current realities are another. Mucianus carried the old guard's dislike of new men seeking to be equals with them and he had had his run-ins with Vespasian before. (It never dawned on Ti that Vespasian would be considered a 'new man.') Only when Ti mentioned his association with Publix - in family and now business, neither of which Licinius had known about before - did he soften a little. In his mind, Publix - not Ti - was his equal even if the old Senator was weirdly different in his business interests. So, Licinius passed the buck about Vespasian and steered Ti over to General Tiberias Alexander who commanded the troops in Alexandria.

'Perhaps he could help you?' Licinius said. But what he really thought was what is this world be coming to when two Jews jockey to wage war against their own people!

And Ti thought: so he's passed the buck to Vespasian's right hand military supporter. Where can this lead to?

*

The Olive Tree synagogue was always cold and dank during Rome's winters, perhaps because it was the largest one. But Volumnus, its ruler and his long dead father's brother, Solomon, who ruled the one in the rich District XII, had to make their decision now, before the spring campaigns began. How could they best use Rome's war against their people to dominate the city's synagogues and then steer Rome's Jews out from under their domination by Jerusalem's Sanhedrin? It wasn't much of a dilemma because it was apparent that their 'Jews for Rome' was the perfect vehicle for expressing their sentiment and channeling their leadership through.

'How can those idiots think they can win? Not even the appointment of this turtle, Vespasian, can stop the Romans! He'll just prolong their agony!'

'Don't let your temper take over! We're here to solve a problem and I have an idea.'

Vol looked at the man whose brains had saved them many times over the past twenty years since people calling themselves 'Christians' started trouble among their people. Vol remembered being shocked at Sol suggesting they encourage it precisely because it promoted conflicts and divisions. 'Chaos and division are our chief allies,' Sol said. 'That's what we've been trying to do with the Sanhedrin and we should continue doing it.'

'People think all Jews are the same, neph. They expect that we'll probably become rebels too. I've heard that Nero has even warned Tigellinus to keep his eye on us. So, maybe it's time we do just the opposite!'

'Support Rome?' Vol's smiled, more and more broadly. 'You mean continue accusing the Sanhedrin of taking Judaism down the wrong path! We could even say their leaders are not only rebels against Rome but against Judaism itself!'

'Has all sorts of possibilities, doesn't it?' Sol said, smiling and smug.

But it was lost on Vol because he was remembering the look of horror on Annas' – his new father in law – face when Vol told him he was returning to Rome instead of remaining in Jerusalem. That was twenty years ago, when the new emperor Claudius was in Britannia and before Sol suggested they wrest control over the Diaspora away from the Sanhedrin.

Sol smiled. He knew what Vol was thinking because he had been grooming Vol to replace him as leader of Rome's Jewry ever since his own son had been murdered during one of the Chrestus riots twenty years ago. He questioned, as Vol did not, the safety of living in Rome rather than Jerusalem. From what he heard, not even Babylonia was as bad.

'Jews for Rome!'

'What?' Vol's voice broke into Sol's meandering mind.

'That's who will save us!'

*

Ti couldn't remember ever having a briefer interview with anyone in such high authority. General Tiberius Alexander told him about Vespasian and his previous relations with Mucianus, and that if he, Ti, could get them to end their animosity and pull together, everyone would benefit. It was a virtual ultimatum. Get the two to resolve their differences or forget it. He didn't say so, but Ti thought he told other contractor wannabes the same thing.

Well, I've been to Antioch and now Alexandria and I'm not dumb, Ti told himself as he walked out of Alexander's headquarters. Go to Caesarea, see the turtle, and try to patch things up between them. Use Senator Publix' name liberally instead of your own. Then we - me - will benefit. Alexander made the old adage perfectly clear: it takes two or more to make a contract.

28

Contracts followed after I smoothed over our relations so I returned to Rome to spend the winter of 66-67 at home. I didn't know that was the same winter that Vespasian and his son, Titus, stayed with King Agrippa and his sister, Berenice, in Caesarea Philippi, and where Titus began his liaison with Berenice. The most valuable lesson that I learned from my meetings with Vespasian was that Publix earned his fifty percent merely by sprinkling his name through my conversations. That's what really got us the contracts. My God!, I thought, he earns fifty percent and isn't even here! Now, that's social power!

But Publix also did me a favor by telling me about Vespasian; and because the turtle (that nickname – and more unmentionable ones - came from his own troops.) wasn't as forthcoming about technical details as Corbulo had been, I focused on trying to understand his strategy. And discovered he was the most methodically thorough military commander I ever met or heard about: which made dealing with him a military supplier's dream. And that's when I realized the rebels really didn't have a chance and the war could be shorter than even Pub thought. So, I had alternative sources of income on my mind when I saw Marc.

'Have you been watching commodity prices in Antioch and Alexandria?'

Marcus smiled. 'Yes. They've been rising steadily. And it's good to see you too.'

I laughed and said, 'I'm sorry. I've been too relaxed at sea trying to get used to be a grandfather. You look good. How's the family?'

'Everyone's well and you're going to be a grandfather a second time.'

'Wonderful! When?'

'We think in June.'

A good month for marriages and births.' But I'm sorry I won't be here again, I thought. 'I don't have to tell you the old adage, do I?'

'Which one?'

'Buy yesterday and sell tomorrow.'

Marcus laughed. 'I have been and we've been doing well. But what about Judea and Jerusalem?'

'What do you mean? I stopped doing business there years ago.'

'I mean in foodstuffs. The more successful Vespasian is in the countryside the higher food prices should climb in the city.'

I stared at my son. My God! He's worse than I am!, I thought. 'You have a point. But how would that work if the Romans control the coastal country?'

'Use the back door. Through Jericho. Where the tenth legion's stationed.'

He was right, I thought, shamefully but excitedly (it's my Titianus side, I told myself once again). 'Prices will be higher by the end of this year and even higher next year.'

"And they'll certainly have enough gold to pay for it."

'Maybe we should play with some calculations about when they'll garrote the city,' I replied.

'You'll be right there in headquarters. It won't get any easier than that, will it?'

I looked at him. Married now; Val pregnant with their second and Tay more ecstatic than I ever saw her. I looked at him: he seems younger and more energetic than ever; and now I'm the one having to keep up. 'But there's also the issue of who commands in the city,' I replied. 'Vespasian's success in the countryside will drive the Zealots into the city and they're so factionalized that--'

'But they'll still have to eat and - hint, hint - they'll have access to coinage.' He knew Ti would like that part. 'But if you take it you'll have to remelt it.'

'I know. But that's no problem.' Marc had a good idea. 'We should also consider who the leadership will be. More Zealots will mean their wanting a greater say in decisions and Zealots never cared much for money--'

'Even when they were stealing it ten years ago?'

That caused me to pause and think. 'You never knew them as I have. They always saw it as nothing more than a means to an end. No, I'm thinking that the Zealots from the countryside will be more radical than any of the city's old leaders. They'll press for an independent Jewish state as never before. And because so many of the Sadducees are abandoning the city, the Zealots will probably win. Next year could decide things.'

'So the countryside this year and the city in 68?'

'That's right. And the more I think about your idea the more I like it.'

I suddenly realized he was staring at me. 'What?' I said.

And he replied, 'then the only question left is who do you know among the Zealots?'

*

But it didn't turn out that way because the northern legions' rebelled against playboy Nero, the Senate's condemn him the following winter, his suicide in June 68 and seventy three year old General Servius Sulpicius Galba's announcement that he was his successor. So, we had to wait a whole extra year.

But Marc and I talked about it whenever we saw one another and especially during the winter of 67-68; only now, the trend in commodity prices had risen even higher. So we decided on insurance by involving the turtle.

That's how I wound up spending April 68 in his headquarters arguing my case for winning the war and enriching ourselves. Happily for me, his capture of the entire province of Galilee made him realize the infinite capacity for factionalism among the Zealots; but it was the dramatic change of Flavius Josephus, the Pharisee commander of Galilee and captured in Jotapata - who then changed his allegiance to the Romans (talk about me being the great betrayer!) in 67 – that made him better appreciate the opportunities offered by the war. I could see the change in him when the army moved south for 68's campaign.

'I intend to sweep the south and prepare to besiege Jerusalem,' turtle said, and I believed him. So I pitched him on that basis: use only half your army and attack them in such a way as to allow as many as possible to 'escape' into the city to swell its population.

He looked at me with his beady fat eyes and replied – as I expected him to: 'do you think I'm crazy?'

'Of course not, but consider this: once inside, their increased numbers and fanaticism will challenge if not divide their leadership and create an unexpectedly huge demand for foodstuffs.' Then, I explained my plan to sell them their needed food in return for the Temple gold which Vespasian and every Roman heard rumors about, but which I knew for a fact – and which, I reminded him - they cannot eat. Fat eyes grew beadier and agreed to the rest of my plan: for thirty percent of my receipts. Of the gross proceeds, he reminded me. Well, sure, I thought. This was gold after all (and proved what I had long suspected: the military was absolutely crucial to the expansion of Rome's future empire). 'Done,' I replied.

*

As far as I knew, Zealots had always used underground rooms and labyrinthian passages like moles, rabbits and the mongooses I had seen in India; but nothing had seemed darker or more dangerous than the entrance into this one, I thought, while standing at its entrance and taking deep breaths to quell my fear. Hard looking, sinister and dangerous men armed to the teeth lurked all around me and I knew more waited inside. But Simon had guaranteed my safety. So, I looked around one last time, drew a deep breath, ducked and plunged ahead, thinking "aren't I getting a little old for this?"

The opening descended into a long, narrow passageway and I followed the wall with my right hand as I had been instructed to do. Slowly, a tiny light at the end became larger and finally my passageway opened into a large room. There sat Simon at a small table with a single candle burning on a piece of broken crockery in its middle. I felt but couldn't see others in the shadows of the room.

'Hello, Judas,' he said. 'It's always good to see you.'

'Hello, Simon. It's good to see you, too.'

'That stool is for you. How can I help?'

'First, this is for you. No strings attached,' I said as I sat down and pushed three bagfuls of coins across the table. 'I'm going to ask you for something but that's yours regardless of your answer.' I nodded at the bags.

'Thank you.' He didn't touch them.

'I'm glad you left Rome.' I said. 'You were right about Paul and I assume you heard about Peter.'

'Yes. I heard he got half-way to Puteoli but then turned back for some reason.'

'That's what I heard too. And I wouldn't have expected it.'

'Me either. That's why I suspect it isn't true.'

That caught me unexpectedly. 'Perhaps we always underestimated him,' I replied.

He just looked at me and said, 'none of us are alone in this world. So, how can I help?'

'I want to go into the city before Vespasian gets too close.' I said. 'Probably in the autumn.' Both of us understood we were talking about Jerusalem.

And he wasn't surprised. 'That's months from now and anything could happen before then. But you have access to Vespasian's headquarters. Surely, you know things I don't. Why--'

'I know what I'm doing and we've known each other for a long time. I'm telling you his big push won't come before next spring.'

'Not until next year? 69?' He seemed genuinely surprised. 'You're taking a chance, telling me.'

'Yes. But as you know, I supply him with various things and this is what I told him.' Then I told Simon what I told Vespasian and Simon listened because we trusted one another. He knew I couched information in my opinions and never carried written documents. 'You can see how the plan makes sense to him. What you do there, of course, is entirely your business. But I pledge to you that I'll deliver twice the amount of foodstuffs that I told Vespasian I will. You deliver the gold. It won't do you or anyone else in the city any good and you can be sure I'll give Vespasian his thirty percent. This isn't, strictly speaking, a military mission and I'm sure you can figure out what he'll do in the field for the remainder of the year.'

He folded his arms across his chest and said, 'yes, nothing because he'll be watching what will unfold in Rome.' He took a deep breath. 'You've been quite candid, Jud. Why do you want to go into the city? It can't be just to rescue Jude and his family!'

I knew he thought he got me but I just looked into his eyes. 'No. I want to rescue the Jesus Papers. You know as well as I do how important they are. I'll take Jude and his family if they want to go and if you don't care one way or the other.'

'Ahhh, yes, the Jesus Papers!' he sighed and sat back. 'So many have died for them.'

'Where we began our journey - yours and mine all those years ago!" He put his forearms on the table's edge for the first time but didn't touch the bags of money. 'So, you haven't changed. I've always wondered why you've helped us over the years.' He hesitated. 'Most people think you severed your connection with him on that day. And I'm sure it must have been very difficult for you over the years. Especially when he never contacted you as he did the others.'

I leaned back and thought, how does he know these things? 'So people have said. Has he you?'

'No.'

'Well, you could say my crucifixion has lasted longer than his. Jesus was my closest friend. Far closer than my brother ever was.

Jesus asked me to tell the Sanhedrin where he would be that night because he feared he couldn't go through with it by himself.' I felt I wanted to explain this more fully to Simon but then realized it wasn't the right time or place. So, I switched topics and said, 'the Papers aren't for me. I intend to turn them over to Matthew. He's already started writing about the Jesus we all knew.'

'I know. Our brothers in Antioch have been in as much trouble since the war as here.'

I nodded. 'And you know Matt: he's been writing about Jesus the man but there's so much that Matt - and everyone of us - missed on our own.'

Suddenly, Simon spoke more slowly and dreamily: 'so, you think the city will fall. Just as Jesus told us forty years ago. That we don't have a chance. That the Romans will take the Temple--'

I interrupted: 'Because they rejected him! You remember his saying that?' I suddenly stopped because I just realized he wasn't a Messianic Jew. But I wanted to be as honest as possible. 'I know I shouldn't say this, Si. But yes, it's the Babylonians all over again only this time I'm trying to help the Jesus followers in the Diaspora. Jerusalem has been as much their center as it has for other Jews.'

He smiled. 'And the Romans don't even know this,' he said.

I leaned my left forearm on the table. 'I didn't come to quibble with you. We've had our differences with Judaism just as Jesus did. But you and I can talk about them and he can't--'

'So, you want him to live as much as Matthew and John do?' he interrupted.

That told me he was wearying of my theorizing. 'And as much as Mark does,' I replied. 'Yes. And now that we're older I realize how insufficient our memory is. How our oral tradition based on secrecy isn't the best way. Paul's writings may be too skewed through himself to give us any sense of what the man was like, but even this quintessential Jew abandoned the oral tradition.'

'I give you that. But about Paul, how else could he be? He never knew him.'

'That's why I want to give the Jesus Papers to Matt. They will be for him what Peter was for Mark.'

'Why? Is this your atonement?'

He touched the nub of it and I considered telling him the truth; but decided not to: it was too personal and only between Jesus and me. So I said, 'I feel badly that so many don't know how to live in the world because they didn't have my experience with him. That's all there's to it.'

Simon didn't say anything; but then he half stood, gripped the edge of the table and scraped his stool backward; then he sat back down. 'We've gone our separate ways since the old days,' he said staring at me, 'but you never answered his call as others did.'

'You mean "as others said he did." If he did call, I didn't hear it,' I replied; and decided to take the chance: 'and you didn't either. Reception is always a problem for those who find it difficult to receive. Remember Thomas? And as for Jesus, he had his doubts about it too.'

Simon didn't answer; instead, he said, 'what I remember is he didn't help my people when we asked him to. He insisted on remaining aloof; going his own way and saying it wasn't what his father told him to do. Well, he wound up alone. And that's why I told Peter, Matthew and John what Jesus told us when they asked me for help.'

I nodded. (I didn't want to call him a liar; after all, how could I even know?) 'Well, all I can say is that you've helped me on many occasions. And I've tried to help you the only way I know how.' I gestured to the money. 'I think both of us understand that friendship is reciprocal.'

Simon slumped a little on his stool. 'I first realized how important friendship was to you when I saw how you were with Jesus. I figured then that as you were with him so you would be with me. And you have been. But I didn't expect you to be still loyal to his memory.'

'I like to feel we both are.'

Simon was silent for several moments, but then he said. 'How do you plan to enter the city?'

'The same way we did the last time we were all together.'

He smiled slightly: 'so, Jericho again?'

'Yes.'

'Do you intend using your real name?' he asked but added hastily, 'I ask because you probably don't know that thousands of Idumeans are with us now.'

It was my turn to smile. 'Perhaps it's our revenge for what Hyrcanus did to us.'

'In any case, you understand that I can't control that situation. But I might be able to help.' He thought a moment. 'I'll tell you what. Why don't we wait to see what happens in these next few months. I'll try to gauge their sequential relationship and when I think the opportunity arises I'll send you a name. No message. Just a scrap of paper with a name on it. You know my handwriting. How much lead time will you need and where shall I send it?'

'Send it to Marcus. Two or three months ahead of time if possible. I'll trust your judgment about the timing.'

Simon nodded and smiled. 'You can count on having the Temple gold because you're right: money doesn't mean as much as goods do in times like these.'

'I know. By the way, I brought seven wagons of provisions which are under the trees on the other side of hill. Take them and the animals. I think you'll find them more useful than that'-- I motioned to the bags as I stood up slowly, not wanting the shadows to come any closer, and held out my hand. 'Thank you, Simon. I only wish I could help you with something more than money, but the most valuable thing I have to give is my judgment about things. May I give some more?'

'Of course.'

'Vespasian's troops gave him his nickname and his political enemies call him the turtle derisively. But don't be fooled by it. He's the most methodical general I've ever known and he'll take the city eventually. Don't be there when he does.'

He stood up in turn and took my hand. 'Thank you. It's strange how what goes around in this world comes around. Keep your left hand against the wall going out and you'll eventually see the light.'

I remembered that scene for years afterward.

*

Nearly five months later, in late September 68, Marcus discovered a small piece of paper with a name written in the middle on it in small Hebrew letters – "John of Gischala October" - under the door of his office at the warehouse. Ti had warned him to expect such a thing and to immediately send it to him in Caesarea, Ti's main port for receiving communications from Rome. Marcus enclosed it with his business reports that he sent each week to Ti in Caesarea.

In mid-October, Titianus was again Judas dressed like any other Jew his age with a prayer shawl over his head leading a long line of carts and pack animals loaded with foodstuffs on the road from Jericho to Jerusalem, and to John of Gischala who commanded the Jewish defenders of Fort Antonia and the northeastern section of the city. Vespasian had ordered Aulus Sulpicianus, commander of the tenth legion to let them pass. They stopped within sight of the city's walls and made themselves highly visible so the guards on top could see them. Judas then walked slowly and alone to the city gate while waving a small pouch over his head. When within hearing range he shouted over and over, 'I have a message for John of Gischala.' As he drew near, the gate opened slightly and four men came out, their swords at the ready.

'Who are you and what do you want?' one asked.

'I'm Judas Iscariot and I have a message for John of Gischala. It's here in the bag.'

The talkative sword carrier took it and asked, 'how do you know him?'

'I'm a friend of Simon also from Gischala. John will know him because he wrote John's name to give to him. He'll know the signature.'

'If there's a reply, where can we find you?'

'Follow the Jericho road about a half-mile out. I'm camped there and you can't miss me. Tell him I have twenty cartloads of foodstuffs for him.'

Three days later, the talkative, sword-carrying man came to where I was camped with a message: 'come alone under your name.' The note was in Hebrew so I knew Simon must have told him who I was and what I wanted.

But that didn't make the venture easier or more pleasant.

'Only fifty percent of the going rate? To what do I owe such generosity?' John of Gischala sneered.

'For helping me to take the Jesus Papers out of the city.'

'We don't care a fig for your Jesus Papers.'

'I know. That's why I'm asking only half price for the provisions. The papers are only important to Jesus' followers.'

'Christians!' He spat out. 'We all know about you and your Jesus! And how he wouldn't join us! Not even the last time he came here when Barabbas tried to help him!'

'No, but the Romans didn't torture that out of him either.' I surprised myself by saying that.

The man's eyes smoldered; they were as intense as Jesus' had been on his last time here, but John's were far more dangerous. I forced myself not to shudder. The Zealot leaders thought they were winning because Nero's suicide and old Galba's succession gave them the false impression that the Romans were weakened by such confusion. But I knew they weren't.

'You and Alexander! Both renegades! How can you make war on your own people!' He stood up so abruptly that his chair fell backward and he stood there glaring at me. 'But then your reputation as a Great Betrayer says it all about you!' He stepped backward and suddenly his tone changed. 'We have thousands of Idumeans here, you know! And they've been waiting for this chance unlike you.'

I saw he was nearly crazy if he wasn't already and I knew it was best to try mollifying him.. 'It's more complicated than that,' I replied. 'I joined Jesus three years before the Romans crucified him and I'm afraid I've been corrupted by his ideas.'

He looked at me. Probably trying to decide whether to kill me or let me go. But my friend Simon was more experienced and outranked him. Besides, he had done equally dangerous things for a lot longer than John did, and they didn't make him crazy. I decided to try to shame him: 'I've known Simon a lot longer than you have and I know he volunteered to lead your second front. So, why didn't you volunteer?'

It worked. He backed down. 'He's one of our heroes, of course. All the young men want to be like him.'

Meaning not like you, I thought. 'And you, I'm sure!' I said. You remind me of how Simon was thirty years ago.' God! I'm shameless! I thought.

He didn't reply. But said, 'a third.'
'Done!' I replied.
'In coin, I presume?'
'Yes.'

'You know you'll have to re-cast it before you get back!'

'I know.'

So many hard, intense men. But such hard, intense times.

*

'We must leave quickly!' I nearly shouted to Jude and Achia, his wife. 'I must take the Jesus Papers to Antioch.' Their son had refused to leave the city.

'He's right,' Jude's wife, Achia, said and turned to me. 'How much time do we have?'

'Three days. Two is better. Power is shifting so rapidly among these factions that safety lies with the shorter estimates.'

I knew Jude's quandary: he disliked me as much as John of Ephesus did, but here I was trying to save his life. I'm sure he hated the situation and me all the more. 'All right,' she said.

'Don't pack much,' I said. 'No more than a bagful each. Speed is most important.'

'You're saying if the Zealots don't kill us the Romans will?' It was one of Jude's stupid intellectual game questions.

'Or the sicarii. You've got to get over thinking the old days will last forever.' I sat back and looked at Achia, hoping she didn't intuit my feeling sorry for her.

'I've been telling him this for years. But not even James' assassination woke him up.' She, too, sat back. 'You think we can get to Antioch all right?'

'We'll take the old caravan routes along the King's Highway. I know them like the back of my hand and the Arabs know me. They'll hide us if we need to.'

'So we won't go near the Romans?' It was a question masquerading as a statement. 'Not west? Or by sea?'

'No. And not west of Lake Gulah. We'll stay east, go through Damascus and on up. Mingle with the overland crowds. Once near Antioch we'll be all right. I know the Legate.'

'I don't know how you do it.' She examined her hands in her lap and thought how different he was from Jude: not the intellectual purist; much more open minded about things and probably far easier to live with. And here he is: offering a diminishing light in a rapidly darkening world.

*

'You couldn't have picked a better time to get Jude and Achia and the papers out, Jud. How did you choose it? Or was it a divine insight?'

We were in the garden at Aaron's house in Antioch in late October 68 with Matthew, Aaron, Hero and Jude. Linus, Cletus and Clement had arrived from Rome a week ago with the latest news and also told us what Sol and Vol were doing. I knew I had to be careful around them because the information I received from Mucianus and Publix's letters was more accurate and recent. So I decided to lie because I didn't want to give Simon away. 'When the Zealots started going into the city during the summer to flee Vespasian,' I said, 'I began preparing things in a staging area near Jericho. Then, after we received news about Nero's suicide I figured the Zealots would attack the last of old priest cast--'

'Ananus?'

'Ananus. And I figured the factions would fight each other for leadership against the Romans. It was as if Jesus opened the door of opportunity.'

'We'll always be grateful, Jud.' Matthew said. 'I never could have done it.' He looked me in the eyes.

'Well, I'm still the sunny side of sixty,' I replied and smiled. 'But I'm afraid my adventures like that are coming to an end.'

'Well, I'm glad the Papers and you are here,' Linus said and nodded to Matthew and Jude. 'We have our work cut out for us in Rome. You know what the 'Jews for Rome' are doing, don't you?'

'Yes, and we need to counter them!' Matthew replied.

'They're banking on Jerusalem's fall,' Cletus said, 'so they can break away from the Sanhedrin and create their new one linked up with Rome's imperium.'

'And lead our Diaspora in following it!' Clement said too loudly. Judas noticed that he always seemed disgusted at something.

'Let's not forget that Jerusalem's fall means our church's fall,' Matthew added quietly.

'Why?' I asked, and everyone looked at me. 'Why should it? Why should Jesus be thought historical, rooted in Jerusalem and past? Isn't what happened in Galilee important?'

'What do you mean?' Jude asked.

'There are two things I don't understand about all this. First is the weight you've always placed on having the church centered in Jerusalem. Jesus spent more time outside the city than inside it. The other thing is all the stuff that's been written about how to follow Jesus as if there's a prescribed way. They all boil down to living life as he did. But how can we? As mere men, I mean. We have so many letters and epistles I can't keep up with them all. But you know what we don't have?' He saw the blank looks on their faces. 'We don't have anything about his life. He was as much of a man as we are. Isn't that right, Matt?'

'Yes, but you can't write his story because no one would believe you,' Silence followed Clement's remark; but I thought he was correct.

I looked at him, then Matthew and said, 'I can't argue with that.' I hesitated but then said, 'I think you should write about Jesus' life, Matt, not just the meaning of his life. That's the real issue.'

'The real issue?' Matt asked reluctantly.

'The real issue is getting your story straight. Where did the resurrected Jesus meet you? In Galilee or Jerusalem? And what happened to Peter after he left the High Priest's house? Did he go to the Essenes?'

Matthew sat bolt upright. 'What are you saying?' he asked angrily. 'You weren't there! Did you hear the call?'

'What call? The one that you or Peter or John or all three of you invented? Made up so everyone could understand the church's development better in opposition to the orthos? And to get stupids like Jesus' brother to go along because of the blood lineage and royalty and all that stuff that appeals to dummies? The Romans have been doing that for generations! But even they distinguish truth from history!' I looked at them. Only Clement was smiling. He knew!

'You would have us let go of our Jerusalem roots? Deny our Hebrew heritage?' Matthew asked. His first intelligent question, I thought.

'I mean use Paul's example. Don't let Jerusalem imprison your minds! Let me ask you. Isn't Jerusalem where you all wound up? Our 'roots,' as you call them are everywhere except' - I almost shouted this word – 'Jerusalem! And I won't be surprised if someone starts saying Rome because of Peter working there!' I stopped and a silence descended on us. Then I looked at Matthew and said, 'you know perfectly well that Jesus considered me his best friend! Who was a better one?' And then I did an unforgivable thing: I said to him, 'how can John claim to have been such a good, such a beloved disciple when he's been such a terrible father?' Now Matthew knew that I knew John's story; and I knew if John were present he would hate me for the rest of our lives.

You could've heard a denarii drop – even a mile away. 'You have to be the most superficial person in the world,' Jude said to me. 'Your highest concern is with friendship. You think that's soooo deep! Well, how superficial can you be? You crave that level of worldly physical and social relations because you're completely devoid of spirituality.'

That's rich! I thought. After he and James led his family's opposition to Jesus' ministry when he was alive? His smoldering eyes reminded me of John of Gishchala's, only smaller and beadier. Probably because he didn't have John's vision. 'I don't think you've ever had a spiritual moment in your life!' Jude continued. 'And your concern about money says it all! I bet you even took money from their common purse!'

Snakes in the room! You could feel their venom in the air. And I was sorry for it. I didn't want it to end this way. So, I said, 'Jude, whatever happened between us has always been on your side of the table; not mine.' I expected - and hoped - everyone would understand the differences between givers and receivers.

But silence fell on us like a humid cloud from the west. Finally, Matthew said, 'I think I understand you better now, Judas. I've never told you this, but I resented you for a long time because you read my accounts better than I did and upside down and from the other side of the table that time. Do you remember?'

'Yes.'

'Well, it took me a long time to get over that. I hated people who were better than me at what I was good at; and it was easy for me to misunderstand the word 'betray' that people said about you. You see, Jesus never told any of us what the two of you talked about and, of course, you didn't either. I'm afraid I took the easy way out and simply went along with what everybody else thought.' He paused. 'I'm sorry, Judas.'

I nodded to him. 'Forgiven. Life is difficult for all of us.' To myself I said, please bless Matthew, Jesus.

*

Three days later, Hero and I were walking along the Orontes river near our home in Daphne south of Antioch and I knew I had a week and a half or two to help him understand the truth of what happened between Jesus and me before I returned to Rome.

'I followed his lead, you see,' I said. 'I always did in these matters. His mind was made up and I knew he was testing my friendship by asking me to help him. He wanted to prevent his human and sinful nature from stopping his spiritual good one from determining his action and didn't think he could on his own.'

'But Peter didn't explain it that way!'

'No. He wouldn't because he didn't know about it! But the curious thing is that he was there. It happened during a crisis. Jesus was depressed if not despondent over why people weren't listening to him. The numbers of supporters and followers were declining and we had just returned from preaching to the Gentiles in Tyre and Sidon; but that wasn't even as successful as a he hoped. That's when he had this crisis.'

'What kind of crisis? Did he become ill?'

'No. Just quiet. But he was bothered by something and we were walking along when, out of the blue, he asked some of the disciples who they thought he was. Put yourself in their place! Here's a man who's been your teacher who all of a sudden asks you who you think he is! Wouldn't you think it's crazy?'

'Did he ask you?

'No. But he asked Peter and when dunderhead said our messiah, Jesus stopped in his tracks and changed completely! He had what those Greeks in Tyre called a Eureka moment! Remember? Then he began saying he was the savior of the Jews and a second Moses who would save the Jews by making them the light to the Gentiles. The promised land was to be his new kingdom of God for everyone and he said Peter was to be the rock on which his church was founded.'

Hero felt he needed to pause; too much was being thrown at him all at once. 'Is that when he started calling himself the Son of God?'

'No, no. That's from <u>Exodus</u> when God told Moses he will be like God to his brother and his people and later says each one of us are sacred to him.' He turned to face Hero. 'You see, he didn't have his ministry planned out from the beginning. It was revealed to him as he lived.'

'He winged it, so to speak? Was he was aware of it? Of his changes, I mean?'

'Yes. That's why he asked me to help him.'

Hero replied, almost as an afterthought, 'so, he was searching for his identity.'

'We all do whether we know it or not. But I think that's when he found his.'

29

WHAT can I say about what followed? I've already said, never say never. But my two week stay in Antioch stretched into a month for several reasons: one was to patch things up with Matthew and Jude for Hero's sake. Although twenty nine now, he was still innocent in the world and I worried about him in ways that I didn't about Marcus. And my stay worked - sort of - at least to the point where peace plastered over any acrimony between us, even though it seemed an uneasy one on occasion.

The other thing was that Vespasian stopped attacking the Jews because he had thrown his own helmet in the ring for the emperorship. 'Why not?' one wag quipped, 'every legion commander seems to be doing it!'

But Vespasian had advantages the other wannabe emperors didn't: he had thirteen legions, all concentrated in the east and under the commands of his two loyal friends, Alexander and Mucianus and everyone they commanded. He may have been furthest from Rome, but his military supporters were concentrated – and in the east where Rome's riches and future lay.

I tried to explain this to Matthew and Jude in late July 69 when Vespasian announced his bid. 'He's already formulated his siege plan for Jerusalem,' I told them, 'and this is just another for the empire. All his son needs to do is follow his script, so it's only a matter of time before the Roman noose strangles Jerusalem.' Not everyone in Aaron's front room believed me or wanted to; but finally they did when I pointed out the realities of our circumstances. I remembered Jesus always encouraging me to do that.

'But what if Vespasian succeeds! Won't he call off the siege and stay in Rome?' Matthew asked.

Grasping at straws in the wind, I thought; but keep it simple and don't reveal too much, I cautioned myself. These people are simple and don't know the world. So I said in a softer voice, 'I don't think so, Matt. He's from a relatively new and undistinguished family and they hate him for living with his common law wife. The only thing he has going for him is the military. If he does get it, he'll leave immediately to consolidate his power there. If he fails, a new commander will probably try to take Jerusalem. I'm banking on his succeeding and that's why I think Titus will crush Jerusalem as soon as possible. It's all laid out for him.' (I didn't mention my information about conditions in Rome and the west came from Publix's latest despatches.)

'So, it's really his plan; Titus is simply its executioner?' Aaron half-asked.

'But I thought Titus was young and inexperienced!' Hero added.

I looked at them and excused them for not understanding because they were the younger generation and was tempted to make of the analogy of Jesus as Son to the Father; but didn't. 'Young yes but inexperienced no. He's spent his life training for this job; and he'll be ruthless about it. And Alexander's here to make sure he does. He's Vespasian's right hand man but Titus is his blood.' I paused, not wishing to appear as a know-it-all. 'You have to remember that if Vespasian succeeds as emperor, the war becomes vitally political and crucial to him and his reign. That's why Titus will have to crush Jerusalem completely and quickly.'

Jude looked at me. 'You're saying the war ceases to be military and becomes political?' He never understood me very well and consequently didn't trust me. And I, it must be admitted, never understood people like that.

'Yes,' I replied.

'Then what will we do when our center is lost?' Matthew asked.

Judas had always liked Matthew's honesty and efforts to cope with the world; but there it was again. That Jerusalem as the center business. 'What I think we should do is get rid of the Sionist disease.' I said.

They blinked. Several times. 'What do you mean?' Jude asked.

'God's chosen people wandered around for a long time after coming out of Egypt. They carried the Ark and lived in tents. Then someone said we need priests, a permanent place to settle, a house for God to live in, and a king to rule over us. Presto! Mount Sion was born. I know this didn't happen overnight. But my point is that we fixed God in place! That's what I mean. It will be deadly if we fix Christianity in a place. The equivalent of Mount Sion that we call Jerusalem.' They stared at me and I could tell they strained to keep their mouths closed. So I said, 'Jude, since you were the last head of the church there, what do you think? Should Antioch become the new center? Or Rome? Or Ephesus where John is?'

'I don't know, to tell you the truth.' Jude responded. 'It's so very different here. So many more Gentiles and Roman power--'

'Who're our bitter enemies!' Aaron nearly shouted. 'The Gentiles hate us for being Jews and the Syrians want to push us into a ghetto like Alexandria's!'

'But the fact remains that if we're to get along we've got to go along,' I replied. 'And, for what it's worth, the same applies in Rome.'

After a brief silence, Jude said, rather quietly, 'I don't think you should have anything to say about our future, Judas. You and the others who didn't answer Jesus' call after his crucifixion haven't suffered with us during the past forty years.' His voice grew louder. 'Now look at you! You dressed like a Jew in Jerusalem but now I'm looking at a Roman! You've turned your back on us and don't deserve a voice in our council!' A pigeon feather falling to the floor would have made a tremendous noise, but Jude had picked his timing perfectly: he knew no one else in the room would challenge him on this.

I looked at Jude and nodded. 'You're right, of course. I haven't been with you.'

Jude glared at me, hoping for another argument I was sure. 'You don't get it, do you? You were never with us even when your body was. Didn't Jesus say as much, Matt?'

Matthew didn't reply. Nor did I.

'Do you really think we should be beholden to you because you once acted as a brother to my brother? These people' – he gestured in a sweeping arc – 'accepted me because I became one of them! Unlike yourself.' He stood up and raised himself as high as he could. 'Or do you think I owe you for saving me from mere death?' he sneered. 'It comes to us all! And will to you as well.' He turned and walked out.

'I have no rebuttal for him,' I said to those who remained. 'I did what I did for the Jesus Papers. So you all can read them and see what Jesus really said and meant; not what Paul or James or Mark or Barnabas or even John says he did!' With that, I got up and left.

Matthew disliked confrontations, was embarrassed by them and tried to de-fuse them whenever they threatened the equanimity of the group he was in. So he switched the subject. 'What do all of you hear about Mark's new Gospel? He's supposed to be writing if from Peter's sermons that he gave in Rome. What do you think, Hero?'

Matthew's tactic worked. But what Hero replied didn't. 'I hear it follows the sequence of his lectures but Mark goes into his life much more because he wants his reader to see Jesus was as much a person as he was the Son of God.'

'Is it true that your father never told you much about Jesus?' Clement asked, acerbically.

'He told me some things. The basics of what all of you did but he never said much about his family or what happened at the crucifixion. He said he left Jerusalem after the Romans took Jesus from the Sanhedrin.'

Matthew nodded. 'That's my understanding of what Judas did.' After a moment he said, 'but I worry about what the story doesn't mention. Peter was always a bit ambivalent about our Hebrew traditions and Jesus knew it. That's why he called him Peter instead of his real name.

*

Joshua was six years old when his older brother, Stephen, was stoned in Jerusalem thirty five years ago, and thirty two when he took over the leadership of his father's -Samuel's - Christian Separatists group after his father's mysterious assassination nine years ago. Samuel's tag, 'Christian,' that he gave to the Jesus Jews in Antioch in the mid-forties stuck and became widely used over the past twenty years, and he never ceased drilling it into Joshua's head that if the Jesus Jews could be persuaded to become fully Christian powder-blue sash emblazoned with two bright red letters - CS - prominently displayed in front and break from the Jews, he could collect their tithes instead of the Sanhedrin. It was just business, Joshua remembered him saying, like any other kind of business. And if you're attentive and patient it's just a matter of time for it to happen. But neither his father nor he, could fully resolve the clashes among the Christians over their identity with Jesus' Hebraic traditions. Until the Jewish War.

Even before the rebellion, Joshua was presented with a fresh opportunity to push for separation under his exclusive leadership when Paul foolishly returned to Jerusalem, was arrested and subsequently transferred to Rome. It ended his expansionary efforts in Asia Minor and Europe with Titus; and Titus was no Paul. Joshua quickly circumscribed (he smiled to himself whenever he used this word, knowing he had to be careful spelling it) his effort by encouraging his evangelism to Crete which buried – in Joshua's sense – him on the island. But it was the war that vastly expanded the scale of Joshua's opportunities when Jews throughout the empire were forced to choose between loyalty to the Roman state or continue their identity as a Jewish sect to a nation in rebellion. Most sought to refuge in an ill-defined somewhere between the two extremes; but Antioch became an exaggerated version of other Jewish centers in the Diaspora because of its proximity to the rebellion. Rome never forgot that it's future lay as its chief outpost pointed eastward. Consequently, Syrian and Arab enemies of Israel used the war to asserted their identity with Rome by attacking Jews.

Joshua's insight in such a context was inspired: 'save the Christians!' Not 'save the Jesus Jews or the Jesus Jews as a remnant of Judaism,' but save the Christians as a separate religion; people who identified themselves as followers of a leader despised and rejected by the Jews! Ironically, Jews everywhere in the Diaspora now had a choice: remain identified with the Judaism at war with Rome, or become Christians as secret 'Jesus Jews.' Defections from synagogues began everywhere but were most severe in Matthew's Antioch and Mark's Alexandria.

Changed circumstances presented this opportunity to Joshua, but he also had a more refined aesthetic sense of identity than his father: Where Samuel opposed the white on white, JC monogrammed dress identity of the Jesus Jews on the grounds of its blandness - 'it won't appeal to Greeks' he was heard to say - Joshua adopted a far more colorful one for the Separatists: an all-white toga with a four-inch, and running diagonally downward, right to left across the chest. In 67, after Vespasian assumed command of the army from Gallus, it was estimated that two thousand were seen in Antioch alone; and Joshua had great hopes for future sales.

It seemed a brilliant idea; until it attracted every hater of Christian as well as Jewish who thought the two were synonymous and didn't care if they weren't. Attacks on them increased. But the turning point came in the spring when the word 'arsonists' migrated from Rome to Antioch as a synonym for Christian. Governor Mucianus sent Roman troops directly to Joshua's warehouse. Stop it tomorrow, they ordered, or we will! That's when Joshua decided to hold this conference of his followers in his warehouse office.

'So, it didn't work! All right! All right! We'll think of something else! How we dress isn't the end of the world!' Joshua finished his opening speech.

'I have an idea.'

Joshua looked at him. 'Let's not wait until tomorrow for it, Micah.'

'Why are we confining ourselves to Antioch? Why aren't we expanding to other seaports?'

Joshua looked confused and then around the table to see if there was interest on the faces of his investors, and replied, 'why don't you explain your idea more fully.'

'I think we should set up a branch of the CS in Rome. All of us have connections there and we all know that Solomon and Volumnus are playing a losing game, trying to replace the Sanhedrin in world Jewry. All those old ways will end when the Romans smash Jerusalem next year and--'

'And it looks like they will!' Jeremiah was young and rich and respect for his father mandated their forbearance of such outbursts.

'As I was saying,' continued Micah, 'we should set up a cell of ours there to act against John and Matthew here and Sol and Vol there.'

Heads nodded and murmurs of approbation told Joshua that there had been talk about this before. 'Who did you have in mind to go there?'

Most of the others sat back in their chairs but two of them pointed to the somber looking man in black and purple and Micah replied, 'Abner.'

*

'Hello, Ti, do you have a minute to talk?'

'Of course,' I replied, looking at Matthew's silhouette in the doorway. It was late, I wanted to go to bed and prepare for tomorrow which I knew was going to be busy; but he had obviously waited up for me and had something important on his mind. So, I followed him into his study before going hom.

'I'm worried about the situation here. Things are bad enough now, but if Titus spends the winter here, it will get worst. Our enemies will try to get at us through him.' I waited. 'I could use Hero's help.'

I nodded. Nothing would make me happier. Not only would I have Hero in more trustworthy hands but Matthew assertion of a greater direction of the church as a whole pleased me. 'I think your idea is a good one. How can I help?'

*

Titianus liked Antioch and liked Matthew but was glad to get away from the relentless religious discussions (he sometimes called them religious dissensions) and felt they didn't solve anything for him. Besides, he never found any profound satisfaction in them. They were, as he once said to Hero, too vague and ethereal for him.

Not to me!, Hero replied.

And Judas quickly retorted, I didn't say they were! I only meant they seem so to me.

We can still be friends and I can still love you as my son even if we're different, can't we?

There were times after his return from India that he thought he said that a lot. He preferred the give and take of business talk; if you're going to spend time and energy arguing and putting on acts and airs then I want something for my efforts, he rationalized. And now, at age sixty, he enjoyed the process even more than the result because Marcus played the more active role in the meetings.

And Amos and Ruth needed consideration. They were retired, and elderly now and without grandchildren except for Hero. Just two days ago, he had to curtail his visit with them because he and Marcus had to meet with a consortium of his business partners which he felt bad about it. Amos protested that he understood: sure, everyone in the eastern trade wants to discuss strategies now that the end of the revolt is in sight. But Ti saw, for the first time, that Amos didn't care as much about business as he once did. And it dawned on him that twenty years from now he won't either. Hero nearby would be a comfort to them.

Ti was glad to have Marcus with him at the meeting of the consortium. He was thirty two now and it was time for him to meet his older peers and they to meet him. One more big step in the path of independent life in international trade; but these were dangerous times and many things could go wrong. He kept coming back to the contrast between the two: Hero was older too, of course; but his sensitivity and innocence wasn't. His spiritual life still mattered most to him. And he felt a twinge of guilt for bringing the poisonous Jude into his vicinity! Ti couldn't help wondering whether he put him at risk by supporting his staying in Antioch.

Such thoughts preoccupied him while walking toward the meeting in his warehouse office that he nearly stumbled into a young, well-groomed Roman who said, 'hello, dad! Good to see you!' Marcus' confident air jolted him back out of his mind into the world and a big smile appeared on his face.

'And it's good to see you, son! Did you have a good passage?'

'As smooth as honeyed baklava. They're all here, but I thought it best to meet you out here first so you can introduce me. I don't want to seem pushy on the first date.'

Ti grinned, feeling proud of him. Putting his arm around his shoulders, they walked into the meeting room where they saw five men - two Jews, two Romans and one enormously large Greek wearing what looked like a very elaborate, finely woven and colorful tent - seated around a large table.

Marcus whispered 'they look so serious' as they entered and Ti removed his arm from Marcus' shoulders and said, 'gentlemen, I want you to meet Marcus my son, partner and successor.'

After introductions, father and son sat down and the oldest man present – a withered, emaciated and pale colored Jew who looked like he wouldn't survive the day, asked: 'without divulging any secrets, Ti, how do you think trade will respond to the end of the war?'

Ti smiled. Of course, he wanted to hear secrets! Obadiah didn't get to be eighty three by being careless and inattentive! But he thought: will I? 'I think we'll have a rush of trade because of pent-up demand. But I expect prices to fall after that initial rush. Demand should be quite high at first and I intend to sell for cash only. I'm not going to sell on credit because—'

Wheezing, old, full bearded Eleazar, who dominated the through-trade of eastern goods to Spain and Gaul interrupted: 'in my opinion, we'll have increasing prosperity for the next decade because Vespasian's first concern will be with those legions and rebellious natives in the north. He'll need to bring both under greater control so he'll keep the legions here at maintenance levels.'

'Vespasian? Did I hear you say Vespasian? Perhaps you have some inside information you might share?' asked Ahab, thin to the point of emaciation which he said was caused by vegetarian diet his doctors put him on; but everyone joked it still didn't temper his greed.

'He now has all the eastern legions who are mainly Italian,' Aulus replied. 'They are his political *testudo*. When it moves west the others - especially those Germans - will flee or acknowledge his superiority and I think it'll be the latter.' Although Ti had been selling goods quite profitably to the military he could never figure out where Aulus got his information from and had given up trying. Business partners were not necessarily deep friends.

'I think you're right. Vitellius' support isn't reliable and they'll give way if that madman, Primus, backs Vespasian.' Fabius, who dominated the Aegean seaports in the trade, said. Ti liked him; and even toyed with the idea years ago that he should ask him to take on Marc as an apprenctice.

'So the vital question is,' Obadiah croaked, 'who has the military power?'

Ti broke the silence: 'the empire is the military power. That hasn't always been the case but I think will be so from now on.' No one spoke for a moment. So he asked, asked, 'what's your opinion, Aul?

Aulus leaned forward. 'The way I see it, we're all in the eastern trade together and' should help one another by pooling information. There's more than enough for all of us. I agree that the military is the backbone of the empire and as it prospers so does the empire.' Then he looked directly at Ti and asked, 'do you think that Vespasian will then expand east?'

Ti knew they were all aware he spent much of time in Vespasian's headquarters and he saw how Aulus parried his thrust and turned it back on him. So he answered, 'he won't immediately. I agree that he'll tighten up and secure his control over the entire army starting in the north and west and concentrate on those legions which supported his rivals. But only then will he turn his attention back to the east.'

'But that could take years,' said Xerses, the big Greek who dominated the trade to Archadia, 'which means we must have peace during that time if we're to make any money.'

'And how can we predict what the Parthians will do?' Fabius said. 'I hear Vologases has been ill on and off. And who knows who his successor will be if he dies?'

Marcus looked at Ti who was deliberately avoiding his eyes.

'You're right,' Ti said. 'That would upset the business. But I wouldn't worry about it at this stage.'

'So, the consensus is that trade will be rushed before it bottoms out right after the war and then slowly rise over several years if Vespasian succeeds? Is that what I'm hearing?' Eleazar asked, looking around the table. When he saw their heads nodding in general assent he said, 'well, then I guess there's only one other question to be decided.' He stopped.

'What's that?' Fabius asked.

'How much money does Vespasian need to solidify his control and what sort of concessions can we expect?'

*

When Ti wrote to Governor Mucianus that evening asking for an audience in two days he also mentioned he wanted to bring and introduce his son Marcus.

But he had no idea what he was getting into. He couldn't have known that circumstances beyond his control had changed again and this time for the worse. So, Mucianus was not in his usual social mood when Ti and Marcus arrived.

'I'm sorry to appear rushed, but events have pushed further and faster than I anticipated since I saw you last, Ti.' He turned to Marcus. 'I'm terribly sorry about this, but I must ask Ti to do something for me that's dangerous but very important and must be done in a hurry.' He turned to Ti. 'It might be best that we talk in private.'

'Marcus is my son, partner and successor, Licinius. He's also Senator Publix' only son. His son-in-law, in fact.' He emphasized the word 'only' and paused to let it sink in. 'I think it's safe to say anything you want to me in front of him.'

'All right,' Mucianus replied. 'Vitellius is in Rome and of course consolidating his power--'

Ti interrupted: 'Publix wrote me that the Senate has recognized him as emperor!'

'Yes. But legal niceties are not power.' He looked down, as if he didn't want to talk about what he was going to say. 'I'm afraid we must move more quickly than I anticipated.' Now, he looked across his desk steadily at Ti and said, 'I'm leaving for Rome next week with legions that I've had to scrape together and I need an urgent favor from you.' He paused.

And Ti asked, 'how can I help?'

'I want you to leave immediately – I mean tomorrow - and go to General Antonius Primus on the Danube. I know you don't know him, but I'll give you all the necessary papers you'll need. You must - and I mean *must* - convince him to support Vespasian and march immediately on Rome.'

Ti took a deep breath. He'd never been involved so directly with the military before. '*Convince him*? To publicly acknowledge his connection with Vespasian before Vitellius can settle in? That's a big step for Primus – or any man - to take.'

'Yes. But Primus is a risk taker and his support will be decisive because whoever controls Rome will be emperor.'

'So you want him there first. I mean, before you get there.' He nodded. 'Which means you must be marching your troops overland.'

Musianus was surprised by Ti's quickness. 'Yes. Along the Via Egnatia. It'll be long and laborious but we must arrive there intact.'

He means concentrated, Ti thought. 'So you can hold Rome for Vespasian. Will he leave from Caesarea?'

'No. He's in Alexandria and has already stopped the grain shipments to Rome. Which is one more reason why I must get there quickly.' He stopped talking a moment and then asked, 'any more questions?'

'No. Just some specific directions where I can find General Primus.'

Musianus stared at him for a minute. 'First I need to say something about him. You're not used to dealing with commanders on the raw frontier like him. You won't find him sitting around his tent planning things like Vespasian does or Corbulo did. Primus is used to operating in the field as Titus does and he's twenty years younger than Vespasian.' Then Licinius stood up and began pacing in front of them. 'Civilians aren't used to dealing with men like him and you don't have time to get used to it. It's enough for you to know that his men love him as a comrade and will do anything for him. He sleeps in the field with them and he's a fighting general in a way that Vespasian - and even Titus, isn't. He can muster probably thirty thousand men which are not many, but they have the impact of a hundred thousand because he leads them. He's like Alexander was in the old days andvital to our support for Vespasian now that it's coming to the fighting stage. I'll bring at least that many but you should think of Primus as the spearhead of our operation.' He turned to Marcus. 'If I were you, I would keep my family out of Rome until things settle down.' He looked back at Ti. 'In fact, this would be a good time for your families to winter in Pompeii. I know you keep a villa there.' He returned to his chair and sat down which signaled the meeting was over and father and son stood up. But Musianus looked up at Marcus and said, 'I'm glad we met. I'm just sorry I've been so pressured by these events.'

Marcus looked at him and said. 'Nevertheless, I'm glad to have met you, too. After Vespasian has settled in I'll be glad to help you in any way I can.'

'Thank you,' Licinius replied. 'Remember what I said about Rome,' and thought, a chip off the old block.

After they left and were in their litter returning home, Ti said 'I think I'll return here after seeing Primus. It shouldn't take more than two or three weeks . But you go to Rome immediately and move everyone out of harm's way. But don't alarm them.'

'Take Publix to Pompeii too?'

'Yes. I'll stay here for two or three weeks after I return to write to Mal and prep for a big spring trade. Then I'll return to Titus' headquarters. I don't want to write you until I return here.'

'Then you expect Vespasian to succeed.'

'Yes.'

PART FOUR

FULFILLMENTS

30

SWARTHY, sixty year old Vespasian looked up and thanked Neptune, Mars, Fortuna, Fides, Felicitas and several others; then he stopped and shook his head. Sometimes he wondered how he could remember them all and thought maybe – but just maybe – the Jews are right.

It was the eleventh day of July 70; the blue sky was brilliant, a back wind drove his ship forward through a relatively calm sea; everything felt right and all he and Titus needed was another month or possibly two. The new emperor looked over the rail of his warship enroute along the coast of northern Africa from Alexandria to Rome via Carthage. Yes, he thought, July is definitely the best month for sailing. And I'll be emperor at sixty one; in time for a new dynasty. We made it. Pound away at them while I'm at Rome, he remembered, thumping his eldest son's chest and saying: "engage every day and kill everyone who offers resistance. We need a crushing defeat to consolidate our power." He pursed his lips.

But the bigger battle lay ahead. The old snobs never liked us. Men on the make, they called us, brawlers and opportunists. Bootstrappers. They did things the social way, behind closed doors out of public sight; and never accepted Caenis. Unforgiveable. But they'll have to now. I have the office and the army, and know how to use them. He looked over the bow and smiled. Bootstrappers win.

He paced to the other side of the ship. Give them order and prosperity and stability and power will follow naturally. Start with those northern and western legions that supported Galba and Vitellius and employ them where victories are not possible but only probable. War contracts and rebuilding programs. Mucianus is good at that and no one has been more loyal than he after we came to our understanding. He's my right hand man.

And Titus. I made it clear: Jerusalem's fall is crucial and must be quick. The timetable is two months; and don't worry over the losses.
You'll be hated regardless because I want you to succeed me. They're tired of chaos. They just don't know it.

While Vespasian was enroute to Rome, Licinius Mucianus, still technically governor of Syria but de facto ruler of Rome for the previous six months, stood on the Praetorian General's portico overlooking the city from the northeast. An arrogant descendent of impeccable family lineage who qualified as one of Vespy's snobs was a maverick; a realist more like Senator Publix than the brash Titianus or certainly the republican diehards he grew up with. Times were changing and he pegged Vespasian as a crude upstart with the quick wit and relentless drive of the peasant for survival.

He didn't like him. But after many clashes and confronted by the Jewish rebellion, he saw the benefits of working with him. Beyond enrichment: Vespasian fit the new times. He wasn't afraid to declare for the emperorship six months ago, a real life or death decision. And after the shock of his winning, he thought, I could help him reshape Rome after Nero; starting with the stability we need. He'll want to secure the army, mop up the last of the opposition and secure his son's succession. I know what people like him want. He's like Titianus but closer to one of us in his origins.

Licinius sighed, turned and walked into in office, thinking it time to map out what needed to be done. So many new men and all so competent. He smiled: just remember to sift the competent from the greedy and merely ambitious.

'Gnaeus,' he shouted.

'Yes, sir.' the aide replied as he entered the room.

'Have you finished that list of Senators with my notes about them? The emperor will want to see it first thing.'

'It's nearly finished, sir. This is what we have so far and I'll have the last scroll to you this afternoon.' He hesitated. 'I thought he wasn't due until the day after tomorrow, sir.'

Mucianus, walked back to his desk. 'He doesn't like to waste time. Things must be ready for him so he can act quickly. Have you finished the report on Civilius yet?'

'Just about, sir. I'll have it for you within two hours. He's clearly backtracking and not going to pursue his Gallic empire now that the Jewish war is nearly over.'

Mucianus nodded and muttered, 'I wish it were as easy in the north as it is in the east. There's so many tribes up there!'

'Yes, sir,' Gnaeus said and left him examining the proscription lists on the table. It was a long one.

*

'We should all worry about the direction our Christian truth is going in,' Gideon began his speech, surveying the large crowd many of whom were wearing his white tunics with the letters CS embroidered in bright red on their left breasts. He knew this speech would make or break him and that Joshua sat in disguise in the back row.

'You all know the Jerusalem church is in shambles! Peter, Paul, James and Mark are all gone! Who is left? John in Ephesus and Matthew in Antioch! Old men who misremember what Jesus told them! But I know what Jesus wants! I know from Jesus and Paul who, together with Joshua's father before he was cut down so cruelly by hand of an assassin, goads me on to fight the Jewish philosophy of the old Sanhedrin! I've fought their priestly, sacrificial and sacerdotal ways! their love of hierarchy and rigidity! their precious Temple! And who taught me that? Who gave me the confidence to? Who stood at my side while my fellow followers fell right and left by the wayside?'

'Jesus!' shouted several white tunics who jumped to their feet with their right arms raised. Unbelieving observers would think they were well orchestrated.

'That's right, brothers! He's been my protection through it all! And Jesus will be yours if you accept him.'

'Tell it, Gideon! Tell us the truth!'

'Look at me! My hairs have grown thin in his service! But my mind and spirit will never be quenched! They will never succeed in denying that Jesus was the Son of God as long as I can draw a breath!'

The room erupted into clapping and shouting, foot stomping and the crying out of hosannas. Gideon held both hands up, palms facing the young men. 'It is not me you should praise, it is Jesus! Jesus who walks with me, who has been my best friend, my Lord and God! He has never failed me!' He looked up then at the back wall and saw Joshua smile and nod.

Again, the room erupted and applause was heard this time. 'But danger prowls our Antioch! It lurks behind closed doors and in darkened cellars! It's the voice of mortal men who diminish the Godhood of Jesus! Who says 'yes, he was a good man. But that's all; he wasn't the son of man any more than he was the son of God! Jesus was merely another Jew; just another one of a long line of men who tried to save the faith of their fathers! Who tried to prevent the reality of what has happened to Jerusalem! No, I tell you! He was more than that! He was even more than a man! He was the Son of God!'

This time the young men in the audience stood shouting on their chairs and two or three danced in the aisle. Joshua let it go on awhile before he raised his hands and said, 'I've invited you here because it's time we establish a new group, Jesus is God, to preach Jesus' message to all people, to the people of all nations. Jesus didn't come to merely save Jews! He came to save all peoples regardless of their blood! And beyond the confines which the so-called apostles tried to establish in Jerusalem or what Matthew and John preach?'

A frenzy broke out! Chants of 'Beyond Blood!' began and men marched from the back to the front along the walls spearing the air with their fists while Gideon let it run its course while he organized his helpers behind him. When the audience grew silent, he announced he had scrolls for those to sign who believed in Jesus, the Son of God; but then he stopped for questions. 'No,' he answered the first one, 'Jesus was not merely the Messiah, as some' - he deliberately didn't use Matthew's name – 'were saying, but was the Son of God and' – he deliberately strung the silence out – 'the Messiah for all people!' At the end of the evening he had more people than there were in the room signed up and he promised to bring more next time.

'So there will be a next time?' One white tunic asked.

'God's work is never done,' he replied gravely: and he waited until he had safely gotten into his curtained litter to smile.

*

When I was growing up near Beersheba, long before meeting Jesus, I discovered two things about myself. One was that I wasn't one with nature; why? because more changes occurred in the world outside myself that were different from those within me; and that I could only then react to them. I first discovered this when I had been away from Idumea for a long time and then returned to find it very different. Why did that happen? Why couldn't I go home again? Then, after thinking about the Negeb, I asked myself why would anyone ever want to return there? I never did.

    The other thing I discovered was that it helps to know what one is looking for. I discovered I couldn't find what I didn't know I was looking for; so, it was both a surprise and yet not a surprise when I found something new and different. I don't have many surprises anymore.

But my interview with Mucianus in late February 71 surprised me. He wanted me to go to Antioch. Titus, Berenice, her brother, and their new hanger-on, Josephus, the renegade Zealot from Galilee, were wintering there and from the reports coming to him, Licinius expected trouble. He knew the city, knew the animosities of the peoples – particularly those of the Syrians - against the Jews had shattered the old, pre-war unities and were reaching a boiling point. Public riots had become commonplace: Jews caught alone or outside their residential areas at night were beaten and four so far had been murdered. Their synagogues and cemetery were repeatedly vandalized and other known Jewish-owned properties damaged or destroyed. 'You know as well as I do,' Licinius said, 'that apostates are the worst. One of them, a Jew who got Greek citizenship has been plaguing me all during the war. And now he's a magistrate who tells the Greeks and Syrians that the Jews fired the city back in November—'

'Sounds like Nero.'

'Yes, and he's made great political capital out of it. The thing is, many public buildings as well as residences were destroyed so it's a highly public issue.'

I stared at him and shrugged. 'What do you want me to do?'

'I want this to stop because he now insists Jews make a pagan sacrifice to prove they had nothing to do with it and my sources tell me he intends to ask Titus to create a Jewish ghetto similar to Alexandria's or banish them altogether to Palestine. Take this – it's Vespasian's - letter to Titus which gives him full authority to stop him. Make it clear that Vespasian distinguishes Jewish political nationalism, which he wants rooted out, from Jewish civil rights in our imperium!' He stopped and looked into Ti's eyes. 'Yes, he insists that they must be protected.'

I said I understood.

'But there is another, more delicate, issue.' Titus himself, it turned out. Mucianus explained how he had spent all his life as a soldier but it was time for his political education as his heir apparent. And he must learn that his hangers-on aren't the best of advisors, Lucinius said. So, I want you to write me every week about conditions there and by 'conditions' I mean what our procurator and Titus'hangers-on advise him. Do this separately. And give me your opinions as well as the facts and remember that peace there is paramount.

As Ti walked down the hall after leaving Licinius' office he thought he heard a low, sucking sound; and feared it.

*

When I reached Antioch I discovered the city was just as Mucianus, Matthew and Hero had said: Rome's gateway to the east – and, of course, I knew this was Mucianus' larger concern – was rift with religious dissensions. Matthew, Hero and Aaron were more concerned about maintaining Jewish unity than evangelizing and this had caused Jude to leave them. At least Matthew's people realized that proselytizing now was the worst thing they could do.

I encouraged them to stay the course while following Mucianus' instructions by sending him weekly reports via the proconsul's weekly dispatches from Selucia. And after two meetings, I realized Mucianus was right about Titus: the son was a political baby who needed political guidance; but not from me. Happily, Antioch's governor, Pompeius Collega, was experienced and astute enough to also realize that and provided a counter weight to Berenice and Agrippa's pro-Jewish advice. But it was providence in the form of the fire that Mucianus told me about in Rome that really shaped matters.

Antiochus' popularity was founded on the fire – similar to the one in Rome in 64 – which had swept through the city in November 70, barely three months after Jerusalem fell. The fire destroyed many public buildings as well as houses – which he escalated into his crisis call for Governor Collega's public inquiry. But after I arrived, Collega's investigation reported the Jews were not to blame and from that point on, tempers cooled as the burnt over district did. Then it was 'leaked,' as politicians say who want a contract to build a new aquaduct – to the public that Antiochus, was himself an apostate Jew who hated his father for converting to Judaism in the first place and his movement lost its momentum. I sent this information on to Mucianus as it unfolded and included my comments on the entire episode. Finally, I wrote saying I had accomplished what I thought was required and intended returning to Rome in April 71.

When he replied – 'see you then' – I thought, oh, I intend to! I now knew what a political creditor felt like.

*

But I didn't go to Antioch merely for Mucianus: I also went because I worried about Hero in such circumstances in spite of Matthew's assurances to me. I had been hearing rumors about Joshua stepping up his father's old dream about separating the Christians from Judaism but didn't know the details of what that meant for Matthew, Aaron, Hero and now two new men, Luke and Theophilus. So I met with all five of them after contacting the people in my political assignment.

'Actually, you needn't worry,' Matthew told me. 'Not only are we holding our own but we intend to expand our efforts.' When I raised my eyebrows he elaborated: I intend to circulate what I know about Jesus and his teachings to buck our people up and we have several new helpers.' The 'we' were Matthew, Aaron and Luke, a new helper who recently moved to the city. He nodded to him. 'He's a physician who knew Paul and knows John's group in Ephesus.'

'I've been helping Timothy for years,' Luke said.

I looked at the young man about Hero's age but dressed and looking like a Roman, and realized he must be, given his occupation.

' John's doing very well in Ephesus and expanding on Paul's early efforts there and in the interior. His idea is create a greater uniformity among all the churches --'

'Of practices and procedures?' I asked.

'Yes. And along Paul's lines so as not to confuse people. But his problem is that many of his constituents are Greeks and Celts and have trouble understanding how Jesus was both God and man. They tend to believe he was a man in touch with God as your old prophets did or as all spirit.'

When I didn't reply, Matthew said, 'and Theophilus here is helping us financially and allowing us to use his home and warehouse for meetings as well. He has many contacts overseas--'

'I'm an international merchant more on the scale of Joshua than yourself,' Theophilus interrupted. 'We know many of the same people and work each side of the street, so to speak--'

'But you don't advocate separation,' I interrupted.

'That's right. Matthew's point is the truth: his people are badly off because of what the war's done to them. Their needs are of immediate concern and I want to help them.'

I picked up on his use of 'his people.' Obviously Greek, it meant he was a godfearer or a Hellenist follower of the Jesus Jews. What else was there to say? I turned to Matthew and said, 'you have things well in hand it seems. How can I help?'

'By taking Hero to Rome with you.'

I looked more intently at him and turned to Hero who was smiling and said, 'he wants me to revive Peter's group of helpers there--'

'They're dormant, not dead,' Matthew said smilingly when I turned to him, 'and Mark and Barnabas are too busy in Alexandria to go to Rome. You know how intent Peter was about establishing ours presence there and Sol and Vol always encouraged him. They know who Hero is and, most importantly, know him as a friend of Peter's rather than Paul's.'

I understood. And he would have my backing. I smiled. 'So, you're gradually pulling me back into it.'

'I don't think you were ever really out of it. Perhaps just strayed off, along a different path. But you never lost his Way.'

*

Titianus and Hero returned to Rome in early April 71, the father happy to be reunited with his wife and tell her the news; the son, not wanting to confront Clement and the others but knowing he had to.

'So he was satisfied with your report about Antioch?' she asked, wanting to know what he had achieved.

'Yes. I think much of Licinius' confusion about Titus' reports were caused by Titus' not knowing the city as well as Licinius does.'

Tay smiled. 'You mean his ignorance. You're sure it wasn't because of Berenice's distractions?'

He smiled too. 'I'm sure. Licinius was stationed there for many years.'

She picked up her comb and began combing her hair. 'But you told him about Berenice's incest with Agrippa?' She saw no point in telling him about her business plan involving Publix - yet. Not until Marcus returned from Parthia.

'I told him about the 'rumor' of incest.' He smiled. 'I don't have personal knowledge of it.'

She turned and made a face at him. 'Is Titus really that gullible as well as stupid?'

Ti sighed. 'Everyone wants to think men in high positions are sophisticated or decadent men of the world. But, between us, Titus is – well, yes, you could say gullible and stupid but it's owing more to his inexperience in the world outside of the military. I'm sure Vespasian knows it and is trying to change it. And yes, he's completely ignorant about women . . . What?' he asked, noticing her raised eyebrows at his last remark. 'Oh, no! I'm not claiming to be an authority on women. But there are degrees of knowledge and ignorance and I'll admit he's very low on that scale.'

She turned back to her table thinking he doesn't have to know about Val's pregnancy tonight. It's only been two months. 'Ti, are you telling me the man Vespasian is grooming to succeed his as emperor is a moron?'

Too harsh, he thought. 'No, not a moron, darling. Only on the slow side. He's spent his whole life in the army. But I don't think he's evil and I can't do anything about it either. It's the old aristocratic idea of the blood line. Vespasian knows the old guard in the Senate will defend that unto death.'

'But won't the brainy ones object?'

'They do.' He smiled. 'But they and the emperor know they can't defy him or he'll cut off their contracts.'

She looked down and thoughtful for a moment. 'And that's why you don't want to become dependent on government contract work.'

'You're half right. Its civilian government contract work that I want to avoid. Military contracting is more of a sure thing and far more profitable.' He stopped and thought, God! protecting one's freedom is a full-time job!

'I hope you're teaching this to Marc.'

'I am. As well as the other aspect to it.'

'What's that?'

'Since Titus isn't very bright, they know they'll get around him easier than they can around Vespasian!'

She laughed. 'I'm glad Vespy wants to mend fences with Ctesiphon.'

'Did I ever tell you how smart I think you are?'

'How did Titus ever conquer Jerusalem!'

He looked at her. 'Easy. He just followed daddy's plan to the letter. And speeded it up when his father told him too. No, he's not very intelligent on his own. He's a nice guy who looks good in a uniform. I suspect Berenice makes mincemeat of him in private.'

'The three of them don't really sleep together, do they?'

'Don't be such a gossip! Remember, he'll be emperor!' He looked into the future. 'And God help us when that happens.'

She put her wine glass down and said, 'Sometimes I think you're too harsh about people.'

'I'm sorry. I only talk this way here when I'm with you.' He seemed to shake himself. 'And I think you should know my true thoughts and feelings. I'm sorry if it upsets you.'

'No. I didn't mean it that way. I shouldn't have said that. I was just being light about our conversation. I want you to always talk to me about your thoughts and feelings, Ti. I want our life together to be as strong as possible and honesty just strengthens us. Nothing we say to one another goes outside these rooms.'

'In that case, I want to tell you what Licinius also told me. He was quite serious about it so we'll have to do this. And I need your help.'

'What's that?'

'He said Vespasian's Triumph is now scheduled for next July and we must – "absolutely must," I'm quoting him – attend and make sure that he sees us.'

'Is that the thing where the emperor parades to that little hill called the Capitol?'

'That's it. From the Forum all along that paved road going up there. He'll ride in a chariot with Titus behind him and Domitian will be on horseback. Caenis will be seated at the family's table. The senators and magistrates act follow as their escorts. Publix will be in his own chariot and many tens of thousands will follow in the parade--'

'So, it's an all day affair with the public orders on display.'

'That's right. His troops will be part of it as well as booty from Jerusalem's Temple and thousands of those poor captives in chains. Licinius said he wants to make this a great public spectacle to get his regime more popularly supported with the people.'

'We're not in it, surely!'

'No. We're just freedmen. The Triumph is meant to demonstrate the great power of the emperor and the divine favor bestowed upon him.'

'Oh, wowee!' she mocked, standing up, reaching for the ceiling and bowing down to him. Then she sat down and said more seriously, 'what did Licinius mean about the importance of our being there?'

'Freedmen can't be part of the parade but we're allowed to build our own stands to see and be seen in the open spaces between the buildings that line the Forum. It's the prime viewing places. Several families pool their resources and join together--'

'We must do it! Have you invited anyone?'

'No. But I've rented a long and large space so we can build a huge stand on it right in the middle--'

'So it will be conspicuous!'

'Yes. Everyone will notice it and I told the contractor it must hold ten or twelve families. I'll take care of those arrangements but I want you to think about who we should invite. It'll be canopied and have three viewing decks--'

'For tables and chairs?'

He smiled at her growing enthusiasm. 'And drinks and delicacies to eat! Oh, I'm having a set of wide stairs erected along one side to get up and down to the decks which are open in the front. I'm also having separate stairs built on the back side for the servants to get all the stuff up and down the decks.'

'But what will you do with the empty spaces on each side?'

'Nothing.' He smiled at the puzzled look on her face. 'I want us to see and be seen. The cost of it will come back to us many times.'

*

Ti's 'Grand Stand,' ' as many called it, was roped off and guards stood with their weapons deliberately visible. But across the Sacred Way was a narrow strip of land too narrow to build a stand on because it would block the House of the Vestals; and that's where spectators stood to watch the parade go by between themselves and the 'Grand Stand.' One man, stood in the middle of their line, hooded in spite of the heat, and intently surveyed Judas' area. It's God's will this happened this way on my fifty-ninth birthday, he thought. Exactly forty one years and four months ago Jesus paid the price for all of us, and I suspect Judas has too. Oh, there go those smug Sanhedrin bastards!, he thought as some of the Jewish prisoners were driven by. I wish their chains were heavier! There goes the old distorted and perverted life that Jesus told us about. Then he glanced at the Grand Stand again: and there's the man who helped pass it along.

Simon watched Judas move slowly from table to table, deck to deck, stopping to talk with his different guests. And Tay and Marcus and Val doing the same, but each on their own. What a family! He thought. Making conversations, giving gifts and ingratiating. Always ingratiating! Simon didn't mean it in a demeaning way; he was the first to acknowledge the man's generosity to himself and his helpful efforts over the years. He also knew he would be asking for more. All those bags he got from Judas were filled with sesterces, not denariis. He felt proud that at least one fellow follower of Jesus knew how the world really worked. Didn't fall for all that wait-for-the-next-world crap. No, he corrected himself, that's not right. It's not that he knows better than I do, he just limits his responses to it, to enable people like me to do my work. Paul was always right about that. Simon stared at Ti: I think Jesus is probably helping him even now.

As he watched Judas maneuvering and giving for future receiving, he remembered when Judas didn't think of giving as an investment to get; didn't know that givers must receive first so that they can gave. He remembered Jud giving alms to the poor, giving all from the treasurer's purse and then reaching into his own for more. The giver inside the giver. Simon never understood why John never liked him; and he thought John was wrong about him. Simon knew the generous-hearted side of Judas; and he was sure that was why Jesus helped Judas by filling his purse as fast as it was depleted. Well, he was going to need a large one for what I'm going to ask him to do, he thought.

Yes, Jesus will redeem all of us; through his instrument, Vespasian, he thought. He's the real Janus-face of Rome. The man of peace deserves a temple of peace; right down there – he glanced left - on Capitoline Hill. Only beware of the Jews, Vespasian! Like phoenix, they plot their rise from their ruin. And in the meantime we have the Druids: the Jewish priests of the west. But never fear! For we will help you!

A voice suddenly whispered from behind him: 'Simon! Jesus' is ready to go!'

31

WHAT Judas, Hero and even Matthew himself didn't know was Aaron's anguish and dissolution over Rome's destruction of Christian as well as Judaic Jerusalem. He grew up in David's city and remembered worshipping at the Temple. But to him, his father's concern with Jesus' Judaism seemed pitifully like a charity that went backward into an unrecoverable past instead of forward into a hopeful future. And his concrete-mindedness made any accommodation with a purely spiritual Jesus like Joshua's Christian Separatists impossible. He felt at odds with himself and in disarray, reflecting how the Christian movement appeared to be as the number of apostles diminished.

There it was under a nutshell: the war changed Aaron far more than it had his father. He was in his early forties during the conflict, became a grandfather twice as he saw radical Jews replace moderate ones, saw his father take a defensive – but do-nothing position in his view – while secretly wishing they did more. They never once talked about volunteering to go to Jerusalem.

To top it off there was Jehu, John's son. He didn't understand him. He came to them from David, Peter's son in Capernaum, and lived with them nearly two years, even marrying his wife's younger sister, and was now talking about returning to Ephesus. Everyone talked about how brave the disciples were but what happened to them? They've become do nothings and their sons ineffectual? Aren't disciples supposed to *do something*.

Then, the end of the war and dissipation of Antiochus' threat brought Aaron his moment of decision: he had learned to thrive against opposition and now needed more of it. So, he invented it where he didn't find it. He went to Theophilus, the most prominent of their godfearers, and proposed a more aggressive stance and actions than his father was taking, not understanding he was repeating what Antiochus had done.

Theophilus was Matthew's age but a more practical man of the world; and he no more understood Joshua's sense of a spiritualized Jesus separated from this world than he did Matthew's of a Jesus taking on the sins of his people. He was still searching for that door to knock on that Matthew said Jesus talked about. What worried him – more than it did the others – was that the end of Judaism and of their Christian church in Jerusalem left them with a fearfully fragmented world populated by John in Ephesus, Mark and Barnabas in Alexandria and Hero in Rome. But, unlike Aaron, he lived in hope because he never tired of telling everyone Jerusalem was destroyed, not God

But Theophilus was also a hard-headed businessman who didn't worry about or question his own psychology or the state of the world beyond his personal opportunities. He quickly saw the larger, international ramifications of the idea; he had known Amos, Titianus' business partner, for years and knew Titianus was Hero's father. So, an 'informal partnership,' an understanding, as he called it to Aaron – it was part of the oral tradition he explained; nothing in writing – was born: Theophilus would fund the entire operation on condition of remaining anonymous; Aaron would create the Sons of God through his like-minded friends in Antioch, and they would slowly develop the organization overseas.

What even Aaron didn't know, however, was that Theophilus had long known Luke through his medical services and planned to be his connection with John's group in Ephesus. In Theophilus' mind, if and when push came to shove, Luke would be his answer to Joshua's Separatists; but it was too early to tell Aaron that.

*

Rome had changed for the worst in Hero's mind: it was meaner and more vicious. Fewer pagans practiced nobles-oblige and pursued their self interest than he remembered. So, he looked for physical anchors that would help his spiritual work. One was his family. As he walked to his first meeting with Peter's old helpers he thought about Judas. Everyone in Antioch told bad stories about him. *But I never doubted he loves me. He's always done everything to help me. I mean really help me; not what he thought would help me.* He remembered telling Matthew that just before sailing from Antioch to Rome with Judas, and thought it strange that this old friend of his father seemed embarrassed; *as if there was something he didn't want to tell me!* Hero didn't understand that. Both he and Matthew knew Judas would help him revive Peter's group of Christians.

Nor could he understand why Jude was so hateful to him; it didn't seem very Christian-like, especially after he and his wife had been rescued Jerusalem's death. Self, Hero decided – that old devil in all of us – defeats our efforts to help one another.

'I called this planning session about what we can do to further Peter's work according to Jesus' plan because it's time we crawled out from under this war cloud. Since there are only four of you to begin with, let me pass around the letters signed by Matthew and John with their suggestions--'

'But these are addressed only to you?'

'Yes, but only because I was there with them; they know me and that I worked with Peter. But it's addressed to all of us in the sense that we all do Jesus' work. I'm not claiming any special dispensations here.'

'But do they understand that we are to continue Peter's work here in Rome, not Hero's and not anywhere else?' Clement persisted.

Some people can be mired about the tiniest of points, Hero thought. 'Yes, they do. Now, can we get on with their suggestions about what to do?'

'It seems clear enough, Hero,' said Pudens. 'We could make a simple list of the points: poor relief, providing food and shelter--'

'And start in the poorest District.' Clement interrupted. 'Look, this is doing pretty much what Peter did.' He seemed bored.

'Aid for widows and orphans and finding medical care are, but these others aren't,' Linus said.

'You mean employment and housing?' asked Cletus.

'That's right.'

'But other things aren't as well,' Hero said. 'There's nothing that's negative. I mean there isn't any 'thou shalt nots' are there?'

'So we can ask for contributions - money, food, clothes, physical help doing things - those sorts of things,' Pudens said.

'That's as I understand it,' Hero replied.

'I don't know about this. The entire thing goes against what God said to Moses about what men can do. He does have rules for how we're to behave.'

Hero could see he was going to have trouble with Clement and he wasn't sure why he was so negative about it all. 'Look Clem, as--'

'Don't call me Clem, please! My name is Clement and that's the name I answer to!'

'I'm sorry. I apologize. You didn't seem to mind years ago and I just assumed--'

'Well, don't!'

'All right! Clement it will be in the future. I was only going to ask why you seem to be in opposition to these things now. I thought we used to work together quite nicely.'

'You mean when Peter was alive and before Nero started burning us alive! Well, those happy days are gone forever!' Clement said sarcastically. 'We all accept that times change! Rome didn't just destroy Judaism, it destroyed our church! Our church! And you don't seem to understand that the Godfearers whom we depended upon to finance us in the old days don't trust us anymore! And who can blame them for not wanting to be tainted with rebellion! Where's our money going to come from? Where's the employment going to come from? It's a different world from what it used to be!'

'We talked about that in Antioch, Clement. Everyone understands we've been thrown back on our own resources and we accept that's the way it is now. If you want to think of it as having gone back to where we started, that's fine. But what's important is our example. We must teach and more importantly live by example so that others may follow us. If we teach one thing and live another people will see the hypocrisy of our lives.'

'Our doing good will help others do good.'

'That's right, Linus. So, let's start in the poorest District and see how it works! What do we have to lose?'

Clement shook his head and sat back in his chair. 'Our lives. Just our lives.'

Hero looked at the others. 'Look. We must face the fact that times have changed and we must change with them. We will probably never be able to fund all of the things we'd like to do but we must keep trying to--'

'Do you have something concrete to suggest or just more blather?' Everyone looked at Clement in disbelief: crudeness was one thing, rudeness another.

'As a matter of fact I do,' Hero replied. 'Many of the people we help have skills. They make things or they can do things. Why don't we offer them for sale to the public--'

'You mean *Christian* goods and services?' Linus asked.

'Yes. I remember people buying and wearing those white togas with the JC embossed on them in the old days. But poor people couldn't afford them. Anyway, they were a consumption item--'

'And a luxury,' Clement snorted.

'Precisely!' Hero rejoined. 'Let's offer simple, cheap and useful items and inexpensive but necessary services. Those things that their providers can feel proud about. At least, let's think about it and discuss it at our next meeting.'

*

They agreed to do so and adjourned the meeting with everyone except Clement congratulating Hero on his idea and promising to give it further thought. Clement thought it a rich kid's business model because his background of growing up on that hard-scrabble farm in Pontus where few Jews lived had taught him that only God provides for everything in life. More importantly, he thought, it was such a *Jewish* plan.

Vespasian followed the traditions of his imperial predecessors in giving free bread to the poorest Romans, but the lines at the public bread dole office (next to the meat markets along the embankment northward and across the Fabricus Bridge opposite the Theatre of Marcellus) had stopped lengthening now, in the mid 70s. But the Transtiberina area of the fourteenth district across the river from the Emporium still remained the roughest part of the city and a potential threat to public order. At least, that's how Mucianus described the situation to Titianus in June 74.

'The problem could be resolved if our grain ships could reach us. But they're held up by the rioting in Alexandria.'

'Can't the Alexanders do anything about it?'

'It's the Jesus Jews who are the problem! They've been rioting in the synagogues again and there's no end to it!'

Titianus knew Judas couldn't admit to knowing much about it. So, he didn't.

'But this is delicate. I want you to go there. Use your business contacts so everyone doesn't think our government is as desperately worried about it as we are. Straighten it out but don't interfere with the locals. The Greeks and Egyptians are just waiting for the chance to be at each other's throats and only the Jews keep them apart! So, we need to solve the problem between the three of them and you know our policy is not to interfere in local matters unless the situation is dire.'

Hrmmph! Ti almost said aloud but controlled his behavior. As if killing Mark and Barnabas' flight weren't dire enough! He looked at Mucianus and asked, 'when do you want me to leave?'

'Yesterday.' He leaned forward. 'I'll have your papers ready in the morning.'

After Ti told Tay about his mission and left a week later, she decided to do what she could to further her family's interest while he was in Alexandria because - as he said - 'he couldn't be sure exactly when he would return,' and it was clear to her that Ti's work for Mucianus advanced the family's interest. But it was also clear that their chief source of income, their eastern trade connections, had to be renewed and strengthened in preparation for what now looked like a long duration of peace. Ti didn't have the time to do it and was too old for it anyway, in her opinion. So, it was Marc's turn because it was a family connection.

Two evenings later, she began her campaign when she said to Marcus and Valeria over dinner, 'I want assess where our family's at so we can decide what our family's next phase should be.' With Ti gone, no one questioned her speaking for the family.

'You sound like dad,' Marcus said, looking at Valeria and knowing she liked these conversations.

Tay smiled and looked at him. 'I hope you know I knew him long before you did. And in different ways.' They all laughed. 'Now, correct me if I'm wrong but our trade with India is currently more profitable and greater than it is with Parthia.'

Marcus nodded and added, 'that's because of the war.'

'Well, I think we should correct that imbalance and do it through our family connections,' she said. 'They're more important than capital. Don't you agree?'

Both nodded.

'It's up to the two of you and me, then. Ti did the work originally but he's in his sixties now. I don't think he has another trip to Ctesiphon and back in him, and even if he could do it, his work with Mucianus is more important at the moment. We need him here while Vespasian establishes his regime on a firmer footing and we acclimate ourselves to it.'

'You mean while we accommodate ourselves to his regime. But we can't do anything about his push into the northwest,' Marcus said. 'You want me to go to Ctesiphon?' Marcus smiled.

'Yes, but I want to talk this out because our situation more complicated than it used to be. I'm going to write him to come home as soon as he's finished Mucianus' assignment and not hang around developing new business in Alexandria. I think you need to take over the field management more and more because it's more important that he keep us connected with Vespasian's movements. Does that make sense?'

'Yes,' he answered, nodding.

Then she turned to Valeria. 'This is where your father comes into it. Pub and Ti made a lot of money contracting for the armies during the war and Vespasian's people know this. Right?'

'Yes, and I think Mucianus' sending him to Antioch is proof of how much they trust him.' Marcus added.

'Yes, but I'm moving on from that now and talking to Valeria.' She turned away from him and back to her.

Val nodded. 'Dad says it's impractical to continue contracting with the armies because of the greater distance to the north and it's far less profitable because it's mainly overland.'

'And he doesn't want to try to get involved in any detail in the new areas--' Marcus started to say.

'I'm sure he doesn't,' Tay interrupted. 'But my point is that our military business is winding down rapidly and Vespasian won't be primarily concerned with the eastern legions again for a few years. But that's where our contacts are.'

Valeria and Marcus looked at her and nodded.

'Well, I think we should use our profits from the military contracting to invest someplace other than in the overland eastern trade.'

'What do you have in mind?' Marcus asked, sensing she already did.

'It's peacetime for us and will be for a while,' Tay continued, 'but we should always remember to stay with businesses we know. Not go off speculating in things we don't. Every day, Vespasian is a little more entrenched and I think it's time Publix proposes some new public works in the city.' Valeria and Marcus looked at one another.

'Especially, if it's stipulated that slaves cannot be used and it's required that they hire freemen.'

Both Valeria and Marcus now riveted their eyes on her. 'But that's a political decision!' Marcus said.

'I know. But Vespasian will politically benefit from it as well as get richer. Pub should argue to him that his new policy of hiring free labor will revive republican ideals and pump wages and spending into the society. That he won't have to raise as much public funds and Publix can begin residential construction and--'

'Where did you learn all this?' Valeria interrupted.

'I've been reading and talking to people--'

Marcus chuckled. 'You hired tutors like we used to do!'

'Of course! What do you think? Jewelry is more important than thought?' Marcus and Val stared at her. 'You'd be surprised what I've learned from life but . . . but that's another matter and until now--'

Val interrupted: 'is that what you do when Ti's gone?'

'Yes. But I want to ask you some serious questions so let's move on to them.'

Val sat up straighter; it reminded her of when she was a girl and dad talked business with her.

'Now, I have two questions for you, Val, and' – glancing at Marcus - one for you too. But I'm saving the biggest one for the two of you.' She faced Val. 'You first. Do you think it would be all right - I mean, he wouldn't think it out of my so-called sphere would he? - to talk to him like this? About business? Even to suggest that he initiate the program?'

Val thought about it. She didn't remember much about her mother but felt she hadn't been interested in business. 'I think he likes you, respects your ideas and how you think. He's always respectful of practical ideas and I suppose he pushed that too much with my brothers. But if you went about it correctly - traditionally, I mean - he would not only listen but seriously consider what you have to say.'

They saw Tay thinking and were quiet. But finally, Marcus asked, 'and what did you want to ask me?'

'About using our profits from the army contracts to put into the public building projects.'

'With father?' Val exclaimed. 'That's brilliant! I'm sure he'd love it.'

'And it would continue our partnership from the army contracts,' Marcus agreed.

Tay smiled. 'But now, Val, here's the big question. Shall I ask him or should you?' She didn't say she wanted Val to.

Val didn't expect that question and had to think it over. She remembered how her father never made fun of girls' taking an interest in business or saying a woman's life should be confined to making and raising babies. And when she shared business talk with him it always made her feel closer to him. It was only a feeling, but she was sure he felt that way too. Baby-making didn't interest him that much. Then it suddenly dawned on her: was that why he was never particularly close to Servius and Julius; they didn't share his business interests! 'I would like to, Tay,' she replied. 'I think it will work better if I do for lots of reasons. But I'll need some details.'

Tay looked at the two of them and thought, there! I did it! They have a future from her side as well as his. She turned to Marcus and asked, 'any problem with that?'

'Not at all,' he replied, turned to Val and smiled. 'It's simple. In my scroll, no women, no family and no future.'

They all laughed and Tay suggested they walk around the atrium to see her new, exotic carp in the pool. It was getting dark and the lamps showed them off so beautifully in the water.

When they returned to a smaller reception room for wine and sweets, Tay asked, 'are you ready for the big question?'

Val and Marc were still thinking about the first ones and simply looked at her.

'Are you pregnant?'

Val and Marcus looked at one another; they never remembered Tay being so direct. 'I don't think so. Why?' Val replied evenly.

'Because Volgases is in his mid-seventies - that's about ten years older than Ti but seventy is far older in Ctesiphon than in Rome. I can't remember even seeing or hearing about anyone in their eighties when I lived there.'

'What's your point?' Marcus asked.

'Whoever succeeds him needs to feel as secure as we do.'

'Any idea who would succeed him?' Val asked.

'My guess is Pacorus, his son who was loyal to him during the Roman troubles. His brothers are too old.'

'How old is he?

'In his early forties now. About ten years older than you,' she said turning to Marcus.

He gave a big smile. 'I think I'm going to dream tonight about riding a camel along the Euphrates and over-nighting in a royal palace.'

It was Tay's turn to smile. 'You got it. Ti's too old for the trip and it's important that you renew your allegiance to the next generation there.'

'How long will you be gone?' Val asked her husband, trying not to let her anxiety show.

Tay sat back in her chair while the two of them looked at each other and replied, 'about a year. Possibly more.'

'Oh!' Val said, turning to Tay with a sudden smile: 'so, that's why you asked if I was pregnant.'

'Yes.'

'You want me to be, don't you?'

'Three children are better than two. You never know what can happen.' Then Tay corrected herself quickly and in a softer voice. "Can' doesn't mean 'will.'

'Do you--'

'Be quiet, Marc.' Val said. Turning back to Tay she asked, 'you never had any more after Marcus did you? Pregnancies, I mean.'

'No. But it wasn't for the lack of wanting and trying. It just never happened. I can only think God didn't want it to.' She looked away. 'But you're situation is different. You've had two pregnancies with Marc and there's no reason not to have a third if God wants it.' She looked back at Val, thinking, I know Ti would agree with me, and paused. 'I know Ti and Pub would want for it.' Then, putting her left hand over Val's right one, she said, 'if Marcus goes,as I hope he will, now is the time to be realistic instead of noble.' She turned to him. 'I've never told you this. But my life with Ti has taught me the difference between the two and that's another reason why I think you should go.' She turned back to Val. 'I was raised in that culture of nobility and self-sacrifice for glory. It killed my first husband; and that's when I realized that's all glory's good for - death.'

Later that night, Tay watched her maid comb her hair reflected in the burnished Corinthian mirror on her table but didn't see her. She was thinking how glad she was that she wasn't a man. What she had just done was her duty to keep the family going while he was away. A duty that gave her no pleasure beyond the relief of being over.

Then her thoughts turned to Hero. He tried to make what he did sound noble and uplifting. But she didn't see it that way. How can Hero feel anything else but relief when his day of serving poor, smelly people who didn't really care about themselves is over" I hope he doesn't do it here. What can he possibly learn from them? What pleasure can he derive from his experience with them? Why wouldn't he come to the safety of the villa with us instead of staying in the dangerous city with corpses everywhere? Sure, he helps people. But so what? I'll give him that he believes in the purity of his motives. But why that? Doesn't it all boil down to the purity of our motives in anything we do? Does what he's doing really have any good effect them? It's like whistling in the wind. At least what Ti does is give them employment.

*

Two months later, Titianus returned from Alexandria and learned that Marcus had already left for Ctesiphon. Three days after that he had an unexpected visitor, his old friend, Simon who filled him in on what was happening within the old Judaism.

Yes, Judas replied he knew Jamnia. That village south of Joppa four miles east of the Great Sea. What's so important about it?

Nothing, Simon replied. What is important is that Vespasian designated it as the seat of the Beth-Din - Israel's new Sanhedrin - just before the war ended. Then he exiled those Sadducees and members of the Sanhedrin who didn't join King Agrippa in Tiberias there. It's now the center for resurrecting Judaism.

'I spent the winter of 72-73 there,' Simon said. 'I wanted to meet the rabbis and see what they're doing because that's what we need, a renewed Judaism, renewed in our hearts and lived in community, all communities wherever we are.' He looked intently at Judas across his desk and said, 'I believe the synagogue must replace the Temple.'

'So you accept what Jesus said about sacrifice.'

'Yes. Replace it with conscience and heart.'

'But does this unify us? If you give up the Temple and sacrificial system and the priests who administer them, what then?'

'Scripture and our Holy Ones. One God, one people, one way of life. That should define our new people. Turn back to the way we were: before Sionism!'

'I remember we all thought that when we were with Jesus.'

'I remember. But the problem was his Way wasn't in the world and that's what defeated him! And just look at where we are today! Hero's people are still so few compared to the Jews who are all over the world even though nearly wiped out by the war!'

'I'm confused,' Ti answered but was really just stalling for time to think about it. 'You mean your new Judaism will adopt Jesus' Way but not abandon our old ones?'

'That's right. Partly because Sol and Vol's idea to regionalize the Temple and sacrificial system was tried by our ancestors and never worked. Don't you agree?'

Ti smiled. 'I do. But it seems to me you're still fighting the world.'

'But why not? Aren't we God's chosen people and didn't he give us dominion over the earth? I never understood why Jesus didn't acknowledge that.'

Ti suddenly realized that Simon hadn't accepted Jesus as *the* Son of God. That he still considered him – as most traditional Jews did – a good man and a prophet who spoke to God as the others had. But Jesus was not the Messiah to Simon. Ti decided arguing wouldn't go anywhere and said, 'then why are you here? Surely, it isn't to give me a lecture on theology! Is it to warn me that the new Judaism will be a threat?'

'No,' Simon replied carefully, not wanting to alienate Ti. 'The new Judaism won't be a threat but those who oppose it will be.'

Ti looked at him and said, 'now, I am confused. Who's the threat?'

'The old hard liners. The ultra orthodox die hards. I don't mean the old men who survived. I mean the younger ones who've yet to fulfill their dreams. Many want to go back. To repeat the Temple and priesthood and sacrificial system. I call them restorationists.'

Alarm bells rang in Ti's head. For one thing, he had long thought that's what Jesus was when he talked about wanting what he thought Judaism was before the monarchy, the centralization of the Temple and sacrificial system, and ritualization of the prophets. But this must also be what Vespasian means when he says Jewishness. 'Do you think it's possible? To revive it?'

'Not in our lifetimes. But perhaps in Marcus."

Ti thought rapidly: how far should I go? 'That's what many said about Jesus but I don't suppose your crowd did.'

'What do you mean? Of course we did! We hoped. . . .'

'I know you did. But I mean Jesus didn't want to merely rid the world of our corrupted leaders, he wanted to change the system entirely. To go back before the monarchy centralized everything in the the Temple and dictated the only ways men could prophesize –'

Simon looked perplexed. 'You mean to when our fathers first came into the promised land?

'Yes. He used to tell me how the promise went wrong. Corrupted by them inventing their own ideas about how to live a Godly life instead of listening to God directly.'

Simon nodded. 'So he opposed Deuternomy. Torah.'

Ti pursed his lips. 'He was the real restorationist and this threatened them. I mean the entire system they had staked their lives on.' He looked away, as if thinking of something else. 'But you're not telling me everything about your restorationists, are you?'

Simon stared at him and thought, he's so like Jesus was. 'Perhaps I should have said in Hero's lifetime rather than Marcus. But we don't agree with them and thing they'll just lead us down the same path we've just been on. We think it's better to renew Judaism in all communities through holy scripture and trust to its interpretation by rabbis. That will replace a central authority with uniformity throughout world Jewry.'

Ti nodded.

'I don't mean to be harsh or threatening about this, but that will isolate the Jesus Jews in the long run and drive them out if they don't go along.'

'And if they don't want to go?'

'Boot them out of the synagogues as they always have been but now more formally.'

Ti thought about how long he'd known Simon. 'You've always been a hard man.'

'You don't know hard, Jud. You weren't there during the war.' He paused. 'It's blood for blood now and Jewish identity is at stake.'

After Simon left and he thanked him for his warning and gave him three bagfuls of coins, Ti thought about what he said. Clearly, it was directed at Hero and his attempt to resurrect Peter's efforts to enlarge the number of followers of Jesus' Way in Rome. That was it: the eternal city; the center of the empire; and that's why Simon is here. He knew the old Zealot tactics: begin with the bottom social rungs; start in the poorest districts and work outward and upward. Provide poor relief, food stuffs and medical help; particularly for widows and orphans. Find employment for those needing of work. He sighed. It was all so familiar.

But he had to protect Hero. But did this mean having to deny his Jewish identity as well?

*

Tay's faith in her plan for Marcus' trip to Ctesiphon had far greater and better results than what she hoped for. It solidified the family's connections with its Parthian branch, showed his Parthian family that their long-range trust and plan in their sister had been correct, and confirmed his own identity as a Roman. She and Ti discussed it several times after his return and agreed to leave them alone.

'You're sure we can miss the party?' Val asked Marcus five nights after his return. She was sitting in a chair in front of the table that Marc used as a small desk in their return rooms.

'Yes. People know we're not political and Publix has already declined attending because of his health. They won't think anything of it.'

'Then I'll use his health as our excuse not to go and you can plan on going to Alexandria next week.' She paused, and then Suddenly said, 'I don't hate Jews, you know.'

He put his quill down. 'I know. But from how Ti and Pub have been talking about it, I gather that it's becoming quite the political issue among the Senators.' He conveyed his concern about what she thought by saying, 'that's all we need be concerned about. Don't worry about it.'

'But I do! Do you realize how much we've moved into public construction since the war? I mean we're like dad was when I was a girl!' She looked down and Marc could see she was in a pensive mood. 'That was the beginning of it, wasn't it? Ti's war contracts?'

'Yes, but it still doesn't equal our overseas trade, Val, which isn't as dependent on politics!'

Feeling insecure or anxious always made her fearful. She was just six when her mother died in that horrible accident which changed her family's life forever; so, not knowing what her mother and father's marriage was like, she looked - listened and watched - what her neighbors did. The closest ones were Marc's family - literally next door, so she took many of her cues from his parents; where Tay held her own and seemed more than happy to pay attention to the daughter she never had. Val absorbed Tay's sense of what a married woman's role was. Consequently, Val and Marc shared many of Tay and Ti's ideas about marriage and family life and what secured it by the time they married. And now, ten years and three children later, they had developed their own married style, especially in private.

When they first married they referred to 'the business of marriage' thinking it was cute to say and expressed how both thought of life in general. But as cuteness confronted the different everyday problems in every marriage, they asked themselves: are we going to relate to one another through our changing culture or are we going to deal with each another in honest, open though episodic ways. How personal are we going to be in our relationship? Because each knew themselves, they talked about it like this, and chose to be honest with each other, both realized that was the only way their marriage could be strengthened, have a future, and not be ruled by social fashions. And they had a model: they saw it work with Tay and Ti.

Val told him it wasn't as much her adjustments as her learning to value acceptance. Acceptance of the changes that cropped up almost daily between them, and then learn how to incorporate them into their life together.

Marc said he agreed with her because that seemed to allow them to become different – and even more confident - people who knew they could be free with one another as long as they retained their individuality. And that their shared life gave each of them a freedom to express themselves which preserved the intimacy of their marriage. It made their marriage, as he put it, a true partnership.

She said she thought that it strengthened and enlarged their love in ways they never experienced before and that it provided them with the resiliency that preserved their newness as they grew from two to now five.

One night, Marc told Val: I married you because I felt comfortable with you and liked you. I loved you; but I didn't really know you. Wasn't that silly and stupid? To marry someone you don't know? So, I asked myself why did I do that? And I realized would grow into knowing you as long as I believed I would. It was a matter of faith and trust; not facts. So, now that we're married with three children we know the world hasn't stopped so, why should we? I've never felt so confident, so in love with you as I do now; so looking forward to us becoming yet more different; and I'm grateful that our children give us an even larger, growing future. I love the changing world; and I love the changing you. He said it with a smile, 'it's like meeting a new you every day.'

That surprised her. Not that he said it, but the depth and way he did. She liked being able to change and felt his affirmation of her freedom to be herself gave her even greater security. She was also surprised at surprising herself this way. And she told him that this freed her from what the other women talked, cried, groaned and bitched about. They dwelt too much on the negative things of life and she was too busy pursuing her own life to bother with anything not positive, not moving toward a goal. She didn't become impolite; just more immersed in herself and realized she could talk - actually talk - to Marc about her fear of the family's becoming too dependent on public contracts. And it would be a real conversation. Meaningful, she said, looking into his eyes, not mechanical, because living that way had purpose beyond the senses.

'I think the reason dad was so successful at his contracting was because of who he was. And still is, of course. I mean his family lineage goes back to Marcus Agrippa, Augustus' good friend.' She paused. 'You don't have that because Ti didn't. I think we should dabble in that world for the contacts and the fun of it, but let's not be confused about its role in our life. Let's not become dependent on it in any way or make the children's future dependent on it.'

'Yes, we can do that. There's certainly enough private ways of doing business.'

'Do you have anything in mind? I mean big mural ideas whose directions go on for years. That will last for the lives of children and grandchildren.'

Marc leaned back in his chair, holding her eyes in his. 'I've been thinking about some things generally. Vespy's what? Sixty six or seven and more intensely concerned with Titus' succession than ever. Just between us, Titus isn't very bright. He's big, blond, likes the good life and his chief concern is being everybody's friend. Well, that's all right if you're a dog; but it could be a disaster if you're emperor.'

'So, you don't think you have much in common with him. Is that what this boils down to?'

'No. There's some other ingredients. Domitian is smarter and I think Vespy has deliberately excluded him from power because he's chosen Titus to succeed him and--'

'You think Domitian's dangerous. You think Titus won't last?'

'Who's to know? One can't predict what will happen and I certainly don't want to paint Domitian as brilliant. Oh, I know his reputation is terrible for whoring around and partying but he has nothing else to do. And Vespy's responsible for that.'

Val shook her head. 'Fathers are so important in shaping their son's lives. They both had the opposite of your upbringing.' She stared at her red lacquered fingernails lying in her lap. 'Tay and Ti knew what the positive things they wanted for you.'

'Yes, but that's not what I'm getting at,' Marcus looked down. 'I'm not trying to beat my own drum. The best thing Vespy did was to have him marry Domitila, Corbulo's youngest daughter. You don't know her, do you?'

'No. I haven't met her.'

'Well, I'm going to arrange that you do. I think she's the smartest of the lot and I want to see what you think.'

'So you're planning even beyond Titus.'

'For the longer term because it's imperative for people like us. If Titus is forced to give Berenice up, if this Jewish business does turn against them politically – and I wish Volumnus and his stupid 'Jews for Empire' were gone - Roman bootstrappers without money will have to look for credit from non-Jews.'

Val's eyes widened. 'You're thinking of going into banking!'

'Yes. It could have a good future if Vespy goes for Tay and Pub's new economy.'

'At good interest rates, I hope.'

'Of course, and to approved borrowers who pledge real property for their loans or for pieces of their business.' He saw her eyes start to shine.

'Let's go upstairs.'

'That's two great ideas you have.'

32

JOSHUA never admitted he wasn't as good at business as his father, Samuel, had been; he found it more comforting to blame others; and for the past ten years, he didn't put his heart or soul into his father's efforts to create a new religion called Christianity separate from its Jewish origins. He glided along; living high on the dwindling profits from his international trade and ignoring the impact that Paul's arrest in Jerusalem and transfer to Rome had wrought upon the Christian movement. Then the Jewish Revolt woke him up and he was forced to re-examine the same old dilemma; that's when he realized how times had changed, that his business had stagnated, that Judaism was gone but the Christian sect was actually growing. If ever the opportunity to push for separation presented itself it was now; and it was the only practical means of reviving his fortunes.

Matthew's sending Hero to Rome was his specific wake-up call. Having visited Rome many times, he always did so as an outsider; it seemed a world unto itself and he had no friends there. But he sensed that Matthew smelled its potential, and that he should follow. It was his time for expansion. But he was like Matthew in another way: he couldn't leave Antioch. What he needed was a Hero. The more he thought about it, the more he settled on Gideon, one of his most articulate helpers, who had just returned from Ephesus. He was perfect as organizer and evangelist and could be active in Rome.

'This is our third meeting and I'm pleased to see that we are attracting new men and becoming better organized. I want to continue what we're trying to do this evening in greater distinction to the insidious lies preached by Mark and John and especially Matthew about BANG--'

A loud noise interrupted him and he, along with everyone else, turned to look at the large man stumbling over a chair into the room obviously drunk.

'Sorry,' said the big, raw boned and incredibly ugly man, Gideon thought, as he sat down.

'As I was saying before the world intervened' - laughter rippled across the room - 'Jesus, my Lord, was the Son of God. He was more than merely a Jewish prophet or even the Messiah. He was sent by his Father to bring the truth and light to every nation. . .to every people! Not merely the Jews!'

'That's right, brother!' exclaimed big and ugly.

I've seen him before somewhere, Gideon thought. I know him.

'Don't believe Matthew or what his 'Sons of God' followers say!' Gideon continued. 'Don't confine him to Israel as they would have us do! His message is for all mankind! His message--'

'Is for all people here in Rome where it's needed most!' big and ugly shouted as he stood up, bobbing and weaving. 'And you know why I know? Because Peter' he surveyed the room and virtually shouted, 'Jesus' designated founder of his church, told us so!' He began clapping his hands and soon every one followed and repeated after him, 'Peter told us so! Peter told us so!' And he laughingly danced a little jig.

And stole the meeting. He went on like this as Gideon watched and approved. Many already knew him and voiced what he was going to say anyway. 'Come up here big' – he caught himself in time - 'man! He looked over the crowd as big and ugly made his way to the dais. 'This is truly the work of the Lord! I feel the spirit in this very room!' The crowd shouted and yelled as b and u climbed onto the dais.

He shook Gideon's hand and turned to them. 'Many of you know me! You know I love Jesus! But I love his Father more! I feel their power! Don't you?' And he threw his hands up to almost touch the ceiling. Some in the crowd started dancing in place; others called out 'Hosanna! Hosanna!' and others remained in their seats, eyes closed and rocking back and forth.

Gideon turned to b and u. 'You are truly touched by the spirit. What's your name?'

'Clement,' he answered.

*

Ti noticed that Hero was quieter than usual at breakfast the next morning and, knowing it was a sign he was upset, asked him what was bothering him.

'I received a letter from Aaron yesterday saying Matt's very upset about John's criticism of his gospel.'

'I didn't know he had finished it.'

'It's only a first draft but he asked John and I to read it over and make comments about it. Apparently, John's were quite harsh. Nearly "vitriolic," is the word he used.'

'John can be that way at times. Jesus used to call him one of the sons of thunder. Did Aaron mention any specifics?'

'He said John called it very "Jewish." That John told him he wouldn't circulate it in Ephesus or his other churches because the people were overwhelmingly Greek and would never become Jews just to follow Jesus' Way.' Hero looked into Ti's eyes. 'John apparently accused Matt of betraying Jesus' Gospel. Can you believe it?'

'Yes. I can believe it. Do you still have your copy?'

'Yes.'

'May I read it?'

'Of course.'

A week later, having read his friend's gospel in its first draft, Ti sent Matthew the following letter:

'Dear Matt,

I hope you don't mind my reading the part of your proposed Gospel which Aaron sent to Hero. I appreciate the situation you've been in for the past twenty five years and can only think that Jesus was sitting beside you, guiding your hand. What you have written is a perfect introduction to Jesus' discipleship. It's wonderful how much attention you devote to man's hope in this world, to all his possibilities for moral rectitude and piety and to how you address his expectations without the certainty of God's reward. You've put your finger on exactly how we need to sustain our hope for it.

It's wonderfully historical and expectational which makes it seem more familiar to our Jews, and therefore a perfect complement to Mark's. His was realistic enough and captured what Jesus said on many occasions, but you have done so more reflectively of our Jewish culture than he did. For what it's worth, I always thought John never felt comfortable with our Jewish heritage and misunderstood a lot of what Jesus said about it and what he thought about it.

What is perfectly true – and what I like best - is how well you've captured his description of the behaviors necessary not for rewards but for hope - the hope of joining the kingdom of God.

I notice you use particular words that have more than one meaning and assume you do that on purpose, to help people of different backgrounds better understand you. Yes, I understand that you mean I identified Jesus to the High Priest's mob when you say I 'betrayed' him. But do you think people will understand your usage of the word 'poor' as bereft or low when you apply it to 'of spirit?' I worry that some of the philosophy-minded will think that means they are impoverished and destitute; they'll think of it in typical Greek fashion as social and economic terms.

I applaud your use of contrasts because they affirm - obliquely and subtlety as they should – our capacity for change. I say this knowing you probably had me in mind.

Lastly, I am amazed at your organization of them which could only have been divinely inspired. I am certainly not among your latter three: but you are. You are the true representative of Jesus; no longer a disciple as we both were, but now an apostle every bit as much as Peter and Paul were.

Please know that I look forward to reading more as you progress.

Your friend,
Titianus'

*

Clement arranged the meeting in secret for just the two of them - with one assistant each — for the middle of the night at the Owl tavern just south of the Ostian gate on the third day of the following week. He told Hero that Gideon just wanted to talk; to make certain facts known to him.

'The center's crumbled, Hero. I don't have to tell you or any thinking follower of Jesus that; there's simply no unity anymore. The number of factions are growing out of control. You see that. The fight between John and Matthew's 'Sons of God' hasn't come to Rome yet. But our faction's fight with Hezekiah's Jews has been growing more frequent and violent. Vol's old order can't preserve the peace and it's chaos! I propose we put an end to it!'

The man in the white toga crossed over with a sky-blue sash with the red CS letters emblazoned on it put his hand over Hero's forearm resting on the tavern table. 'You know the best way to restore the unity is to preserve our Christian center totally and separately. All followers of Jesus under one roof, so to speak.'

Hero understood perfectly. But he didn't want to tell Gideon about the terrible arguments he had been having with Clement because he figured Clement already did. Besides, he would always be loyal to Matthew; but he understood that it was only a matter of time before John's split from Matthew eroded his own backing to the point where it didn't make sense for him to even continue in Rome. He shook his head because Gideon may be right: the so-called apostolic age may very well be over. But Clement's win really means Gideon's Christian Separatists winning; and that really means John winning over Matthew. So, the issue comes down to how I can help Matthew.

Gideon's voice broke into his consciousness: 'both of us know there's another dimension to this, a racial one. Don't you agree?'

Hero nodded.

And Gideon continued, 'we're both Greek. I mean I know you opted to leave your father's ways but now you and I share an understanding of oneness better than the Jews ever did! They've had their day. But it's over now. Surely, in your heart of hearts, John's interpretation makes more sense than Matthew's does!' Gideon looked into Hero's eyes and raised his eyebrows.

So, it was decision time to Hero. But he wasn't ready to give up. 'What makes you think we'll reconcile our differences over Jesus by simple separation?'

'Reconcile? Who said anything about reconcile? That's only a first step. After that, our growth will itself be reconciliation! That's what growth means: a harmony of interests. Their articulation. And no one will be able to stop us!' He smiled. 'Besides, Gentiles far outnumber Jews.'

'Because of the war?'

'Of course! But my point is that they defeated themselves by division!'

Hero smiled. 'You sound like my father.'

'You mean Judas? He's no failure? I hope we're talking about success here!' He saw his argument winning on Hero's face and continued. 'But until we can make our own decisions we can't go forward, you understand. As long as we're tied to Judaism our hands are tied and we won't have the freedom that Jesus wants us to have!'

Hero understood this as he knew Clement never would. What Clement probably hoped was that his affiliation with Gideon's group with it's emphasis on Jesus' spirituality would enable him to his refusal to accept Jesus' Jewishness. This was a possibility; but one that would never happen as long as he drew breath.

Gideon suddenly saw his victory recede.

'What's the matter?'

'I was thinking about Greek myths. The Trojan horse in particular. But I must leave now.' And he got up and did.

As he watched him go, Gideon sighed. He only had one recourse left. If Hero were out of the way Clement could step in and take Peter's group into the new order. And he was a lot easier to manipulate than Hero.

Stepping outside in the cooler but humid and stinking air not far from Titianus's warehouse on the river, Hero thought about Aaron's letter delivered to him this morning. Luke had asked his advice because Timothy had written to him– not about his health complaint – but about his John one; and asked him to come to Ephesus. Luke wrote that he told Aaron he didn't want to go but felt he had to defend his friend. Aaron advised him to write Timothy immediately and tell him that he couldn't leave Antioch for two months. Then he wrote to Hero and pleaded with him to come at once.

Hero just decided to.

*

One of Rome's many things that Titianus never got over was that they usually burned their dead instead of burying them; especially since he remembered them doing that in India and adding still living wives to the fires. But this afternoon, watching from the shaded portico of the Temple of Apollo, he had to admit it was a spectacular funeral. All of Rome's Jewish elite accompanied the bier as did many of Rome's godfearers. And he saw the gossip ripple through the onlookers. The question in nearly everyone's mind was who did it.

The big man, dressed in black and leading the procession, did too. He had found his uncle slumped over his table in his synagogue office covered in blood and his head nearly severed from his body. But the mystery was nothing was taken! Even the bagfuls of money had been left untouched!

Clearly assassinated! But by whom? And why? Then a revelation came to Volumnus: if no one claims responsibility I'll assign it! He glanced at Solomon's family walking two steps behind him and particularly at Isaac, Sol's son, heir and now the new ruler. They deserve answers. And so do I.

It should be easy, he thought. Starting with those Jesus people - Joshua's growing network of Christian Separatist cells scattered around the leading seaports of the empire - Amasa in Antioch, Jeremiah in Ephesus and now Gideon in Rome. None of them are here. And now the same for Matthew's Sons of God. At least, we got Mark. Maybe Hezekiah's right.

*

Licinius Mucianus' funeral was as intensely private as his life had been because he willed it: he hated notoriety and wished his life to be remembered merely by his family and close friends. That's why very few attended and why Vespasian and Titus couldn't help noticing Publix and Titianus in attendance. They nodded to them. But Vespy didn't see, when he nodded, that the Chief Imperial Priest who presided to invoke the proper gods, noticed his nod. The fact that no one smiled meant merely confirmed the reputation of the deceased as a peerless Roman.

'It was good of you and for you to attend, Ti. Especially given how busy you are this time of the year,' Publix said, sitting across from him in his library over wine later that afternoon in October 75.

Ti stared into the bit of swirling wine in his glass. 'I always thought of him as my good friend, Pub, not merely a source of contracts. I hope you'll believe me when I say I loved him and will miss him. He helped me in so many ways.' He looked up at him. 'And he taught me so many things. That's why I came. Not to be seen.'

'Oh, you were seen. Everyone there was noted.' Pub sensed Ti was in a reflective mood. 'Actually, I asked you to join me because I want to talk about some things with you that I shouldn't but feel I must.'

'I'm flattered, Pub,' he replied 'And rest assured that I would never repeat anything we say between us. As for hurtful things, true friends always forgive hurtful things said because they know they're not really meant.'

Pub looked through the window of his dining room as he now called it and replied, smilingly, 'it's like how marriage should be, isn't it? There's two parties involved and it has its ups and downs but if both parties want it to succeed it will.'

Ti looked at him and understood the motivation behind the luncheon invitation better. 'We're in agreement about this. So, let's also agree that enough's been said about it.'

'Agreed.'

'So, what's up on the political front?'

'I could use your help.'

'What about?

'It touches on what we've talked about before. But let me recast it in a different light. Vespasian needs the Senate to fund his expansion program in the north—'

'Against the Druids!' he laughed. 'The tree livers.'

'This is a far larger than that. Much larger in scope. He intends to go against their center at Mona--'

'In Britannia? But that's so far away!'

'He intends to send Agricola there with huge support and we expect it to take two or three years.' He paused.

Which caused Ti to sense that Pub was trying to tell him something important. 'So it will be very expensive and he needs the Senate's funding all the more,' he said, thinking he was filling in.

'Yes. But there are other issues involved. That's what politics is all about. All the other issues that touch on the main one. He also wants Titus' accession to his office to be automatic when he dies.'

'And many Senators won't accept a Jewish empress.'

'I'm among them.' Pub said this looking steadily at Ti so there would be no mistaking his position. 'And Titus has agreed to give her up.'

Ti stared back and said, 'I always thought he would because it's the most sensible thing to do,' while thinking, he's got something else on his mind. So, he stabbed at the dark: 'look, Pub. I am Titianus. I make my annual obeisance to the emperor. You've seen me do it and articipate in our public civic rituals many times. Judas was my old life and it's gone. Completely.' He hesitated, debating how strong he should say this. 'And I'll say one other thing about your son-in-law on this topic: he has absolutely no interest in Judaism whatsoever.'

Pub looked down for several moments and then back up into Ti's face. 'What I find interesting – and a little baffling - is that you've spent your life escaping from one identity into another while I haven't been able to hold onto mine because the world won't let me.'

'Perhaps confronting change is one more thing we have in common, then. We've only gone about it in different ways.'

'Yes, I can see that. And that's is why I want to tell you this. The Senate will give Vespasian the funding he needs and the full backing he wants. But he wants more—'

'No one wants to go back to the bad old days of Nero.' Ti looked away and then back. 'Since we're telling our secrets let me tell you something about myself.'

'What?'

'I've never tried hanging on to something until recently. I've always tried to go forward into what's new and different. But in an inclusive way. By incorporating it into what I'm doing or who I am. This has worked for me. I think it's wrong to try and preserve things because that's beyond the scope of myself – my individual self, I mean. So, to me, Pub, you're fighting a losing battle. Surely, Vespy will expand the Senate to get around you like so many others have before him!'

'Yes. That's where I was going in this conversation. To tell you that he intends to expand the Senate from outside Italy. As Caesar did. And he's looking particularly to the east.'

Ti looked at him, intrigued by Pub's line of conversation. 'If I understand you, he needs friends in the east who will allow him to concentrate on his northern and western problems until they're settled.'

'But many old guard Senators oppose appointing non-Italians.'

'Do you?'

'No. Not on the grounds of nationality. But the old guard fear the new appointees will be his political creatures, beholden to him for their new status and look to him for direction and protection rather—'

'That they won't be or can't be independent from him.'

Pub suddenly realized he better be careful here, not play his hand too early, so he said nothing.

'I'm not a politician but don't I remember hearing that kind of talk several years ago?'

'Yes. Piso used to rail about the foreign dogs as he called them. But what Senators now fear is that the Titus accession is just the mask for what Vespasian really wants.'

Ti scrunched up his eyebrows and smiled. 'They fear he wants to make the imperial office hereditary. As the Senate has become.'

Pub smiled and tipped his wine glass in salute. 'Got me!'

Ti sat up straighter. 'I'm not trying to. I'm trying to understand this in my own terms.'

'Your terms. I'm glad we're having this talk. I'm glad we're neighbors. I'm glad we're friends and share being fathers-in-law. But now, do you trust me as much as I am going to trust you?'

Ti felt bewildered; which was unusual. Then he remembered his conversations with Jesus after their northern trip. 'Yes,' he said.

'You still keep a residence in Antioch, don't you?'

'Yes.'

'Vespasian knows you. I mean who you are and what you've done for him and Rome.'

'I'll take your word for that. I'm sure he knows about my work with Mucianus. Why?'

'I wonder what kind of Senator you'd make.'

Ti stared at him. 'I don't know what to say! I'm speechless!'

Pub twisted around in his chair to see his sideboard and said, 'if you'd like more wine please help yourself. You're right about my trying to hang on to the old verities and you're right about things changing outside and in spite of myself.' He put his glass down. 'I concluded that I'm not going to able change the direction that things seem to be going in. Vespasian will expand the Senate which will expand the empire. I see that and know I can't stop it. But I also see that having the right kinds of men approved for appointment is crucial. I'm not a reactionary. We're alike that way and, speaking for myself, I want men we can trust and, given my age, especially those with sons I can trust.' He looked off –

And into the past, Ti thought; and he suddenly realized Pub's two sore points. They had never gone away. Ti also realized that's what they all wanted - Vespasian, Pub, and himself, a future through their sons. He sighed and thought, God!, It comes back to blood every time. My people, Esau's people, were right. So why did Jesus rebel against that? Because he read it in Deuteronomy?

After a short silence, Ti asked, 'what are you saying, Pub? I need to know in plain terms.'

Pub turned back and look into Ti's eyes. 'If I nominate you with the support of my friends in the Senate and Vespasian's known favoritism to you, you would be a shoo-in. The question is whether you want it: not whether you can get it.' He paused and then said, 'remember Marc.'

Ti got up for a little more wine, and asked 'refill?' Then he handed Pub's refilled glass to him and sat back down, he said, 'I'll have to talk this over with the family, of course. It would mean completely restructuring our life—'

'Of course. I understand.' He added, almost as an afterthought, 'but for what it's worth, Valeria grew up in a political household as well as a business one so I'd be surprised if you had any objection from her.'

'Thank you, Pub. Your offer honors my family more than I could ever dream of.'

Publix looked at him, nodded his head and said, very seriously, 'but it's still only a possibility. I don't have to tell you what you must do before you can even be considered for this to become an actuality, do I? And I don't have to tell you that he's been saying things that will sink both of us.'

It was clear in a flash to Ti what must be done. 'No, you don't have to say it. I know what I must do,' he answered.

33

Two weeks before Pub's talk with Ti, Volumnus had a revelation about what he must do: his replacement of Solomon as leader of Rome's Jewry would be more firmly established by his stopping the 'murderous sects of Jesus Jews' – as he had taken to calling them – from their rapid proliferation since the war; but only if it could be done at the same time by ridding his traditionalists of the taint of treason the war had tagged them with. He decided to do this through the 'Jews for Rome' because that might also return – or at least start - the vital godfearers support to him.

So, he prevailed on the rulers of the synagogues to allow him to present a series of free talks on 'The State of Rome's Jewry Today,' donations to be encouraged at the end of each talk. They began in his own Olive Tree synagogue.

'Ladies and gentlemen, I've been asked for my opinion about this so many times that I feel I must now speak out about it. Once again, we are under attack by the so-called Christians. You have probably all heard some of the lies that Matthew of Antioch is now writing about Jesus.' He looked at the expectant faces in the crowded Olive Tree and up into the galleries. 'And let me begin by reminding all of you of what a renegade Jew Matthew is! Jesus may well have been a good man; perhaps even a holy one. But he was no more of a man than any of the others in the long history of our people who have talked with God!' Murmurs of agreement and nods of heads confirmed that he was on the right track. Jacob, his prompter, sat directly in front of him and silently mouthed the word 'Matthew.'

'But I want you all to know that Matthew confirms the same lie that Mark told us: that Judas betrayed – BETRAYED is the word both use – Jesus. But now, I ask you: who is the betrayer here, Judas or Matthew? Let me go even deeper than this! Who was the better Jew here? Jesus, the secretive, rebellious, troublemaker to our faith, who couldn't even accept responsibility for his evil deeds on his own? Who was too weak to stand up and be responsible to himself and to God?' He paused and looked around. 'Or Judas, his friend, whom he begged to help him by telling the authorities where he could be found?

I'll tell you who the better Jew was! It was Judas! It was he who agreed out of the loving bonds of friendship to tell the authorities where to find Jesus where he and his so-called disciples cowered under the trees of a thick wood! To find this Jesus who refused to stop preaching his rubbish when even his entire family walked from their home to Capernaum to plead with him to stop his lies! Who preached the destruction of our Law! And who led a mob to destroy the Temple! And who then even went against our Law by refusing to allow his brother to care for their mother when he knew he was dying!' Hoots and shouts of praise for Vol arose from his audience and Vol stepped back in mock appreciation of their approbation.

After a moment he held up his hands to quiet them. 'Romans! I repeat: who was the better Jew! That sniveling, cowardly rebel Jesus who *begged* Judas to betray him! Or the manly Judas who agreed to help him! Who was the better friend? That weak and spineless trouble-maker who lacked the courage and fortitude that is instilled in every Roman boy? Or the more manly and righteousness Judas?'

Shouts of 'Judas! Judas!' came from the gallery by Vol's plants as he stepped to the side of his lectern to emphasize his height and girth behind his rich and sonorous voice. His left arm in the sling no longer hurting because of the three glasses of wine he took before his speech. Then he stepped back to behind the lecturn and continued.

'What man among us exemplifies the loyalty, the trust and the confidence that Judas demonstrated to help his weak friend in his hour of need? What man among us is brave enough to bear the stigma of BETRAYER - that even Paul, their equally spineless turncoat who was not even a witness to the proceedings? Paul the weakling who complained about a tiny thorn in his flesh! Yes, Jesus died! But we all do! What's the point of repeating the obvious? That's neither new nor significant! What was new was Judas' willingness to live the rest of his life with that stigma! That, ladies and gentlemen, is real courage! That demonstrates real Roman fortitude!' And as he slowed his speech so he also slowly spread his right arm out wide to look like a huge, fat half-cross. Silence followed for a few seconds before his plants began the applause and shouts that increased and rippled throughout the building. 'Well done, Vol!'

'Thank you,' he put his arm down, saying to himself, God that hurt! Then he turned and paced to his right. Suddenly he stopped, turned to the people and bellowed: 'and we should remember one other thing. We should be eternally grateful to him because by fulfilling his word – and I hasten to clarify that it was not his obligation! - Judas saved the Christians from extinction!'

'Yes! His so-called betrayer's role allowed them to reinvent themselves under Peter, the sniveler's designated successor. If Jesus had not gone through with his crucifixion where would he – or any of them - be today? Just another in a long line of unredeemed martyrs remembered for nothing but their own vanity! Yes, I say unto you, Judas made Jesus what he's become today! I don't mean God; I mean an alleged holy prophet of God!'

'Oh, my God! Wait 'til the godfearers hear this!' Jacob said, when Vol stepped down from the dais.

'Why?'
'Don't you know who Judas is?'
'No,' Vol pretended to look blank.
'Titianus.'
'No!'

*

'My goodness! I didn't expect you today!' Tay was genuinely surprised by Publix' unannounced visit, a violation of social protocol which was a sin in his eyes.

'I know and I apologize if I've inconvenienced you. But I have an urgent matter that I need to discuss with you.' She thought it was about the resident in the small, portable cage that he carried.

It was the two days after Vol's speech when Tay lead hm into her small reception room where they sat down and wine and nibbles was provided.

'We may have a problem that I hope to circumvent.'

'Yes,' Tay said, her defenses activated by his use of 'we.'

'Volumnus intends to cement his leadership of Rome's Jewry by going around to the different synagogues lecturing about how Judas didn't betray Jesus, but that Jesus betrayed him. He gave his first speech the day before yesterday and claims that Jesus convinced Judas to prevent his weak nature to go through with his crucifixion but never reciprocated. Never paid him back so to speak--'

'What does that have to do with me?'

'It has to do with all of us. Please hear me out.' She nodded, wide-eyed. 'What's potentially dangerous is his saying Judas was the better Jew than Jesus was. And yes, that's part of what he wants to do. Vol knows that denigrating Jesus as the son of God is popular among Jews and Romans, and that's part of the bridge he's building to re-ingratiate himself with the godfearers he lost during the war. What's important about it is that he says Judas has all the ideals that Romen men should have and he identifies them with Titianus. It's only a small time before everyone figures out Judas is Ti. Or Ti is Judas—'

'Oh, hello! I'm sorry,' Marcus said, walking in while reading a small scroll in his hand. 'I didn't you were here, Pub. I don't mean to interrupt.' He turned to Tay and said,

' I'll see you another time.'

'Please stay,' she replied and looked at Pub. 'Would you mind? He may as well hear since he's part of us.'

'Yes, of course,' Pub replied and repeated what he just told Tay to him.

'Yes, I can understand how it's damaging,' Marcus said after Pub finished, 'but you know we're not public people. How can it hurt us?'

Pub took a deep breadth and realized Ti hadn't spoken to them about it yet. 'Because I suggested to Ti that I nominate and get my friends to support him for the Senate. But you know what a political issue Vespasian makes out of being anti-Jewish! Ti won't have a chance now.'

Tay nodded.

But Marcus said, 'that means you and your friends who support him will be tinged with Vespasian's same anti-Jewish brush.'

Publix looked at him. He belongs in the Senate, he thought. But he just nodded.

'How much time do we have?' Tay asked.

'No more than a week,' Pub replied.

Marcus stood up and said, 'I know what to do.' He turned and left.

*

'First grandfather, then father and now my uncle! I can't believe they assassinated Volumnus! These Christian bastards are nothing but common murderers! We must pay them back!' Jacob, Isaac's son, harangued the half dozen men assembled in the small room on the benches along the side of the Olive Tree.

'I'm sure it's one of the Antioch group.' Joab said. 'Their people here are too timid to do anything like--'

'Unless a new group has formed! Has anyone heard anything?' Amos interrupted.

The others shook their heads or said no.

'Then I say let's go after that Antioch group!' Jacob said.

'Whoa! Not so fast!' Amos replied. 'I'm not opposed to it but I've been thinking about it since you mentioned what you wanted to do a few days ago. First of all, Jacob, are you absolutely certain they were Jesus followers?'

Jacob came to attention in his chair. 'Who else would do it?'

'I wouldn't put it past the Jamnians! And Hezekiah's 'Young Judaists' make no bones about hating us. We all know they're backed by the Jam heads.'

'Yes,' Jacob replied; calmer now. 'That's all possible.'

'Maybe we should consider a completely different approach, at least in the beginning,' Asa said. Everyone looked at the coolest head around the table.

'Elaborate,' Amos almost demanded.

'Consider this: instead of going after them directly, maybe we should form small groups of our counterparts in Antioch and encourage them to go after them?'

After a brief silence, Jacob said, 'Vol always said it shouldn't be difficult to find defenders of our traditions.' He was thinking that Amos and Asa may be right about thinking of this in longer range terms. Maybe it would be better if others elsewhere did it.

'Anywhere, for that matter.' said Amos, noticing Jacob becoming calmer.

'But this will take months!'

Amos, Asa and Jacob looked at Micah. He was the youngest and a hothead. Like the others, he inherited his ruler's office from his father and, so far, his child-like impatience was tolerated only because it enforced their own beliefs. But he was understanding the need for deliberation more and more. Old Amos remembered Asa actually telling him one time that it was like weaning a baby.

'What do you think, Jehu?' Amos asked.

'I like the idea of establishing a group in Antioch for two reasons. One is that Micah's observation that it's taking time could work to our advantage. Like a calming period while we whip them up to a--'

'I heard just yesterday that John and Mag fled Ephesus after hearing about Solomon's assassination,' Nathan interrupted. 'His people probably expect repercussions.'

'That's my point, Nathan,' Jehu continued. 'Let's allow things to cool a bit. In the meantime, we can build up a small group of supporters in Ephesus as well as Antioch.'

After a short silence, Aaron said, 'I think we only need only four or five young men. Maybe six. But intensely loyal. And we should think of this as just a beginning. Let's create a network of such groups in all the major cities--'

'And under our direction!' Jacob exclaimed, remembering Vol's old dream. 'Vol's assassination could be the issue to achieve it and serve as a memorial to him!'

'And to Solomon as well as your father! I hadn't thought of that this way,' Aaron replied. 'That's an excellent idea. Memorials to martyrs of our faith!'

'May I make a suggestion?' Asahel asked.

'Certainly,' Jacob said smiling, pleased at the direction the discussion was going in.

'As we refine this project further, we should think about finding support from among the sons of the Zealots and the sicarii. Now that the Sanhedrin are completely out of the picture it's be a good time to give them a home to go to!'

Jacob remained seated after the meeting ended and the others had gone. It had gone far better than I had hoped. And in a new and broader direction than he originally conceived. A lot of things need to be worked out yet, but it's a start to realizing the old dream he heard about all his life. He smiled. So Sol and Vol really do live!

*

I admit I was lax, wasn't thinking. Three nights later, after the dinner, I stopped briefly to pick up a scroll from my ground floor office where I was surprised to find Marc and Pub in deep conversation. They stopped suddenly when I walked in and looked at me. I knew something was up.

'Discussing me?'

'We were agreeing that you shouldn't say anything more about what happened to Vol,' Pub replied.

'Part of our Roman way,' Marcus said and smiled. 'It'll just deepen speculation about your origins. The more mysterious the more they'll love it. The power of innuendo and rumor.'

But that made Ti mad and he glared at his son. 'You know that's exactly what I don't want! People talking about us!'

'I told Marc about their attempt on your life, Ti,' Pub said to defuse the tension, 'because I think he should know about it. There could be others in the future and you were lucky this time.'

'I gather you don't want the ladies to know.'

'That's right. I'd rather they didn't worry about death. I think it's enough for them to worry about life. What profit is there in worrying about certainties?'

But Ti knew he lied as he walked up the stairs to his return rooms. The strangest thing about the discussion of Vol's assassination was that Tay never talked about it. Did she think nothing of it? Maybe she thinks she's done her duty as wife and mother and that's enough? So, do I really want to ask her about it? I don't think I will, he decided. I owe her so much all ready.

*

'Tell us you didn't do it! That you're not behind it! We can't live with a murderer!'

'Val, on my oath as a father-in-law, husband, father, and grandfather, I swear I had absolutely nothing to do with it.'

'But everyone in Rome thinks you arranged his assassination. Who else would want him dead?'

'What about those four men I told you about?' Marcus asked her. 'The heavily-armed ones who came from Antioch together?'

'You never told me about them!'

'I can't remember to tell you every little detail that passes through my life!'

'They must have done it,' Marcus replied, 'they're members of the group of radical Christians we've been hearing about and who everyone says assassinated Matthew. They won't tolerate people saying Jesus wasn't completely divine. They're mistaken followers of John.'

They were in Ti's main reception room and Publix was thoroughly enjoying discovering this new aspect to his daughter's family. 'And was he?' He asked.

'He?' Ti asked.

'Jesus.' Pub answered. 'Was he God or just his son?'

'Always the devil's advocate, hey Pub?' Ti answered, feeling beleaguered. 'Well, the short answer is no. The man I knew was fully human. If he wasn't he wouldn't have needed my help. That spiritual dimension was claimed by Peter's crowd after his death to fit in with the story they told about his resurrection.' Then he noticed everyone was quiet and looked around. 'Oh, don't mistake me: he talked with God as much as Moses or Elijah or Job or Isaiah or any of our prophets did. But he was definitely a man. What people find difficult to understand is that he lived here on earth as the human incarnation of God.'

'So, you knew him that way?' Pub persisted.

'Yes. That's why I agreed to help him when he asked me to.'

'And the others: did they see him that way?' Marcus asked.

Ti looked up at the ceiling. 'Not completely. I mean, most of them didn't understand his incarnation. I think John still doesn't and that's why he hates me so much.'

'Then you're saying these radical Christian spiritualists are wrong?' Val asked.

'Not merely wrong but dangerously so. As I said, I knew Jesus the man and those who didn't know him can only know him through their imaginations--'

'Like Paul, you mean? He didn't know him and he yet mentioned your betrayal of him in one of his letters!' Marcus interrupted.

'That's true. But only after Peter and the others created Jesus' church and Paul talked with them after he returned from Damascus. I'm sure his experience of Jesus was genuine. But there was another problem that Paul raised in his ignorance. Because he claimed to know Jesus the same as they did, he was the first person to raise the issue of whether you can know God and his son on your own independently from the apostles. You see, all of us were *selected* by Jesus; he *chose* us; we didn't choose him; that was certainly true of me; and that's the road Paul went down. But right after Jesus chose us, John and a couple of others thought of our discipleship like priests-in-training – like mediators between people and God - and I don't think they ever got over that.'

'Well, it always comes back to how we receive what we're told in this world!' Everyone turned to look at Pub who seemed unusually vehement.

'Have you become a secret Christian? You seem to know an awful lot about all this,' Ti asked.

'No, but I'm a reader and a thinker. And when I think about those radical Christians they're dangerous to me exactly because they live in their heads.'

Ti nodded. 'I agree: the head is a far more dangerous to live in than in the heart.'

34

SINCE his first heart attack three weeks ago, Vespasian had Titus simply announce at the public rostrum that he was temporarily ill but was expected to resume his public receptions any day now. He always intended for Titus to succeed him, but now that his time had come, he couldn't quite admit it enough to even tell Titus. But finally, on the eighteenth of June 79, after several days of progressively more painful attacks, he summon his Roman stoicism to prepare Titus for what he would have to face.

'Death comes to all of us, Titus. There's no point fearing it.' Vespasian was having a good morning: he was sitting in a chair near the window to better feel the breeze and watch the rising sun on the eastern slopes of the distant hills, his favorite view.

Titus noticed the beads of perspiration on his ashen grey-colored face. He looked like a grand mural of a Roman aristocrat sitting in his chair waiting for death. Gods, what will I do when that happens? he thought.

At sixty nine, Vespasian had suffered two extremely painful heart attacks in the spring and the doctors told him he would 'probably' not survive a third one of such intensity. But he was determined to make one last push to put his house in order before that happened.

'Beware of Domitian. He's clever but ambitious and he's always been jealous of you. He's always begged for a role in my administration but I never gave him one because I wanted you to succeed me. But it will be different with you. Give him something because the succession of our family must be assured and he'll need to know something about governing.' He put his right hand over his heart as if to protect it. 'But minimize his role.' He paused and rested his chin on his hand before continuing. 'Look for men having large perspectives on life. Their loyalty, trust and friendship is far more important than cleverness or even the money and perks you give them. Cleverness is tactical at best and such men usually think more of themselves than for the good of all or what you're trying to achieve.' He stopped and looked into the distance, wishing it was the future. 'And never fear personal conflict nor think it permanent. My best friend turned out to be Mucianus and I couldn't have achieved what I did without him. Yet, we started off enemies. Eprius too. If I've learned one thing as emperor it's to be a friend to the right kinds of people and they, in turn, will find their right people. You see how things are connected?' When he saw Titus nod, he looked up at the sunlit hills and said, 'I'm tired now and want to lie down.' He watched his handsome son stride out and felt a twinge of sadness and fear. Such a faithful, good boy, he thought, and I've done what I've can for him. But there's such a nest of vipers out there.

*

On the twenty fourth of June, three days after the announcement of the Senate's affirming Titus' succession as emperor, Ti and Marcus were in their warehouse planning their moves in what they expected to be a relatively peaceful and prosperous few years.

'I think the succession will go smoothly,' Ti said. 'Titus has the army behind him and has been training for the office for nearly ten years. Besides, Pub says he likes the idea of using public works projects to build political support.'

'Sort of like me.'

Ti smiled. He discovered he more and more enjoyed his talks with Marcus and frequently reflected on the old adage of children being the joy of their parents. 'Yes, sort of. But Domitian is no Hero. And don't underestimate him. He's clever, willful and frustrated as small minded people are, but he'll be ruthless now to achieve his ambition. Watch out for him.'

Marcus raised his eyebrows. 'To be emperor?'

Ti sighed. 'Yes. I suspect Titus' reign may not be a long one.'

'Really? He's only forty!

'But he's not as clever as Vespy was and doesn't have his drive.'

'But he *is* a good man.'

Ti looked at son in his half-serious way. 'Never overestimate the power of goodness in this world. Which is a backhanded way of saying never underestimate the power of evil.'

'Did Jesus teach you that?'

'In a manner of speaking.' He looked down at the papers on his desk without seeing them. 'Maybe I should have said God doesn't want us to be naïve about this world or the next.'

'So, cultivate Domitian?'

'That's what I would do if I were you. He's only a few years younger than you, but if he gets the power--' Ti looked at Marcus and raised his eyebrows. 'avoid politics if you can!'

*

A week later, court hangers on reported a violent argument between Titus and his brother in the public reception room of the imperial palace.

'No, I will not appoint you to a command on the Danube! Why do you want to be so far from Rome?'

'But I want to help you, brother! You've never been emperor before!' Dom really meant 'never made an imperial decision before' but didn't say it.

Titus looked at Domitian and thought, twenty eight with no military experience. I had to wait 'til I was thirty but had trained for it for years. Only then did father appointed me. And guide me. Dom's appointment would be disastrous. And remember his warning. 'Why don't you stay here and observe how things go.' He paused. 'I'll confess that I never knew how intricate politics can be.' Titus' problem was not that he knew he wanted to be everyone's friend but didn't know why; and didn't want to.

Dom suddenly realized this was his brother's weakness, not the military he was trained for. Back off, he told himself, and see where the winds will shift because they always do. 'All right. I won't press you about it or anything else. But remember, I just want to help you.'

*

A month later, rumors about what the new emperor would do and the many disputes between him and his brother still buzzed about the city and delayed families from going to their summer residences until the wrangling was resolved. But now, in mid-summer, the wives and children were gone while most men of power and influence remained; Ti and Marcus among them.

In the last week of July, even they had had enough and decided to join their families in their Pompeii villa. They talked about different things as they finished packing the last of the business scrolls to take with them. Taking a break, Ti was standing looking out the window when Marcus entered carrying several scrolls to put into the small, traveling chest on the table. Ti glanced at him and said, 'I love you and Hero in different ways, you know. You've been a perfect son in the sense of most like me and I couldn't ask for any higher compliment from God.'

'Do I detect a "but" coming?' Marc asked with a smile.

'No, no. Not at all. I was going to tell you that many years ago, long before I met your mother or you were born, Jesus told me that spirit was more important than blood and you've proved it. I feel you're my true spiritual heir.' He paused. 'But what's even more important to me is that I feel we're more than father and son, we're friends. Jesus knows I've tried to be yours.'

Marcus placed the remainder of the scrolls in the little chest and looked at him. 'You know I love you, dad.'

'Yes, and that's why I want to warn you about Domitian. Don't ever cross him and never be hostile.' Marcus observed him look away, high on the wall over his head. 'He'll be seriously plotting against Titus now; and, unfortunately, he's smarter than Titus.'

*

But that summer away from Rome wasn't as happy an interlude as previous ones had been. The heat, water, sand, wine, and neighbors were all the same, but the time spent there was shorter and more pressured. Titus' new reign was really going to begin in the fall, earlier than usual because there was so much to do and so many new people involved. And Titus was nothing if not social. So, Tay, Val and the grandchildren returned on the 22nd August to begin putting the house in order and Marcus returned the next day to ready the business and warehouse office for Ti's and Publix's return the next week.

'So, do you feel abandoned now that everyone's gone?' Pub asked. 'I remember you had your old friend, Simon, visit you last year. He found my telling him about Spartacus grouping his men around here fascinating.'

'I don't feel abandoned as much as pressured,' Ti replied. 'I wish it wasn't time for the family to start our town season so soon. I would have liked us to have had a longer summer season.'

'Of course. But you have to admit it's been an unusual year so far.'

Ti nodded. 'Val says the social season is starting earlier this year because everyone wants to see Titus and he's planned many public fetes to make himself available.' He shook his head. 'There's so many new people.'

Pub laughed. 'I probably shouldn't say this, but he's always been far more fun than Vespasian.'

'Maybe the rumor about his new amphitheatre being finished earlier than expected is true.'

'That might be.'

'You seem more thoughtful than usual tonight, Ti.' Pub peered at him from under his bushy eyebrows. 'You've been getting so more and more lately, you know.'

'Actually, I've been thinking about us. You and me. Do you realize we've been friends now for nearly twenty five years?'

'I think it's grown beyond *amicitia*.'

'Certainly beyond the conventional. I'm genuinely grateful for all you've done for me and my family.'

'Thank you. I feel that way too and I trust you. And I'm glad that Titus is going to formally enroll you in the Senate in the fall. I'm only sorry that Vespasian didn't live to see it.'

'That's kind of you to say. I'm looking forward to it too.'

'Perhaps you'll feel even more Roman now.'

'What do you mean?'

'We Romans value our public life. That's why we grade free men into classes based on money. You must have the material ability to live the public life; and you do.'

Ti nodded.

'I always thought you're wanting a private life was a form of hiding, perhaps even escape. From society, I mean. After all, so many assert themselves for their own benefit instead of society's.'

'But surely I'm not hiding! I live in one of the few domus' in the city. My retainers are dressed in the best livery and carry pennants with my colors. They're all badges of identification of who I and my family are. Everyone knows me.'

Pub smiled. 'Yes. But isn't this just your ego peaking out?' He wanted to avoid saying that he always wondered what Ti was hiding from; perhaps it was something anti-social like a criminal act? Some guilty secret?

'I don't think so. You know as well as I do how much you've helped us become Roman. I know Tay has always appreciated it.'

Pub nodded while John Hyrancanus' subduing the Idumeans and forcing them to be circumsized, flashed through Ti's mind. Those Hebrew bastards. Racial purists. 'Jews have long memories, you know. Even longer than Romans do.'

Pub's brow knitted. 'What brings that to mind?'

'That we've never ritualized our relationship. Or is that more Greek than Roman?'

'It is. Does it bother you?'

'No. I always thought we shouldn't ritualize it. For your sake. I don't have your status and only money distances me from others. But it's curious to me that you've become less and less concerned with how you appear to people.'

'And you haven't? I remember when we first met and I thought what a foreigner! Trying so hard to be Roman!'

Ti chuckled. 'I remember that too.' He paused. 'My! How I tried to fit in! Watching and observing how it all worked.'

'And how did you live in India? As a Jew, a Syrian, a Roman or an Indian?'

'As a Roman, I admit. India was. . . well, just too different for me.' He paused. 'But I think the real reason was that I knew I wasn't going to stay there. I knew I wanted to live and die in Rome.'

'So, in the end you identify yourself as a Roman.'

'I've thought about it quite a bit and I've asked myself many times,' Ti replied, '"what is a Roman?"'

'And?'

'And I've concluded that there's several kinds. I wasn't born and raised in the circumstances you were, so I'm not your kind of Roman.'

'You mean you think that how people wind up is more a result of their conscious experiences than of their birth?'

'Yes, to a degree. I believe some men are self made by their consciousness. I think my friend Jesus was that way. But it's not common and I've never understood why some have it and most don't. And I think Jesus didn't understand that either. He never understood why men didn't follow him.'

Pub looked down in thought. Finally, he said, 'I notice that you've been talking about Jesus more in the past year than you ever did before. Does it have anything to do with Simon's visit last year?'

Ti stuck his chin out. 'I don't know. Perhaps. But it's strange to me how I seem to be starting a new life this autumn without escaping my old one.

'But you understand change because you've lived with it all your life. You've even changed because of it.'

'I always thought I understood change because of him.'

'I want to ask you a personal question about that,' Pub said looking intently at him, 'but I don't want to jeopardize our friendship. So don't answer if you think it will.'

Ti looked into his eyes, intrigued. 'I'll tell you if I think it will.'

'There you were, a Jew. Then you travel around with Arabs, marry a Parthian and wind up here, a Roman. What happened to your Judaism? I've never seen you practice it as I've seen others do.'

Ti thought about what Jesus did nearly fifty years ago. That the most important things in life are the choices you make, and he wasn't sure he consciously made the ones he did. 'I'm like most people. I can feel sad about all the might-have-beens in my life if I want to. But I refuse to because I believe that's what life is, one choice after another.' He hesitated. 'But to answer your question. Jesus taught me that life is a matter of form. I left the form that Judaism had become at the time I became consciousness of it. That's how I explain why I followed Jesus. I was a seeker as much as he was. We realized our heritage had been taken in a direction we didn't want to go in. Jesus preached how our leaders had betrayed us beginning with Deuternomy's defense of monarchy and centralization. Everything had gone wrong in his view.' He stopped and looked into Pub's eyes. 'I suspect the same thing has happened here in Rome and I think you understand what I'm trying to say. In any case, Jesus understood it far more than I did. I'd never stopped believing in God but I did in the form our belief had taken. That awakened me to the whole realm of culture and history and differences among people that I never knew about. I used to argue with John over it. He still thinks that spirit is more important than the material and therefore the cultural forms we live in really don't matter.' Ti sort of shook himself and laughed. 'So we carried our beliefs in different directions.'

'Then what about our Roman gods? You must have been shocked by their images but especially by your household altar when you first moved here. When I was growing up our household gods were far more important than they are now.'

Ti smiled. 'I admit I was shocked and I'm ashamed to tell you that I responded by flight. Since I couldn't tear the altar down, I avoided the room; I didn't go into it anymore.' He hesitated. 'You see, Pub, I'd learned long before how my selectively ignoring things can be very helpful.' He hesitated again. 'But I want to be completely candid with you. To me, our friendship doesn't depend on the fact that I'm circumcised and you're not. How I treat you is more important than what I merely believe. Creedal definitions make our minds our life and I've learned that there's more to life than my mind.'

Pub nodded and looked away. 'That's being honest but what about your salvation that I've heard about? Isn't your Jesus returning for your final judgment?'

'Perhaps. He talked about it on that final trip to Jerusalem but I associated it with his talking about his atonement. Those were our darkest days. All the exuberance, the light, the hope and optimism were gone by then. I'm sure he knew it. And it was like our last ditch stand. It changed us forever.'

Neither spoke for a long moment. Then Pub said, 'I don't mean to offend you, but I want to ask one last thing.'

'Yes.' Everyone wants to know, Ti thought.

'Did you really betray Jesus in the sense that most people understand that word?'

That's the first question everyone asks me, Ti thought. It's interesting that Pub saved it for the last. 'No. Not in the sense that many think now - and as even Jesus predicted they would. But if you think about it, who was I disloyal to? Certainly not to Jesus. Mark has the story pretty much as it happened because Peter, who was there, told him. But I think Matthew understood me better. I just wish he hadn't caved in so much to what John thought.'

'I'm sure you're tired of re-telling the story. Don't if you don't feel like it.'

'I'd like you to know, Pub. But because it's so simple and sensible, no one believes it's true. Jesus was a holy man. We've had many of them in our tradition; and I think we'll have more in the future. But all are men like us who may or may not be touched by the divine. Jesus took his life to a level far beyond what the holy men did before him, however. He had this final idea of his entire life serving as an example. Others only flirted with it at best—.' He noticed the smile on Pub's face. 'Oh, you're probably thinking of Horatio at the bridge or those Greeks at Thermopylae as the same ideals of sacrificing one's life for the community. Only it wasn't the same; he didn't think of it as for any small community but for all humanity. Throughout the world and from when it was created.'

Pub stared at him. 'I've never thought about it on such a broad level. It's overwhelming!'

Ti smiled. 'It was! So much so, that most people - including myself - couldn't really grasp it. But he asked me to help him! He asked me to personally help him! Not to help make some large cosmic idea manifest! He merely wanted me to help put himself in a position where his human nature couldn't back out of it. So, he would have to go through with it.' He stopped. 'Does this make sense?'

'Yes. I can understand that. All of us need help from the gods.'

'But what made him such a truly understanding man to me was that he warned me what would happen to me. That I would be hated and despised for doing it.'

'So that's what Volumnus was talking about. And which you accepted?'

'I was his best friend and most beloved disciple. Everything that's happened to me I owe to him.'

'But you've been remarkably successful! You can't deny it!'

'I don't. But, you have to realize it wasn't of my own making and lately I've been thinking this was his way of reciprocating our friendship. At least, I hope it was.'

Publix nodded. 'Let me speak about the others first. They all have something in common: they all talk about God and Jesus. I heard that he appeared to Paul and many other people. Did he appear to you?'

'No. He never did. But I want to tell you that he also taught us that the divine is within each of us because God created us. God blew the breath of life into us and we carry that with us while we're alive. Jesus talked quite openly about our ends being there in our origins and how we had to look within ourselves in order to realize the divine within us.'

'Don't I remember you're saying something about your friend, Thomas, saying that?'

'Yes. But others have too.'

'But not you?'

'No, probably because I'm less certain of how exclusive that is. But as you've observed, I've been thinking about it more now that I have some time to think about my life. And what Jesus said.'

'Have you written anything?'

'No. Just a few notes to jog my memory.'

'I hope you do write it down, Ti. We need all the help we can get.'

They were quiet and Ti drank the last of his wine.

'Feel free to have more,' Pub said.

'No, I've had enough. But thank you, old friend,' Ti said and stood up. 'I'm going home now.'

'Stay here tonight, if you wish.'

'Thank you but I want to get up early in the morning and do some writing as you suggest. You've evoked some ideas that I've been thinking about and I'd like to explore them more fully now.'

'Well, come over whenever you feel like it, friend.'

35

TWO days later, Rome's Forum was ablaze with excitement that had spread rapidly across the city and shocked everyone. Posters were nailed everywhere and people in the streets talked about nothing else. But Tay, Val and most of the household hadn't heard the rumors. What shocked Tay and Val who followed her into her reception room, was the sight of Marcus, standing in the doorway, leaning against the jamb, his face ashen white and holding a parchment. 'I ripped this from the public news board,' he said faintly. His eyes saw but didn't see them.

Tay went up to him and scrutinized face. He didn't move and seemed to look into another time. She took the parchment from his hand and read:

25th August 79
TERRIBLE DISASTER AT POMPEII AND HERCULAEM !!!
> Various reports are coming in as dispatch riders arrive hourly at the imperial palace.

According to eye-witnesses, the eruption of Mount Vesuvius started yesterday about noon and worsened during the course of the day. Some claimed a column of flame and debris reached a height of twenty miles accompanied by very dense and rapidly rising clouds. It was also recorded that the bright flames at the beginning became darker and spotted with earth, cinders and other minerals. People as far away as the naval base of Misenum, about twenty two miles across the bay, said they saw it quite clearly.

Day turned to night and the night became a nightmare as many people tried to flee under a rain of hot chunks of rock of different sizes, killing some outright and injuring thousands of others in spite of their tying pillows over their heads. People used torches and lanterns to get to the beaches but they found the waters roiling and the poisonous, sulphuric gases becoming thicker. Worse for them: the wind shifted from its normal southerly direction so sailing became virtually impossible. Escape became impossible; and daylight did not return for two days. Molten lava poured down, covering Pompeii, Herculaneum and the surrounding areas. We will never learn exactly how many thousands were killed nor will we recover their bodies.

We will keep you informed as we receive further news.

Below are the known dead but we expect the numbers to increase hugely in the days ahead:

Pliny the Elder, newly appointed commander of the fleet at Misenum

Agrippa, son of Antonius Felix and nephew of King Agrippa II of Judea

Marcus Publix Agrippa, well known public benefactor

Titianus, a private merchant

Tay fainted.

THE END

Other novels in the Apostles Series published by BCB Media Group include:

PAUL

By

Gary Browne

What drove Paul to kill, maim and torture Christians in Jerusalem? *And then join them knowing he may well suffer what they did?* What lay behind his compulsive obsession to always travel, always be on the move to new people, new locations and new locations? Using the latest historical and psychiatric scholarship, Browne reveals the man's darker secrets - why Paul never settled nor seemed able to, never married and blamed his irregular life on the 'thorn' that God had given him – his ultimate secret! Read and learn why Paul wrote more about 'will power' than any other early Christian writer!

ISBN-13: 978-0-957058217 (BCB Media)
ISBN-10: 0957058217

www.ingramcontent.com/pod-product-compliance
Lightning Source LLC
Chambersburg PA
CBHW070713160426
43192CB00009B/1178